THE McGRAW-HILL INTERNATIONAL SERIES IN SOFTWARE ENGINEERING

Consulting Editor

Professor D. Ince
The Open University

Titles in this Series

Further titles in this Series are listed at the back of the book

PEOPLE AND PROJECT MANAGEMENT FOR IT

Sue Craig • Hadi Jassim

McGRAW-HILL BOOK COMPANY

London · New York · St Louis · San Francisco · Auckland · Bogotá · Caracas · Hamburg
Lisbon · Madrid · Mexico · Milan · Montreal · New Delhi · Panama · Paris · San Juan
São Paulo · Singapore · Sydney · Tokyo · Toronto

Published by
McGRAW-HILL Book Company Europe
SHOPPENHANGERS ROAD, MAIDENHEAD, BERKSHIRE, SL6 2QL
Telephone 0628 23432
Fax 0628 35895

British Library Cataloguing in Publication Data
Craig, Sue
    People and Project Management for IT.—
(McGraw-Hill International Series in
Software Engineering)
I. Title II. Jassim, Hadi III. Series
005.10684

    ISBN 0-07-707884-5

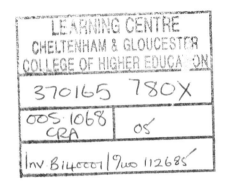

Library of Congress Cataloging-in-Publication Data
Craig, Sue
    People and project management for IT / Sue Craig, Hadi Jassim.
        p.   cm. – (The McGraw-Hill international series in software
engineering)
    Includes bibliographical references and index.
    ISBN 0-07-707884-5
    1. Software engineering – Management.   2. Industrial project
management.   I. Jassim, Hadi.   II. Title.   III. Series.
QA76.758.J38   1995
005. 1′068′4–dc20   94-23473
                                                          CIP

12345 CL 98765

Typeset and illustrated by TecSet Ltd, Wallington, Surrey
and printed and bound in Great Britain at Clays Ltd, St Ives plc
Printed on permament paper in compliance with ISO standard 9706.

CONTENTS

ACKNOWLEDGEMENTS

We have been lucky enough to receive a great deal of support from our friends and colleagues in Logica and KPN. We thank in particular Nicolette Kok, Terry Coombes, Arnoud de Vos, Phil Jones and Henk Smit. Martin Ashton, Mike Jerome, Peter van Es and Wim van den Berg have all given us important insights into aspects of project management over the years. We are also grateful to Peter Callender, Jenny Gent, Peter Lindvald Nielsen and Bernt Svihus for their constructive criticism and suggestions for different parts of the book. Rupert Knight and his colleagues from McGraw-Hill provided the right direction and support to enable us to meet our deadlines.

Writing this book during one of the busiest periods of our lives would not have been possible without the encouragement and support of our families. Duncan, Gill, James, Katherine, Sami and Niall, we love you.

Special thanks go to Duncan Craig, who reviewed all the chapters, supported us when we got stuck and contributed his own valuable insights for the key sections of the book.

Hadi Jassim
Sue Craig

1

OUR STARTING POINT

1.1 INTRODUCTION

You can use this book in several ways. You may want to read it straight through, for a thorough understanding of project management. Otherwise, if you are busy right now with a current project, you may prefer to skip to a particular chapter or section, in order to get fast access to ideas and guidelines which you can apply directly at work. You will find an overview of the structure of the book at the end of this chapter. Once you have read the book we hope you will find that individual chapters will be useful reference material, to support you when you need help in a particular area of project management.

This chapter explains our approach to the key concepts of project management, and how this book can help you to extend and refine your skills. We start by outlining the range of capabilities which a project manager needs, and describing how you can use the ideas here to support you in your role as project manager, client or user. We then define what we mean by the term 'project', and describe the sorts of project organizations which exist in the current marketplace. Finally, we give a skills checklist to help you to assess your strengths and identify the areas of the book which will be most relevant for you.

We will start by looking at the capabilities which a good project manager should have.

1.2 THE CAPABILITIES OF A PROJECT MANAGER

Which capabilities does a project manager need in order to do his or her job effectively? In this section we offer our view; see if you agree with us.

Project managers are, above all, *problem owners*: they have a strong sense of personal responsibility which enables them to confront problems with persistence, assertiveness and courage. They accept that their job is complete only when the business objectives have been achieved.

Project managers create, maintain and communicate an *overview* of the project whatever its technical, commercial or contractual complexity. More skills-oriented colleagues will get distracted by the excitement of producing technical marvels; the good project manager stays focused on the end target.

To maintain the overview the project manager must be able to *abstract key ideas* and information from the contributions of others. He or she is not afraid to ask the 'simple' questions in order to get to the heart of the problem. Moreover, he or she will also be prepared to dive into details if these are required for an important technical decision.

Project managers must be able to live with (and even enjoy!) *tensions*. They will face conflict continuously and will often be under pressure to come to a decision quickly. The project manager must continuously strive for the 'win–win' outcomes which reconcile the needs of all parties. At the same time he or she must be prepared to make realistic 'trade-offs' in order to maintain progress: a difficult balancing act.

The team must have faith in the project manager. This is an area of concern especially for the younger project managers who will need to build credibility with their staff. We suggest that the project manager must reach his or her staff first as human beings before attempting to reach them as professionals.

The project manager is dependent on the skills of the team, and must know how to use and develop those skills. This is another balancing act: on the one hand, the project manager must hold realistic expectations, on the other, he or she must *focus on the individual's current and potential strengths* rather than on weaknesses and past failures.

Staff development is often the key to staff loyalty. The project manager should be *generous* with his or her time and expertise: not easy when you are under pressure. The project manager must understand that the more you teach others, the more you learn and develop yourself.

The project manger should have a strong intuitive sense of the progress of his or her team. One project manager described this as '*the third ear*', which is tuned into the team as a '*super-organism*'. Ordinary ears are for careful listening to the individuals; the 'third ear' hears when the team energy is dropping and signals the project manager to intervene and revitalize the team.

The project manager must be able to build *a network of constructive relationships* with all the key people associated with the project, and in particular the users, the client organization and the project manager's own line management.

The final and perhaps the most difficult quality to acquire is a *healthy level of self-esteem*. A high (but realistic) sense of self-esteem is a vital ingredient which gives people the strength to take the necessary risks in life in order to face challenges – even with a smile!

You can probably think of other qualities and capabilities to add to the list and you may not agree with all that we have written here. Moreover, no one will have all these qualities in abundance – so much depends on the personal style and on the project and organization. Nevertheless, we assert that project managers should be working towards acquiring this as a 'mind set'.

1.3 WHY THIS BOOK IS FOR YOU

Our approach

Successful project managers need a very broad range of managerial, technical and interpersonal skills which they have to use in combination in their daily work. Most books focus on only one aspect of these skills, and few project managers have the time or energy at the end of the day to read all the literature and to select the relevant ideas.

In this book we have done our best to provide you with an *integrated approach*, which offers you insights, ideas and suggestions for the most critical areas of managerial and interpersonal skills. The chapters follow a roughly chronological sequence, starting with planning and ending with project close-down. In practice, however, many processes run in parallel (you will be building your team at the same time as you are working through the planning process, for instance) and so we have dovetailed the more 'technical' chapters with the chapters on people management.

Each chapter invites you to step back from your day-to-day routine and check *why* you should be focusing on this particular aspect of project management, so that you can put activities into context. The detailed suggestions we offer are intended as examples rather than as 'cookbook recipes'. Once you understand why you are doing something (or why you are supposed to be doing it!) you can select for yourself the approaches and techniques which best fit your style and the way you like to run your projects.

How you can use this book

Terms such as 'user' and 'client' can mean different things in different parts of the Information Technology (IT) industry, particularly if you are working in a large organization where these relationships can become very complex. We will define how we use these terms throughout the book, and then explain how you can use the book in different ways according to your role in your organization. Our definition of the relationship between the user, the client and the supplier is shown in Fig. 1.1.

Throughout the book we use the concept of 'client' to mean the part of the user organization which is responsible for delivering value from the investment that has been made in your project. This concept of how to deliver value is currently attracting much attention and debate in organizations with large IT departments with very big budgets. We use the term 'user' to mean the end user – the people or part of the organization who will make use of the system so that the organization as a whole will get the business benefits from the investment.

The user and the client are usually in different parts of the same corporation. In a large organization, for instance, there could be a supplier, or development department which produces the delivery, perhaps with the help of external suppliers such as systems houses.

We have written this book primarily though not exclusively for project managers who are responsible for supplying the system in accordance with the client's specifications. The project managers could be working for an external organization such as a systems house, or for a development group inside the client organization. In either case, they will be using the skills described here to enable their team (and perhaps their subcontractors and other partners) to deliver the system. When we talk about the project manager's 'line

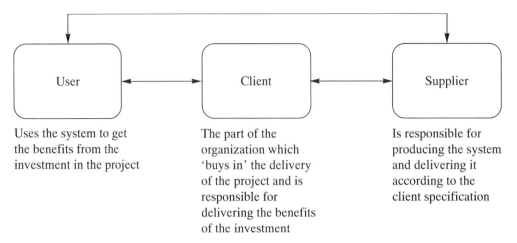

Figure 1.1   The relationship between the user, the client and the supplier.

management', we mean the managers who are responsible for that project manager's employment contract and for the development of his or her career.

Much of the focus of the book is on the relationship between development project managers and their client and end-user organization. We hope therefore that you will also find the ideas expressed here useful if you are managing a project from the client's standpoint – looking at the relationship from the other side of the fence. Similarly, if you are a user this book will help you to understand the work of your development colleagues, and give some suggestions on how you can best work with them to achieve your goals.

1.4 PROJECTS AND PROJECT ORGANIZATIONS

What is a project?

A project is any activity with a defined scope of requirements, time scale and budget. This is a broad definition but many projects which face difficulties tend to be unclear in one or more of these parameters.

Organizations generally set up projects when they are faced with challenges that fall outside their normal stream of activities: activities with which the existing organization cannot deal without a change to the organization itself. Changes to the organization may be the answer if the activity to be undertaken is a permanent feature; otherwise a project team or a task force is set up to carry out the activity. The project team or the task force is then dismantled and absorbed back into the organization when the project is completed.

Terms like 'task force' originated in the military world. Military organizations have relatively fixed structures which are often faced with 'tasks' that need to be carried out by dedicated resources which are borrowed, from different parts of the organization, for the duration of the task. Once the task is completed the resources are returned to their more permanent owners. This temporary organization, or project, is managed by a task leader or a project manager.

In the commercial community, enterprises evolved and developed their own core business, building internal specializations with varying degrees of dependence on each other. This interdependence encouraged the idea of projects to spread like wildfire. Organizations can now be set up in the form of project organizations involving internal and external experts. These project organizations can be dismantled when the project objectives are achieved. Sometimes whole projects are carried out by external resources hired in for the duration of the project under various types of commercial and contractual constructions.

When the specialist skills required are not readily available in the buying organization a set of requirements in the common business language will be defined. The first task of the specialist organization is to translate this set of requirements into technical specifications and designs which enable the specialists to deliver the required product. This model is very common in the IT industry.

Types of project organizations

There are two key aspects of project organizations: the way the project organization fits in with the overall organization of the user and the other suppliers involved in the project, and the organization within the project itself.

We will look first at the way the project fits into the overall organization. Team members in project teams usually belong to different business or functional units or departments where they report to their line manager. For the duration of the project, these team members may report on their activities in the project to their line manager, project manager or to both.

When team members report to their line managers only, as in the matrix type of organization, there is no clear single point of control over the project. When team members report to the project manager only for the duration of the project, such project managers will have full control over the resources within the project and over the way they are used. This is the task force model. Various hybrids of these two types of organizations also exist with corresponding advantages and disadvantages.

In this book, when we talk about a project manager we mean *someone who has full control over the resources in his or her own project*. Reporting on any part of the project to the outside world, in this type of project, takes place exclusively through the project manager.

In a typical project organization in the automation industry we expect to see the following roles:

- Project manager
- Technical manager
- Integration manager
- Team leaders
- Administration manager/assistant
- Team members

We will now identify the functions which are performed under each one of these roles. Depending on the complexity of the project, more than one role may be played by one person while in other cases more than one person may be needed for a single role.

The project manager

The project manager is the person who is responsible for ensuring that all necessary actions are carried out to achieve the project objectives within time and budget, to the required quality standards and to the client's satisfaction. One of the first and most crucial tasks the project manager does is to produce a plan, including a quality plan, which identifies and schedules the resources that are needed to complete those actions. The plan is then agreed with the rest of the project team, with higher management and with the customer. This plan will form the frame of reference against which the project manager monitors progress and reports to the outside world. Other aspects and functions of project management will be covered briefly in the later parts of this chapter.

A project manager can be a very senior appointment, as in the case of large and complex projects, or it can be a technical supervision task for a well-defined activity with a well-defined product and a process to arrive at that product. One of the difficulties project managers have is that virtually anybody can be called project manager: this is why the term is over-used worldwide. This difficulty is not unique to project managers since titles like engineer, consultant or even manager tend to get over-used the world over. When we use the term 'project manager' in this book we are referring to someone with a professional discipline, a wide range of skills and a firm commitment to achieving the business objectives of the project.

Technical manager

The technical manager is the person responsible for some or all of the technical and quality matters in the project. Typically, the technical manager is responsible for ensuring that specifications and designs are produced that will meet the customer's needs and requirements.

Integration manager

This is the person responsible for ensuring that the various parts produced in the project are integrated into a working whole. This person often takes the responsibility for configuration, version and documentation control in the project, possibly with a dedicated team set up for this purpose.

Team leaders

These are individuals who are responsible for managing the work within a pre-designated part of the project. Team leaders are responsible for supervising members within their teams.

Administration assistant

This role becomes significant in large and complex projects. Whether or not the role is fulfilled by an experienced administrator, from outside the project, will depend on the personalities, experience and styles in the project team.

Team members

These are individuals who have specific well-defined tasks to accomplish.

1.5 SELF-ASSESSMENT – WHAT SKILLS DO YOU NEED TO DEVELOP?

Good project managers have a sound, realistic appreciation of the skills which they bring to the job. If you are clear both about your strengths and your weaknesses, you can:

- Find your position in teams easily.
- Build self-esteem in yourself and others.
- Increase your resistance to stress.
- Organize your self-development efficiently.
- Succeed in your assignments.

You will also be able to set up teams in such a way that you capitalize on your strengths and compensate for your weaknesses. This increases productivity and gives other team members a chance to demonstrate and use their capabilities.

The self-assessment process depends on two main sources:

- *Self-perception* your own honest analysis of past and current experiences, in the context of your future aspirations
- *Feedback from others* unbiased, constructive information and opinions from your managers, your clients, team members, colleagues and perhaps family and friends.

If your organization has an effective appraisal system, then you may simply refer back to recent appraisal reports. If you have not had a structured appraisal recently then we suggest that you read the following checklist to see if there are particular areas of skills which you feel you need to develop.

The checklist below addresses some of the key areas of the project manager's task. Can you answer a confident 'yes' to all the questions? If you have any hesitations, you will find suggestions for tackling these areas and other related topics in this book.

1. *Planning* Do you allow enough time for the planning process? Do you fully understand the purpose of your project? Do you think your project through to the end? Do you break down tasks into smaller ones?
2. *Estimating* Do you have a clear estimating methodology? Can you use estimating tools and techniques? Can you assess project risks at the estimating stages?
3. *Relationships* Are you able to build constructive relationships with all the key people associated with your project – especially your client, your line management and your users?
4. *Team building* Are you able to select team members to get a balanced team with a range of technical and personal skills? Can you develop team spirit?
5. *Delegation* Are you able to develop your staff through wise and carefully planned delegation? Are you able to delegate without 'dumping' or being overly controlling?

6. *Motivation* Are you able to recognize and develop your staff's individual strengths, so that they perform to the best of their ability?

7. *Meetings* Can you get a lot done in meetings? Do staff come out of your meetings feeling more enthusiastic than when they went in? Can you create a constructive 'team culture'?

8. *Monitoring and control* Do you have a reliable system which is consistently implemented? Do you always know what your team members are doing? Are you able to help them effectively when they get into difficulties?

9. *Feedback on performance* Can you give feedback in a way that motivates your team members to improve, without causing offence?

10. *Reporting* Do you know when to ask your manager for help? Do you know how much information he or she needs?

11. *Quality* Are you able to build a quality system which is simple, workable and effective? Can you use quality procedures to motivate your staff and create an inspiring 'quality culture'?

12. *Coaching* Are you able to help your staff to develop their skills with a structured approach?

13. *Counselling* Can you help your team members when they come to you with personal or work-related problems that are affecting their performance?

14. *Influencing* Are you able to 'sell' your good ideas effectively? Are you confident about your use of presentations, reports and meetings to influence others?

15. *Conflict handling* Are you able to reach consensus in groups? Can you reconcile different positions and expectations – with your client, your team and your own manager?

16. *Priority setting* Can you balance long-term goals with short-term objectives? Can you organize your day? Are you able to prioritize and make effective decisions when you are under pressure?

17. *Stress management* Are you able to spot signs of stress in yourself and your staff? Do you have your own strategies for dealing with stress so that it works for you, not against you?

18. *Managing risks* Do you know how to cope with tight time scales, user expectations and performance problems?

19. *Integration* Can you maintain momentum at the closing stages of the project? Are you able to integrate your products successfully into the user organization?

20. *Project close-down* Can you close projects in an orderly, stress-free manner? Are you able to plan future needs of the user, after you have your products? Are you organized enough to document the lessons and help your team to learn from their experiences on the project?

21. *Planning your career* Have you developed a clear vision of where you are going in your organization? Do you feel satisfied and happy in your job?

More detailed checklists for each subject area and each chapter can be found in the Appendix.

1.6 A ROUTE MAP FOR THE BOOK

If you can see straightaway that there is a particular area which you would like to read more about in this book here is an idea of how you can access information quickly.

Chapters 2 (Planning), 3 (Estimating), 4 (Project set-up) and 5 (team building) are particularly relevant if you are currently setting up a project – either as a project manager or as a line manager.

Chapters 5 (Team building), 6 (Staying on track), 8 (Coaching and counselling), 9 (Influencing and conflict handling) and 10 (Managing yourself) cover the 'people side' of management and are therefore of general interest to anyone responsible for running a team.

Chapters 6 (Staying on track) and 7 (The fundamentals of quality) are particularly relevant if you are now half-way through your project and interested in how to achieve high performance. If you are worried about progress on your project, you may also want to read Chapter 2 on planning.

Chapters 11 (Managing common risks), 12 (The finishing touches) and 13 (Project close-down) focus on the often-neglected final stages of a project, so if you want to maintain motivation and momentum or if you are currently bringing your project to a close you may like to scan those chapters first.

Chapter 14 (Planning your career) is a chapter written from the heart, especially for project managers but also for line managers who are wondering whether to switch to project management or who are working with project managers on their career development.

In the next chapter we are going to tackle one of the most difficult and important areas of project management – project planning.

2

PLANNING

2.1 INTRODUCTION

The reasons for planning

Planning is a crucial aspect of projects and project management. It is the means we employ to work out how we will achieve the project objectives, who will help us to achieve them and by when and for how much. Planning is also the means to identify the project risks and to be prepared to deal with them. It is our chance to create or ask for the conditions and circumstances that we and our team need to do the job well and with a smile. Partnership (with our management, the client and all those involved in the project), a clear project vision and a fired-up team are healthy indicators of effective and successful planning.

Planning will help you to stay in control. A plan helps you to stick to priorities, use your resources, stay on schedule. When you and your team get tired, a plan acts as a simple reminder of what you should do next. If you plan ahead you will create for yourself the mental and emotional space to cope with some of the problems which inevitably crop up unexpectedly; this reduces unnecessary stress for all the parties concerned. Your plan will enable you to demonstrate progress, and that keeps everyone motivated. And the very process of planning builds cooperation.

What should a plan cover? The details will depend on the complexity of your particular project, but a project plan has to answer, as a minimum, the following questions in the following sequence:

- The 'why?' question: the purpose of your project, the objectives and the criteria for success

- The 'what?' question: the scope of the project – the products, services, etc. which you are required to deliver
- The 'how?' question: the description of the process to make the product. This is sometimes called the methodology
- The 'who?' question: the project organization and the key skills needed
- The 'how much?' question: the project budget
- The 'when?' question: the time scales.

Summary

A plan enables you to:

- Verify that what you have been asked to do is feasible.
- Set priorities and stick to them.
- Form a partnership with the other stakeholders in the project.
- Understand risks and plan for them.
- Create and maintain the 'big picture'.
- Identify the skills and the kind of organization you need to do the job.
- Answer the questions why, what, how, who, how much and when.

The process is just as important as the document.

Paul was excited when his line manager asked him to take over a client's $4 million project to build a warehouse control system. Since his last project had ended he had been reading documentation in the office, and was feeling more than ready for a challenge. The manager told him that the project was in trouble; the client had asked for the previous project manager to be removed following an audit. The client thought that the project was about 50 per cent complete – but when the line manager had politely questioned him further, the client admitted that he had no evidence to back up his assumptions. So Paul was alert for problems when he went along for his first meeting at the client's site.

'I asked about the project plan – it seemed the logical place to start! Eventually, someone in the team rooted out a single sheet of paper. On the paper was a bar schedule, and a handwritten paragraph referring to a specification document. "Is this it?" I asked. "I assume so," said the team member, "We didn't even know it existed." Neither did the client.'

Paul's next step was to find the audit report. By this time he was not surprised to read the following conclusions.

- The scope of the project was not defined.
- No formal project organization existed.
- Project status reporting was in the form of memoranda which were *ad hoc* in terms of frequency and reporting agenda.
- No completion criteria existed for any of the project activities or products.

He was going to have more than his fair share of challenges for some time: the project was completely out of control.

The barriers to planning

So why is it that some managers fail to plan – or fail to plan adequately? One reason is the time pressure which they come under at the start of the project, when they are being required to do so many things in parallel, such as recruiting staff into the project, positioning the project in the organization, defining the scope and agreeing the budget. Under such pressure planning can go to the bottom of the pile.

Another reason is that the very process of producing the planning document can seem complicated and bewildering. People get confused by trying to plan at too detailed a level when the necessary information is still not available to anybody. Even if you have standards to follow it can be difficult. Here is a case from a senior line manager, who had been asked to help Patricia, a junior project manager who had run into problems on her first real project.

She was two months into the project but was not producing anything – there was no sign of measurable progress. My task was to review the project and help her get it back on track.

I asked Patricia for the plan – which she produced rather hesitantly. 'I got stuck,' she explained. 'I tried to follow the company guidelines, but I couldn't get past the Methodology section. And then everything started piling up on me.' By that time she was in a vicious circle: the more time pressure she was under, the more she was reacting rather than planning, and the less progress she made.

We sorted the problem in two days. I worked through the planning document with her, and explained that it was the process, not the paperwork, which was important. She started to cheer up. Once she'd made a plan she could believe in, she quickly got her project back under control, and she completed it successfully.

Patricia was lucky to get support – perhaps a little late, but still in time to learn and recover the situation. Some organizations cannot offer this kind of help because they do not have a 'project culture' which encourages and insists on project planning. This can be another reason for the reluctance of certain project managers to plan.

Other organizations might emphasize the plan but, like Patricia, overlook the importance of the planning process. The main objective of planning is not to produce a document and simply file it. We have seen projects with beautiful, elaborate plans which have been carefully stored as works of art, certainly never to be defiled by updates. Plans made in isolation and locked in cupboards do not help anybody, least of all the project manager. The objective of planning is to find the answers for the main planning questions and we can only do that if we consciously go through a well-thought-out planning process.

Summary

Project managers often fail to plan adequately when they:

- Feel under time pressure
- Don't understand the benefits of planning

- Don't understand how to produce a plan
- Get overwhelmed by the activities at the start of a project
- Are not supported by their organization
- Work in isolation, and file the plan away.

2.2 THE TWO STAGES OF PLANNING

Planning is essentially an iterative process. When you begin, you can't know whether what you have been asked to do is feasible – you can only feel confident that it's feasible when you have actually completed the planning process. This is essentially the barrier Patricia encountered – where on earth do you start?

The approach we recommend is that you divide the planning process into two stages. The purpose of the first stage is to help you to form a rough picture of how you're going to approach the project and broadly the kind of organization and staffing profile you will need. To draw this picture you have to assume that the scope, budget and time scale you've been given are feasible.

The second stage is to take this picture and to work out in detail how you're going to run the project, how much it's going to cost and when you're going to deliver. If you're lucky, these outputs from Stage 2 will match the assumptions you made in Stage 1. Normally, however, life is not that easy, and they won't match. The rest of this chapter explains how to produce the overall plan (Stage 1), how to produce the detailed plan (Stage 2) and how to reconcile the almost inevitable discrepancies.

A general overview of the process is shown in Fig. 2.1. Where you start in this cycle will depend on your current situation. You may simply want to get a feel for how much a project would cost, in which case you would do a quick estimate by comparing it to a similar project that has been completed recently. You may be asking management for a budget because of a major change in your project or you may be assessing how to deliver within predefined budgetary and time-scale constraints. In all these cases you will be going around this cycle although you may be starting at different points in it.

Note that we are talking only about planning. Scheduling, which is working out the timings of the project activities, will be covered in Chapter 3.

2.3 OVERALL PLANNING

Check the purpose of your project – ask *why?*

Overall planning starts with the definition of the purpose of the project. Why is your project in existence? Why have your stakeholders approved the budget, and made other resources available to you? These may seem very obvious questions, but many project managers fail at the outset to set their project in a meaningful wider context – and this can cause considerable problems later.

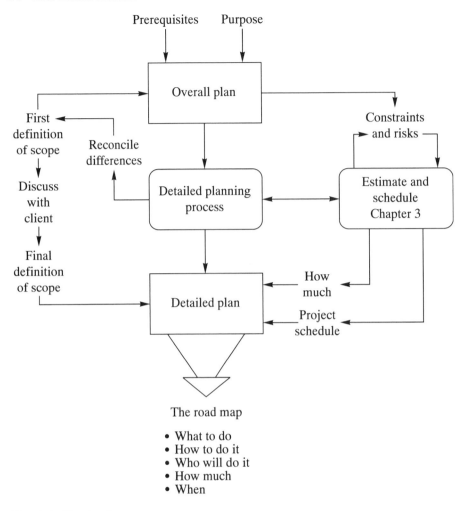

Figure2.1   The planning process.

I was working on a tank farm project some years ago. My starting point was a ten-page Requirement Specification, which described the ways of estimating the amount of oil in the tanks, the problems caused by inaccurate measurements, the methods for checking that the flow was balanced, and some information about an algorithm used to correct errors in the flow metering equipment. Right at the end of the document was a short section describing the reports which the operators had to produce.

It was all interesting stuff. I had a team of very bright programmers, and we sat down to plan. We worked out that we would need to put a lot of effort into the user interface, because this was to be screen-based for the first time. We'd also need some sort of database, and some way of pulling in the algorithm and picking up the measurements. It was technically challenging – just what my team enjoyed.

How did it work out in the end? It was a nightmare. The technical problems were enormous – we'd been far too ambitious. At first that didn't put us off; we worked evenings, weekends, you name it. And do you know what I found out in the end? The *whole purpose* of that system was to produce those reports – they didn't need all the advanced technology which we'd sweated to produce. They had redesigned the operators' jobs, because they didn't have the time or the working space to produce the reports by hand.

When I look back on it I wonder why I didn't *talk* more to the client at the start. Of course, my manager made the same mistake – and I still see project managers now who dive into technical details and miss the point. The advice I give them now is simple – don't start planning until you know the client's answers to three questions:

- Where is the money for the project coming from?
- Where will you get the payback?
- What return does your organization expect to get on your investment?

If I'd asked those questions myself I'd have found out what the real purpose of the project was – and saved myself a great deal of worry.

Resist the temptation to take a worm's-eye view of your project. Step back from the technical details, get away from your desk and start asking questions. Otherwise you run the risk of producing a system which no-one will thank you for later.

All projects have a context. Perhaps yours is one of a number of projects, which are coordinated to produce a bigger end result. You need to understand the interface between your project and the others. If you don't identify the context early you probably won't have the energy, the opportunity or the inclination to do so later.

So ask your stakeholders why your project has been set up; check with your line manager, your client, the users, and anyone else who can help you to gain a proper insight. Be alert for the hidden agendas – the personal motives, the political background which can play a determining role in the success of your project. Often if you invest time early in the project in friendly, informal relationships as well as in your formal professional relationships, you can pick up clues to the real objectives and the criteria by which your client will truly judge your project. Here is another example of the importance of checking all the agendas – including the hidden ones.

My job was to deliver a system within six months, to coincide with the opening of the client's new building. He told me that it was crucial that we should stick to the time scale, because if the building were left empty that would be very costly to his organization. My relationship with him was very formal, and he wasn't an easy man to chat to, but I didn't worry about that at the time because I was rushed off my feet pulling together a number of projects which had not been well coordinated.

My team were working very hard trying to meet the deadlines. Suddenly I heard from someone else in the client organization that the opening of the new building had been delayed by three months. We were all delighted – now we would have some valuable breathing space. I went off to the next meeting all prepared to propose how we could make the best use of the extra time.

I was very taken aback when my proposal was met with an icy response. 'I told you you had to meet the deadline, and nothing has changed,' was the message. I couldn't understand it – his reaction just didn't seem to make sense.

Later I discovered that his reputation was on the line – and that had nothing to do with the opening date for the building. The shareholders in his organization had given him an ultimatum – either he got the project in on time or his career was finished. Of course, he would never have told me that in so many words, but there were enough rumours floating around: trouble was, I was so busy with the project that I didn't listen to them. We got there in the end, because the team worked so hard, but I'll be more careful with those hidden agendas next time round.

Understanding the 'why' gives you a basis for making sensible trade-offs later in the project, if you need to choose between the classic requirements of staying within budget, to specification and within the allotted time scale. If you don't fully understand the context, you may make a proposal which does not meet with enthusiasm from your client.

Your description of the context is an essential part of the briefing and induction of your team and your management. It will enable you to gain wider support within your organization. For that reason you need to write it down, and perhaps convert it into overhead slides, in anticipation of meetings where you will want to communicate it as clearly as possible. The context will form an important part of what we call the 'big picture', and you will update it as you progress through the project.

The context is also the broad framework within which you will start to specify the objectives for your project. The more precise you can make these objectives, the easier you will find it to complete the planning process. The SMART acronym can be a helpful tool here; formulate the objectives so that they are:

*S*pecific
*M*easurable
*A*chievable
*R*easonable
*T*ime-based

In your discussions with your client, check that you have defined as many as possible of the delivery criteria. Some of these will be specific measures, others may be more subjective. If you have the patience and the communication skills to identify the more subjective criteria, you may also pick up clues about the hidden agendas.

Here is a list of questions which can help you to pin down the purpose:

- Who are the key stakeholders – the people who stand to gain or lose most by this project?
- Where has the budget come from?
- Why have the stakeholders invested in the project?
- What do they expect to get out of it?
- What are the key business, organizational and political issues at stake here?
- How does my project fit in with other projects?
- How does it fit into the overall purpose?
- What are my priority objectives?
- What could be sacrificed if we had to make trade-offs?
- How will all the different stakeholders measure the success of this project?

Prerequisites and external risks

At the beginning of any project you would be asked to achieve a set of objectives and deliver the products within given budgetary and time-scale constraints. Beware not to take the responsibility for every factor which is critical to your project success! Some of these factors will be partly or wholly outside your control and you will need to negotiate with your 'external environment' (your client, your own organization and other suppliers) to make sure that they have accepted their responsibility for their part of your project. Before you agree to deliver within these constraints you should analyse the environment of the project to identify the following planning elements (see Fig. 2.2):

- Prerequisites and conditions that must be satisfied by other people outside your team
- Risks, which tend to fall into two categories – prerequisites and conditions that may not be satisfied and likely events that will disrupt the progress of the project (e.g. a key member of your team falling ill)
- Exclusions, by which we mean the objectives, deliverables or actions that the outside world may expect to be part of the project and which we want to keep explicitly outside the scope of our project because we have no control over them or because they are not feasible within the given constraints.

A useful outcome of this environment analysis is an identification of the project's friends and opponents. Having this information will help you define strategies to obtain resources and skills outside the project team. This is particularly important in large organizations where the project is dependent on departments and teams which don't fall under your control. Environment analysis can be represented as in Fig. 2.2.

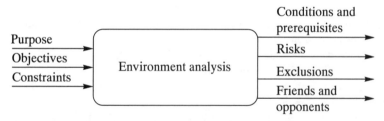

Figure 2.2 Project environment analysis.

As we pointed out earlier, the process of defining these elements is an iterative one. The outputs may lead to tuning of the inputs until stability and agreements are reached between the project team and the client and management.

Identify the production process – ask *how* and *who*

Sit with your team, and explore the concept of your project as a production process. Be prepared to take a couple of hours over this. If you get stuck, invite a colleague to join the brainstorming process until you can identify all the production process elements:

- The final products
- The semi-finished goods

- The process of making the products
- The completion criteria for the final product and for its individual components
- The machinery and tools needed to make the products
- Working practices and procedures
- Tools and procedures to monitor and control the quality in the production processes.

Defining the production process is the answer to the 'how' question.

At this stage you must plan the integration of the semi-finished goods at a high-level to form your delivered system. We will describe the integration planning in more detail in the next section.

Pay particular attention to the people side of your production process:

- The organization required
- The tasks of each team in the organization
- The interfaces of each team to other teams and to the outside world.

Use arrows in the organization diagram to indicate the formal communication lines within the project and between the project and the outside world. This approach will help you to assess the effectiveness of the communication of the project both internally and with the outside world. If you are not happy with the communication as represented by your diagram, reorganize the team.

You will now have answered in broad terms the 'who' question. The details of the specific individuals who will be assigned to specific tasks will be covered in the section on detailed planning.

Working on the 'how' and 'who' with your team offers a number of benefits:

- The process of talking about the product and the steps which you will need to follow helps you to identify the methodology.
- Because the team is involved in these discussions right from the start, they will have a much better joint understanding of the production process.
- Team members can identify for themselves the parts of the process which best match their personal strengths and technical skills.
- This information enables you as project manager to set up an appropriate project organization, making full use of the talents available within the team.
- You will be able to assess, at an early stage, the communication within the team.
- You will also be able to identify all you need, in terms of organizations and resources, to make the product or products.

Produce the overall plan and communicate it

You should now be ready with your team to produce a first overall plan. The main focus of this plan is the production process and the organization needed to achieve the objectives. The purpose of the plan is to set directions and define the vision of the project. Remember, at this stage we still do not have a detailed schedule or even a detailed definition of the scope of the project. Be creative: don't get unduly worried about the constraints you have to deal with. Even small improvements at this early stage will pay dividends later in the project. You must now start presenting your ideas to your team and the outside world. Be prepared to accept new ideas at this stage even if it means a drastic change to your own ideas.

Having written down the answers to the 'how' and the 'who' questions you may, depending on the time you have, proceed to produce other sections of the plan as described later in this chapter. The cost and time scale (schedule) sections can only be high level; more details are only possible when you have been through the estimating process. Now you must start sharing your ideas with all the relevant parties.

Consultation is an essential part of the planning process. You must get the agreement of the client, your project team and management on your ideas and approaches before you present them in writing. Project managers who confront their client with ideas which have not been carefully prepared will find their project and their relationship getting off to a shaky start. The exact style you adopt will depend on the personalities of the individuals concerned but in any case you should prepare your initial meetings carefully and ensure that they are lively and enthusiastic. Dull discussions produce dull results.

The planning process is your opportunity to build a *common vision* of the way forward. To do this you must work interactively and creatively with *all* the relevant parties on the project: the client, the team, the line managers, and potentially your subcontractors. The very process of planning helps you to build your team; the overall plan document produced should synthesize the key ideas of all involved. This requires considerable skill on the part of the project manager, who must be prepared to consult, negotiate, sell, explain and occasionally compromise, until all the different parties can come to clear agreements and hopefully a consensus.

When you have decided on your plan, distribute it quickly. Again, this will depend on the complexity of the project, but we suggest that the first version of the plan should be produced within one week from reaching agreement on the basic ideas. If it takes any longer then you may be trying to plan at too detailed a level too early in the project. Leave the detailed planning until a later stage, when the organization is well defined and you can plan interactively with your team.

Summary

Your overall plan:

- Must answer the 'how' and 'who' questions
- Identify the main project risks and prerequisites
- Must be discussed with all the relevant parties, right from the start
- Helps you to build a common vision via consensus
- Must be produced quickly.

Planning the system integration

Overall integration plans are produced early in the project and should concentrate mainly on defining the integration strategy. More detailed plans would be produced at later stages as the team gains more understanding of the system and the way it is going to be built. Some planning details can only be realistically defined close to the integration itself.

When the system integration is thought through well, at the beginning of the project, it will determine the order in which the system components will have to be manufactured. This is of particular importance for larger systems as integration often takes place in steps and with each step leading to a unique system baseline. The order in which baselines are delivered and the way they are incremented is determined by users' needs, availability of system components and the project's technical realities. When you define your integration strategy at the beginning of the project and have a clear plan of the way the system is going to be built you can save yourself and your team many of the unnecessary frustrations associated with integration at the end of the project.

We realized that the integration phase would make or break the project. By the time we had designed, coded and tested the software we would only have a few weeks for the total system integration which was hardly enough. We had to do something different, not follow the conventional integration lines to achieve our plan.

During the planning phase we appointed an experienced integration manager. His task was to ensure that the system was fully integrated and working by the given deadline! The first step he took was to define the integration strategy where he determined the order in which the main components of the system would have to be built and delivered to him. He effectively positioned himself as the client to the other team leaders in the team. In return, he would define the acceptance criteria for each part of the system which he agreed with the respective team leaders.

The planning phase became very interesting. The integration manager and I had to work very closely to ensure the feasibility of both the integration and production plans. The proposed integration strategy was that of continuous integration which meant that the system components would be integrated with the current baseline as they became ready. The integration team had to have a detailed knowledge of the internal working of the system to allow them to evaluate the various possible integration scenarios. This knowledge became more and more necessary as some planned scenarios became less likely, because the associated system components were delayed. In such cases we had to act quickly to keep the integration progressing, by proposing alternative scenarios to minimize the impact on the overall schedule. We went on swapping and changing integration scenarios until the final objectives were achieved.

Planning the integration early in the project was one of the main reasons this project succeeded against the odds.

2.4 DETAILED PLANNING

Some people are good at overall planning but have more problems with the 'nuts and bolts' of detailed planning; others are good at the details but lack the overview. Perhaps you are one of the lucky few who can manage both! We have covered the overview in the previous sections, so for those readers who are not sure how to progress from here, we now offer our suggestions for the step-by-step production of a plan.

Different levels of plans

Embarking upon a project is like starting upon a journey you have not done before. Your destination and the expected time of arrival may have already been decided for you and now you need to decide the means of getting there. You have a set of constraints such as the amount of money you can spend, the latest time of arrival or the means of transport that are available to you. You then consider the risks such as the traffic conditions and the likelihood of breaking down.

Suppose you decide to take your car and drive it yourself. You would start planning the route to get there by first identifying the main towns or cities you would go through. Then you would plan the exact turns and exits to take by consulting more detailed maps of the relevant places along the route. You would probably identify landmarks that would give you a quick check of your precise position.

The analogy is not perfect but you can see the need to have an overview as well as a detailed plan, and the need to identify landmarks. You can also imagine the complex interactions between the time and the cost consideration in making decisions on how you get to your destination. When you make these decisions, risks and constraints play an important role. Planning a project is very often much more complex partly because the choices you make are dependent on those made by your management, the client or your team.

A common planning problem in projects which are large or complex, or very fast moving, is the difficulty in producing plans to cover the activities at the lowest levels. Sometimes the plans cannot keep up with the changes; sometimes you may find that the information needed for planning at the lowest level is available only within the production teams. The result is that your plans may be already out of date by the time they are produced and this will have a detrimental effect on the credibility of the plans and the team's motivation.

The head of the snake

The answer is to produce a high-level plan and get the team's commitment to it. This high-level plan is what a senior project manager called the 'head of the snake', because a snake's head continues in a straight line while the body moves all over the place.

Your high-level plans may contain very large work packages (e.g. several hundred person-days or more) at the lowest level. This plan will act like the high-level map which shows the main routes in a book of road maps. If you want to see more detail of your route you need to look inside the book!

This way of planning will also help you to organize your delegation better. Very large work packages may represent projects in their own right, delegated to your team leaders who have the responsibility for planning the package and keeping it under control. The team leaders should produce their own detailed plans for these work packages including monitoring and control mechanisms that clearly relate to your high-level plan.

When you start the detailed planning phase check you don't get bogged down; remember the head of the snake! The production of a detailed project plan encompasses a number of steps, which are summarized in Fig. 2.3. The rest of this chapter will describe each part of this model in some detail, but the following are some general points.

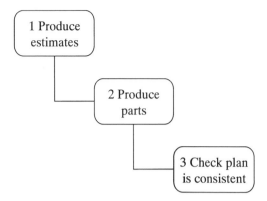

Figure2.3   Stages in the detailed planning.

Produce estimates

Armed with the outputs of the overall planning, you can start estimating. Estimating is a large topic, and we cover it in the following chapter, in order not to lose track here of the overall planning process. When you have completed your estimates, you will have the following:

- The project baseline and the agreed scope of supply
- The production process description
- The organization
- The cost estimates
- The effort estimates
- The risk analysis
- Prerequisites
- Contingency estimates.

If these elements are not available, *stop*! Don't go any further until you can convince yourself that you can do the job with confidence.

Produce the parts of the plan

Get your team members involved early in producing different parts of the plan themselves, according to their skills and expertise. Early delegation will help you to get their commitment to the completed plan. In larger projects, team leaders or managers will be responsible for planning their parts of the project, and then the problem is more how to coordinate the process so that it does not become too compartmentalized.

What should the plan look like? Here we give an overview of what each section should cover.

A summary and introduction

This should define the context of the project and the position of the plan in the planning hierarchy (see later in this chapter). The introductory section should also present the plan revision history and future revisions as well as the related documents.

The scope of the project and its objectives

This should define what to deliver and when; it is the key part of the plan, and must be expressed very clearly in terms that the various parties involved will easily understand. Use active verbs in formulating the project objectives and the project success criteria, for example:

1. Produce a functional specification using the User Requirement Specification, reference CQM0302.04, dd.mm.yy as a baseline. The document to be agreed with the client no later than dd.mm.yy.
2. Deliver a system acceptance plan and specification, to the user department, for comments, by dd.mm.yy.
3. Deliver the user-accepted software for final integration in the production process by dd.mm.yy.

This section should also define the prerequisites and conditions that must be satisfied to achieve the project objectives. Take particular care to remain positive and constructive; your users and management will not be happy if you define conditions that are impossible to satisfy. If you have such a case then you may have a risk that is impossible to manage.

Define the project exclusions. Again you must be constructive; don't exclude a product that the users need. The estimating activity (Chapter 3) should provide you with a realistic list of exclusions.

The methodology

Many methodologies are available on the market with exotic names that undoubtedly serve a purpose in the right circumstances, and may even be mandatory in your own or the client's organization. A methodology, in our view, should be expressed in simple terms which everyone connected with the project can understand. For instance, the methodology for producing a document may read as follows:

> The production of the document will be divided into three phases. Phase 1 is the planning and set-up; the main outputs from this phase will be the project plan, the acquisition of all the relevant documents and a meeting schedule with the users and others. Phase 2 is when the bulk of the work will be carried out. Each individual part of the document will be produced, quality controlled and agreed within the team and with the user. The individual parts of the document will be integrated, in phase 3, into one document. The main objective of the integration activity is to ensure that the individual parts that have been individually produced are consistent with each other. The integrated document will be reviewed internally within the project team against the quality criteria defined in the quality plan. The fully reviewed and internally agreed document will be presented to the client for comments and final approval.

In practice, some of these phases and some of the activities within them may be described in much more detail in order to avoid potential misunderstanding at later stages in the project. Remember to discuss and agree this and other sections of your plan with all the relevant parties.

The organization

This part of the plan should answer the specifics of the 'who' question by describing the project organization which includes the client, other suppliers, the subcontractors (where applicable) and the interfaces to the outside world. You should describe the functions identified in the project organization, giving the main tasks per function and the interfaces to the other functions.

This section should also provide information on the project staffing profile from start to finish. This information is needed by your line or functional management so that they can make allowances for current and future project needs. The project staffing profile also helps you to keep track of your staffing needs as the project progresses through its various phases.

Quality

The project plan should define the general principles of quality application in the project such as the overall criteria, quality control, completion criteria and product certification. Depending on the type and complexity of the project, a separate quality plan may be produced to define other aspects such as the organization, standards and procedures. See Chapter 7 for more detail.

Monitoring and reporting

Here you define the way you will report on the progress of the project and the frequency of reporting. You should also define the structure you will use in your reports unless there is a common and well-understood reporting standard. You may also want to define the different levels of reporting, unless the report structure caters for different levels such as the team, the user and client management and the management of your own organization. In this part you should also define the regular project meetings such as weekly team leaders' meetings, fortnightly meetings with the client and monthly general meetings.

Progress reports should include a risk management update. The plan should define how the project is dealing with the risks identified in the project.

The monitoring mechanisms should also be defined in this part of the plan. Such mechanisms should help you to have the visibility and measurability you need to have a sense of where you are in the project You can read more on this in Chapter 6.

Documentation

The project documentation set should be carefully planned and well publicized within the project team at the beginning. If you do not do this in your plan you may get overwhelmed by the amounts of paper that accumulate very quickly, and you may have no space to store it. Bigger projects may be lucky enough to have an administration support who may help to keep some order around the project. However, most administrators do not have the project experience to assess the project filing needs and hence they are dependent on you to define your needs in terms of documentation storage and retrieval.

One of the main benefits of having an effective documentation set is that you will avoid duplication of parts of the set in your project. Duplication is a dangerous source of inconsistency, as well as being a waste of time, creativity and resources.

Check that you define the standard, format and layout of documents such as project reports and memoranda unless this is defined centrally in the organization. Include documentation control, configuration and release management procedures in this part of the plan.

Change control

Document and get agreement on the way in which changes to the scope or constraints on the project will be handled – how the change and its impact will be assessed and authorized.

Time scales

Most plans tend to concentrate on the time scales and ignore the other parts we have described here. In reality, without knowing the scope, the methodology, the organization and so on it is not possible to make realistic assessments of the project's time scales.

First, you have to decide what the major project milestones are. Starting with the project scope and supply and the project methodology, you should be able to make reasonable assessments of the major events and deliverables in the project. These points in the project may be selected to be the major milestones because they provide you and the outside world with tangible results that would allow you to measure progress in the project. You may want to associate other attributes with deliverables such as user acceptance and quality department sign-off or senior management approval and so on, to qualify them to be major milestones.

The other input you need for assessing the project time scales is the Work Breakdown Structure (WBS) which we describe in Chapter 3. The estimates you inherit from the estimation phase are often based on functional decomposition. At this stage of the project you need to produce a process-based WBS: instead of estimates against functional units you may want to break down the work into design, coding and testing work packages. Alternatively, in large projects, you may produce the first-level plan on the basis of the original functional decomposition and produce lower-level plans for each part of the project using other types of work breakdown.

Now that you have the WBS, milestones and estimates per work package you can produce the project schedule, in the form of network diagrams, bar charts or any other form you feel is suitable for the project and the parties involved in it.

Should you use one of the different types of project-scheduling packages available rather than non-automated methods such as the pencil and paper? The danger of starting with one of the packages is that they can swamp you with information. We have seen project managers feeding large volumes of numbers into these packages only to be confronted by tens of pages of information and thousands of numbers that are difficult to process. Here is a case to illustrate the point.

I was asked to review a project which the client suspected was not under control. This was a four-man project which was scheduled to finish within 8 months. I walked into the meeting room where I had agreed to meet the project manager and was surprised to find him putting together a matrix of four by four of project schedules which he had just printed out. There were sixteen A4 sheets in total – certainly impressive!

We discussed the intimidating-looking schedule for a while; I don't think either of us understood it. We then moved to the whiteboard. An hour later we agreed on a schedule fitting onto one side A4 – at that point we started making progress.

Don't get carried away by a package. Like any other tool, if you know what you are doing it can be useful, but it will not do the job for you. We suggest that you first produce a schedule using the tried-and-tested pencil and paper, and then use the sophisticated scheduling packages to produce a neat presentation of the schedule, and as a means of cross-checking. You can use a package to test your 'what if?' questions, for instance. It will also help you to plan the project hierarchically, so that you can produce many schedules. The highest level will be the master schedule which may have been produced during the overall planning stage. The master schedule will be broken down into many lower-level schedules each giving the details of one portion in the master schedule. Some scheduling packages maintain the relationship between these various levels of schedules.

Cost plan

When you take over a project you agree explicitly or implicitly to achieve the project objectives within the three constraints of the scope, time scale and budget. These are the three classical project goals. We have already dealt with the first two; now we deal with the budget.

This part of the plan should document the project budget and how you plan to spend this budget. Where relevant, it should also define an invoicing plan, relating as closely as possible to the project milestones and to the contract, if you have one. If you are using a project-scheduling tool you may want to use the extensive facilities available within these tools to plan and track your project charges and invoicing.

Success party

Don't forget to plan how you will celebrate the end of the project. Present it as the party to celebrate your success and advertise it in advance. In this section you should also plan other project close-down actions such as staff reviews, clearing the project area, archiving project documentation and documenting the lessons learned.

You may argue that a success party should be outside the scope of the project at least in the commercial sense, and you could well be right, depending on the particular situation your project is in. However, we see this as one of the things the project manager should do to focus the team's attention on the final objectives of the project which will bring real benefits in terms of motivation and commitment.

Risk analysis and contingency planning

We said earlier that scope definition must be accompanied by defining the project prerequisites, conditions and exclusions. Going through this exercise and carrying out structured estimating will help you make an adequate assessment of the project risks.

During the planning process you should separate the activities to cover these risks from the normal project activities. You should also plan how to monitor these risks and how to report to the outside world on the results of your monitoring. The objective is to eliminate or at least minimize the effect of these risks on the normal project activities. If these risks persist and develop into real problems for the project, requiring additional effort or materials to deal with their effect on the project, then you must dig into the budget you have reserved for this purpose.

We realize that this may demand additional discipline and perhaps additional administration, but we believe it is worth it in the long term. One very important benefit of this approach is the increase in your awareness and that of your team of the risks facing the project, and this contributes to better management and control of these risks.

Another form of contingency planning is the way you spend your project budget. Reserve some of your budget for unforeseen activities. We are not proposing that you should keep secrets from your team, but you may want simply to agree with them certain budgets for their respective parts and also, at the same time, procedures for making adjustments to these budgets. Perhaps you want to ask your team leaders to follow the same planning, risk analysis and contingency planning discipline we have described here. Chapter 11 also covers some techniques for managing the most common risks in IT projects.

Check that the plan is consistent

In this phase of the planning you bring the various components of the plan together to ensure internal consistency and common understanding of the people involved. In very small projects where the plans are simple documents produced by one individual, over a period of a few hours, this step may not be necessary although it is always a good discipline to stand back and review your plan before you present it to the outside world.

When you get your planning team together differences of perceptions will emerge. Resolving these differences at this early stage in the project will save a tremendous amount of time and energy later. Your team must be fully aligned at this stage with the overall project objectives, united by a common vision. Small differences at the early planning stage will be amplified with time if they are not recognized and dealt with within the team.

2.5 RECONCILIATION

The result of the planning would be a hierarchy of plans as shown in Fig. 2.4. Subplans will have been produced by different individuals or teams. Although the high-level plan should help to ensure that subplans are generally consistent with each other, nevertheless differences of perception or simple misunderstandings invariably arise and must be reconciled.

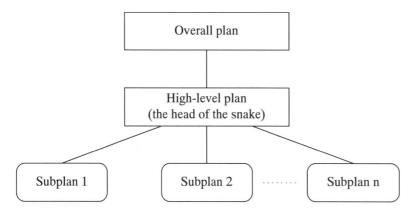

Figure2.4   Different levels of plans.

The process of reconciling can be difficult, but it is also an opportunity and a catalyst for team building at this early stage in the project. Don't become unduly worried about minor irritations, arguments and tension. They are part of the formation of a common vision and the creation of the super-organisms.

The most common area where reconciliation will be needed is the communication and boundaries between teams. Ideally, teams should have some overlap. If there is no overlap then this is an indication of no communication, while a high degree of overlap would lead to conflicts and disputes over areas of responsibilities. You may find the process we described in Sec. 2.3 a useful way to resolve this discrepancy.

Another common area for attention is that some products of some teams cannot be completed until products of other teams are finished. To resolve this conflict you will need to get a clear picture of where these products feed into each team's work. You will need discussion, negotiation and creative thinking to come up with resolutions that satisfy the project objectives defined in the higher-level plans.

The level of ambiguity that project managers may allow to exist during planning the lower activities, in complex and large projects, will depend on the experience of the team leaders. With more experienced team leaders you may allow a greater degree of ambiguity to exist which would save you time and will stimulate team building through working together to resolve these ambiguities.

Present and sell your plans outside your team

The essential final stage is to present your plan to all the parties concerned with your project and, in particular, the stakeholders as well as the critics of your project. Don't think that simply distributing it is the answer; you must check that all the key messages have been fully understood and accepted. Sell the ideas and solicit feedback from all relevant parties outside your team: your stakeholders as well as your project critics. Criticisms at this stage can enable you to take corrective actions; criticisms left unspoken can be much more dangerous for the project later.

Formal presentations can be very useful. Involve all the key players from inside and outside your project team. Prepare well – Chapter 9 contains suggestions for planning and delivering presentations. Encourage questions from your critics as well as your stakeholders. Stimulate discussion so that the audience gives you as much feedback as possible. Don't be tempted to hide in your office and shove the plan in a drawer. Of course, you will be very busy at this stage of your project, but making time to sell your plan will pay dividends in cooperation later.

Summary of planning

1. You plan in order to:
   - Check that the project is feasible
   - Set priorities
   - Create the 'big picture'
   - Answer why, how, who, how much and when
2. Plan in two stages.
   Stage 1: Overall planning
   - Check purpose (why)
   - Identify prerequisites and external risks
   - Identify production process (how and who)
   - Produce overall plan and communicate it
   - Plan system integration
   Stage 2: Detailed planning
   - Produce high-level plan (the 'head of the snake')
   - Produce estimates
   - Produce parts
   - Check that plan is consistent
3. Reconcile overall plan with high-level plan (head of snake) and subplans.
4. Present and sell.

A PLANNING EXAMPLE

The following is a plan for a project to produce a Functional Specification. The project followed the production of a User Requirements Specification project and led to another project to build the system to be specified in the resulting specification document.

The main challenge that was facing this part of the project was to produce a specification document that would enable building a system within very short time scales due to the unexpected pressure the client was under. It was important to define the 'minimum system' first and then specify other functions that were required but were not absolutely essential for the client's operation.

The resulting product was a specification document that indeed defined a minimum system that was built within the required time scale. Many other additional functions that were defined in the document were added to the minimum system after it went into operation.

This project was under severe time pressure. The project team had to recognize this constraint in order to put in the extraordinary effort required to achieve the defined objectives. It was also a prerequisite for getting the commitment of our stakeholders to give us the flexibility we needed under severe time pressure.

Table of Contents

1 Introduction
This plan covers the activities within the Functional Specification (FS) phase which followed the User Requirement project.
1.1 Revision history
dd1.mm.yy   First draft for discussion within the project team.
dd2.mm.yy   Second draft for discussion with the user representatives.
dd3.mm.yy   Issue A of the plan.
No other issues are planned.
1.2 Definitions

User Requirements Document (URS)	This is the final document produced in the last phase of the project, entitled nnnnnnn dated dd.mm.yy.
dd.mm.yy	Indicates a date.

1.3 Scope of the system to be specified
The scope of the system to be specified is defined in the User Requirement Document (URS). Changes to this scope will be subject to change control as defined in Sec. 9 of this document.
1.4 Planning Hierarchy
This document is a subplan that fits under the master project plan issue A, dated dd.mm.yy.

2 The Project Objectives
The 'what' question
The main objectives of this project are:

- Produce a first draft of the FS by dd.mm.yy. This draft should contain the specification of the Distribution Functions, the Remote Data Entry and the links to the external systems.
- Evaluate the first draft with the users' management with the objective of defining the scope of the 'minimum system' that can be implemented and integrated with the existing systems by dd.mm.yy.
- Rework the draft FS on the basis of the users' recommendations to produce the final document by dd.mm.yy.
- Produce estimates and plan for the implementation phase by dd.mm.yy.
- Set up a kernel implementation team by dd.mm.yy. This minimum team should include the Technical manager, the Integration manager and the Database team leader.

3 Organization
The 'who' question
The project organization will be as represented in the diagram on the next page:
3.1 Project staffing
There will be three groups of staff in the project: users' consultants, users' EDP staff and other team members.
3.1.1 Users' EDP staff
Three team members will be involved in the project on a part-time basis to pass on their knowledge of the existing systems.

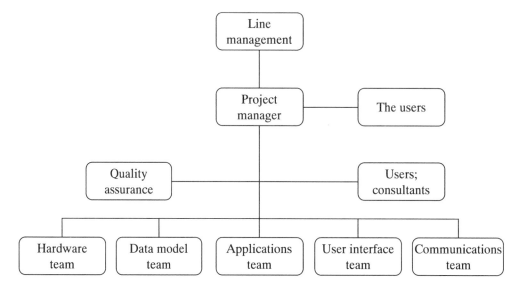

The project organization.

3.1.2 Users' consultants

Two consultants will be available on two to three days per week to advise the team on operational matters and to assess the feasibility of any proposed ideas before they are presented to the users themselves.

3.1.3 Other team members

The remaining team members will be responsible for producing the specification sections in close cooperation with the users, their consultants and their EDP staff.

4 Methodology

The 'how' question

This section describes the methodology which the project will adopt to achieve the objectives defined in Sec. 2 of this plan.

4.1 Production of the FS

The most important aspect of the methodology for this activity is the role of the users. The users must remain actively involved throughout this process. The way the project intends to do this is as follows:

- We all have to remember at all times that a system with the minimum functionality should be ready and working by dd.mm.yy.
- The users' nominated representative in the team must take an active role in all the functionality decisions.
- We must organize weekly presentations to the users' management and document the resulting recommendations.
- We must produce the main sections early in the project to allow the users sufficient time to consider how well the defined functionality matches their needs and wishes.
- A simple and efficient set of change-control procedures will be used to allow the users and the team to assess the impact of proposed changes to the scope defined in the User Requirements Specification document.

There are two main areas of functionality:

- Data model
- System functions

4.1.1 Data model
The logical data model forms the basis for the specification of the system but would exclude any details or design restrictions. The standard Personal Computer (PC)-based package currently being used by the users' consultants will be used by the project team to produce the data model documentation.

4.1.2 System functions
Functions will be specified using textual descriptions and Data Flow Diagrams (DFDs). The text will include the functions to be defined, description of the inputs and outputs and the description of any associated algorithms. It will also include specification of the required hardware and the expected performance.

4.1.3 Interfaces to other systems
Specification of the communication links to other systems will include, as a minimum, the data to be exchanged, the type and structure of messages, communication protocol, error handling, recovery procedures and the required hardware for each interface.

5 Monitoring and Reporting
The project manager will be responsible for the monitoring and control activities in the project. This will be carried as follows.

Once a week the project team will meet for one hour to discuss the following:

- Activities of the previous week
- Outstanding actions
- Objectives for following week
- Risks management
- Any other urgent matters

A weekly report will be produced which will be distributed to the users, QA and line management of the users and the project.

Once a month, the project manager will take part in the steering committee meeting involving the project managers of all other related projects.

6 Quality Control
All documents produced within the project will be quality controlled before they are distributed outside the project. The quality control allocation will be as follows:

Documents produced by:	Will be checked by:
Team members	One other team member and the team leader or technical manager
Technical manager	Project or integration manager
Integration manager	Technical or project manager
Project manager	Technical or integration manager

The producer will agree the quality control criteria with the controller. Quality control records of the external deliverables will be maintained in a project log-book.

The final FS document will be quality controlled by the project manager and technical manager before it is delivered to the QA department for the final quality approval. Following the QA approval, the document will be delivered to the users for acceptance and final sign-off.

6.1 Applicable standards
The following standards will be mandatory in the project:

- Document production standard
- Functional Specifications standard

7 Documentation
The project documentation set will be maintained by the project office according to the documentation standard referred to in Sec. 5.1 of this plan. The project documentation set will be as follows:

File Number	Description
0	Documentation index, plan, standard and distribution lists
1	Users' Requirement document
2	Project plans
3	Progress reports
4	Minutes of meetings
5	Correspondence (IN)
6	Correspondence (OUT)
7	Project accounting, estimates and costs
8	Working papers
9	Quality control records
12	Steering committee matters
13	Change control documents
14	Staffing matters

Note
The internal organization of these files will depend on the internal standards, the team working style and the administration support available to the project.

8 Configuration Management
Three levels of document will exist during the project:

- Working papers which are at the lowest level and will not be issued outside the project. The purpose of these papers is to allow team members to share their ideas within the project without following the formal project lines.
- Specification papers which are documents that are intended to become parts of the FS document.
- The Functional Specification document which is the main product of this project. It is a collection of specification papers integrated together to form a consistent document.

All documents will start as first drafts. As the document changes, the draft number will be increased until the document is formally issued. The first issue will be denoted by the letter A, the next formal issue will be B and so on.

9 Change Control

Change-control procedures will be applied when the project is requested to deviate from the scope of the FS as defined in Sec. 2 of this plan. The purpose of change-control procedures is to allow the project to implement changes of the scope in a visible and a controlled manner. We will do this as follows:

- The required change is documented describing its nature, details and the reasons for it. The initiator of the change will then discuss it with the project manager who will allocate a change request number.
- An impact statement is then produced by the project manager and discussed with the users and line management.
- A decision is then taken on whether or not to go ahead.

10 Work Breakdown Structure (WBS)

The Work Breakdown Structure will be very similar to that of the previous phase, the User Requirements Specification. Only the high-level or super-work-packages are listed below; the lower-level work packages will be defined in consultation with the team leaders.

Phase	Work-package number	Description	Effort in person-days
0	0000	Scope definition	Complete
1	1000	User Requirements definition	Complete
2	2000	Functional Specification	This phase
	2100	Project management	
	2200	Data model	
	2300	Distribution functions	
	2400	Logistics functions	
	2500	User interface	
	2600	Links to other systems	
	2700	Hardware matters	
	2800	Other activities	
	2900	Spare	
	3000	Design	Future phase
	4000	Implementation	Future phase

11 Time Scales

The overall project schedule is given in the figure on the next page. Detailed schedules for the individual super-work-packages will be produced by the team leaders.

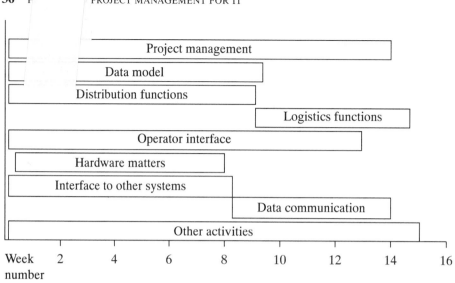

Overall project schedule.

Project Milestones

The following milestones will be used to monitor progress and report to the outside world.

Milestone number	Planned completion date	Description completion of:
1	End of week 8	Data model
2	End of week 10	Hardware design
3	End of week 12	Operator interface
4	End of week 16	Definition of all functions
5	End of week 17	Deliver final FS

12 Delivery Criteria

The Functional Specification will be considered to be complete when:

- All quality control actions for all the document parts are closed.
- QA and line management approval is obtained.
- The users' explicit agreement is obtained on the final draft.

The delivery will be documented and formally announced to the users, team and management. (For simplicity in this example plan, the sections on Costing, the Success Party and the Risk Analysis and Contingency Planning have been omitted.)

3

ESTIMATING

3.1 THE REASONS FOR ESTIMATING

IT projects can go dramatically wrong. In 1986, T. Capers Jones published the results of his analysis of IT projects in 200 large organizations in the United States. Twenty-five per cent of these projects were never completed. Of the remaining 75 per cent many of the products were never actually used. If the managers of these projects had begun by making realistic estimates of the effort, time and budget required many of the projects would not have been allowed to start; others might have been much better managed. Certainly, a great deal of money and many careers would have been saved and the clients would have had considerably more value for their investment.

The main reason we estimate, as we saw in Chapter 2, is to answer the planning questions 'how much' and 'when'. Unfortunately for project managers, estimating is not an exact science and we do not yet have a guaranteed, foolproof method for making realistic estimates. You can only make an accurate assessment of the effort, budget and time needed after you have completed the project. By working methodically and combining the techniques described in this chapter you will have a better chance of making realistic estimates, but the process of estimating remains frustrating and can cause even experienced managers much anxiety. Some project managers will conclude that estimating is more trouble than it is worth. In practice, estimating in a methodical, disciplined way provides a number of benefits for the project manager, line management and the users. First, estimating enables you to identify risks and uncertainties so that you can plan for them. Second, estimating helps you to learn – from successes, and from mistakes. Even if your estimate turns out to be very different from what the project actually costs, you will be able to go back and assess where you went wrong, in order to learn from the experience. You can then use your learning to improve your performance on your next project.

But estimating offers another crucial advantage which is often overlooked. As one project manager put it:

> The reason I estimate is to build my own confidence . If I can produce a plan which I can believe in , then I feel ready to tackle the project – and I can motivate my team, my management and my client to tackle it with me.

The process of estimating should give all the parties concerned the confidence that you are going to succeed. Clients need to be convinced that a project is feasible before they will give approval. Project managers need to be convinced themselves before they take on the task, because running projects can be a lonely and stressful business. You only have to listen to the 'war stories' of the veteran managers to hear things like 'I kept asking myself why I had accepted something so difficult', 'I felt so lonely' and 'I swore that would be my last project'. Many managers have the feeling – rightly or wrongly – that they are only as good as their last project.

Once you have an estimate which you and your experienced colleagues are convinced about, you will tackle the job with more courage and more commitment. And this commitment is contagious: if you feel you will be successful, your team will feel that too. If you are nervous about the project we suspect that your mind set alone could contribute to a greater chance of failure. If you are realistically confident you will be able to transform an ordinary team into a super-organism which can achieve extraordinary results: you set up a self-fulfilling prophecy.

Summary

You estimate so that:

- You can identify risks and uncertainties, and plan for them.
- You can build a sense of realistic confidence for yourself, your client, your management and your team.
- You can learn and improve your estimating skills for your next project.

In this chapter we suggest a range of techniques which can take some of the frustration out of the estimating process and help you to formulate your own successful approach.

3.2 PLANNING YOUR ESTIMATING

Step 1: Preparation – define the scope

Before you start estimating the cost and time scales of any project you must have a reasonable definition of the scope. Even a vaguely defined scope is better than nothing, because the scope forms the baseline for your estimates. Without the baseline, you will never be able to get your estimators to converge.

This step will produce the general list of the products of the project. The list is a good starting point for estimating the whole project, but it is not sufficient on its own. There will be other important activities during the project which will not result in deliverable products, and these activities must also be estimated. Examples of such products are functional specifications, project plans and user-accepted software. The completion of these products often coincides with the project milestones.

Document the scope and agree it with your client and with those who have the end commercial responsibility for the project. Now you can start planning to estimate.

Step 2: Identifying the materials and project expenses

Together with your team produce a draft List 1 of all the materials and expenses in the project. (If you would like an example, read the case study at the end of the chapter.) The draft List 1 specifies in detail all the required materials including machinery, tools and miscellaneous items. Some items on this list, such as computer systems, may require a considerable specification and design effort involving specialists perhaps from external organizations such as the computer manufacturers. The sizing of the hardware is often underestimated in the early stages. This can lead to unpleasant surprises either at the end of the estimation or even during the project.

The materials required during development of the product are also often underestimated. Too few terminals, insufficient computer resources or even inadequate office space are some of the common complaints in project teams. Experience shows that line managers and financial controllers are very reluctant to allocate additional budgets once the project starts. Don't be tempted to cut corners at the proposal stage. This is often a false economy because the indirect costs incurred in the moaning and groaning that follows far outweigh any direct savings you may make.

The output from this step is a final *List 1* of all the materials and expenses required in all the phases of the project right from the outset and up to the final defined objective.

Step 3: Identifying the activities

Now we need to identify the activities that will lead to the final product, in a top-down fashion. Start by breaking the whole project life-cycle into a number of more manageable chunks, which we will call phases. Phases are periods in the project which are clearly distinguishable from each other, just as during a person's life the baby, child, teenage and adult phases can be distinguished.

If you only look at the end products of the project, you might overlook an activity. By focusing on each phase in turn, you can get a complete overview of all the activities needed during each phase. Make sure that you design the products from each phase so that they are certifiable or auditable by organizations outside the project, such as a quality department or the client. *The process of phasing, and identifying activities, will also form the basis subsequently for your detailed project plan.*

If your project is a straightforward development project (as in the case study at the end of this chapter) then your project phases will probably be specification, design, code and test, etc. If your project involves the simultaneous development and modification of many systems, then the division into phases will be much more complex, and will require much more attention.

Each phase should be broken down into its subactivities; each subactivity should be broken down into smaller activities and so on. The lowest-level activities should be well defined with clear completion criteria. Use the team members who have good system design skills to do this effectively. The more detailed this analysis, the more accurate your estimates are likely to be.

The output from this step is a complete list of all the activities that will be carried out in order to achieve the project objectives. This list is often called the *Work Breakdown Structure (WBS)*. Work Breakdown Structures can be expressed in different terminologies, according to which stage of the project you are in and to the person who is producing them. For instance, at the start of the project you will be talking mainly about the user requirements, so the WBS will be expressed in the users' terms. Later the specifier or designer writing the WBS in more detail will be talking in more process-related terms such as design, code and test. We call the WBS the list of activities (*List 2*).

Lists 1 and 2 represent the *estimating baseline* which should contain all the materials, expenses and labour costs in the project. The estimating team should review this baseline against the scope of supply which was defined at the very start.

How about your choice of estimating tools? You will find that there is an enormous array of tools and techniques recommended by your colleagues and in specialist books. Some project managers will be advocates of the semi-analytical tools such as Cocomo and FPA, for instance; others will speak of 'top-down' or 'bottom-up' approaches and so on.

Most tools and methods are crystallizations of the experience of project managers. Entire books have been written about estimating tools, so consult the Further Reading at the end of this book for sources of more details.

Estimating tools are a double-edged sword. Reliable estimates come with experience and if you have the experience you will be able to use these tools and methods effectively. But if you don't have much experience, how do you estimate?

First, you need to be creative in applying the experience that you do have. For example, you may be able to break down your project into a number of smaller ones, each comparable to a project managed previously by you or one of your colleagues. The sum total of the costs of these smaller projects will give you a good idea of the cost of the project you are estimating. Your experience and that of your colleagues will also help you to assess the risks your project will be facing and the impact of these risks on the costs.

Second, you need to draw on the experience of others to help you to understand the project challenges, how to estimate the resources to deal with them and how to use these tools and techniques to structure your thoughts. The output from this process will give you and your team a common language and starting point, and enable you to reach a conclusion which will give you all a sense of realistic confidence.

Summary

When you plan your estimating:

1. Define and agree the scope.
2. Talk through the production process with your team (processes, people, tools and techniques) and make a draft List 1 (overview of materials and expenses).
3. Identify materials and expenses in more detail – final List 1.
4. Identify activities (WBS – List 2).
5. Scope + Lists 1 and 2 = the *baseline* for your estimating.

6. Consult the specialist literature for an understanding of any tools and techniques recommended in your organization: check that you understand the advantages and limitations.
7. Plan to use your own experience and that of colleagues, backed up by a combination of tools and methods.

3.3 PRODUCING THE ESTIMATES

The estimating team

The estimating team should consist of at least two members, with relevant experience of the estimating method used. The team members must estimate completely independently of each other, so that you will get a variety of estimates which you can use to challenge, cross-check and finally consolidate your final numbers. The estimating team must also agree on a set of assumptions before they start estimating. For instance, they must agree whether or not to include effort for quality control and reviews as part of the production estimates.

Use as many relevant estimating methods as possible. Producing as many estimates as possible (two to eight) by more than one estimator per method is one of the keys to producing the best estimates.

Consolidating the estimates

Consolidating the estimates requires a considerable degree of skill and discipline. We have to remember that consolidating is not a simple process of averaging or horse trading over differences in opinions. The team have to realize that there is no obvious right or wrong answer: any one estimate is potentially correct!

Start by comparing the estimates very carefully in order to identify any large differences between them. If you discover considerable variations from the norm, check carefully with the person who produced the estimate to see if the variation is due to a different interpretation of the estimating baseline or whether it is the result of different assumptions. If there are any differences remaining, set up a team meeting in order to arrive at a consensus. (See Chapter 9 for suggestions on consensus building.) If you cannot achieve consensus, the team leader should be prepared to make his or her own decisions and to justify those decisions to higher management. You may find that your management want to come to an agreement with your customer to do the work for a lower or even higher budget than you have estimated because of some commercial considerations. This is fine, provided that you believe in the budget that has been allocated.

The end result is one set of estimates with a consolidation report explaining how you arrived at them. The degree of variation between the estimates will give you an idea of the reliability of the final result and the level of estimating error contingency you have to reserve. This contingency will partly depend on the accuracy of the definition of the estimating baseline and on the scope of supply of the project. For a typical software development project the estimating error is a function of the estimating baseline. If your baseline is a system design you are likely to produce estimates that are up to 90 per cent accurate. If the baseline is a functional specification your error can be as high as 30 per cent assuming, of course, that you have a 'good' functional specification. This is expressed in Fig. 3.1.

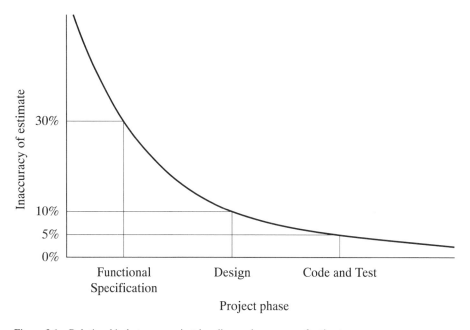

Figure 3.1 Relationship between project baseline and accuracy of estimates.

The consolidation process often has a useful byproduct: the identification of risks and risk analysis which we need to tackle more methodically.

Risk analysis and associated contingency planning

The estimating process and the consolidation of the estimates in particular will have highlighted most if not all the estimating-related risks facing the project. We suggest that you should next organize a brainstorming session to evaluate these project risks and to assess their impact. The output of this brainstorming is a list of the risks, together with an estimate of the costs of dealing with each risk if it becomes a problem. The cost items will be functions of the possibility of that risk becoming a problem and the full cost required to cover it.

Take care that you don't accidentally allow for risks twice over. For instance, suppose you are concerned that the hardware may arrive late; you might identify this risk, separate it out as a project risk, and allow for it. However, one of your estimators, who is also aware that the hardware may be delayed, may have already inflated her estimates. Separate out risks such as hardware delay and allow for them centrally.

The output from this step is a list of risks, each with a cost figure associated with it. The total may also be presented as a percentage of the total estimate. We suggest that it is better to estimate the cost to cover each individual risk separately.

Estimating may be an iterative process if you are producing estimates with the objective of meeting constraints on the budget, for instance. If your initial set of assumptions produces estimates that are too costly you may need to try some different scenarios: reduce the functionality, in consultation with the client, or find a way of planning which enables you to use your staff more efficiently and thus reduce your time scales.

3.4 A CASE STUDY

We set up a team consisting of a project manager, two consultants and a system analyst, to estimate the cost and to plan the replacements of an existing traffic monitoring and management system. The user requirements were documented in a specification document which referenced the technical documentation of the existing system and which gave an accurate record of the users' needs and wishes.

Step 1 was to document and agree the scope of the current project resulting in the following general list of products:

- Functional Specification document based on the user requirement specification. The functional specification document would be used as a basis for the final plans for the rest of the project
- Project and quality plans for the activities following the Functional Specification phase
- Test Specification document including an acceptance test schedule
- The application software as specified in the Functional Specification
- System acceptance testing
- Delivery of the system to the users and the installation of the system in the users' environment
- Site acceptance of the system using the acceptance criteria defined in the Test Specification document but using real operational data
- User training – two weeks for up to ten people
- Internal system documentation, operator manuals, system administration manuals.

List 1 – Overview of materials and expenses

We planned to estimate the following items:

- Computer system hardware and standard software
- Additional equipment for the software development environment of the project
- Labour
- Expenses for meetings, brainstorming sessions
- Travelling and accommodation expenses
- Miscellaneous expenses.

In *Step 2* we identified our *list of project materials and expenses,* with the help of system specialists. *List 1* represents the system hardware, the development equipment and the associated standard software. Some analysis had been done, followed by some design work, and this resulted in the items in the following lists:

Item	*Price*	*Comment*
Main computer equipment		CPUs, memory and power supplies
1/4 cartridge tape		
Kit for CPU upgrade		Standard with main computer
Expansion box		
Expansion kit		
Mass storage controllers		Two units
Disk drives		Two units
High-capacity disk drives		Two units
Communication package		
Communication support package		
Communication hardware		Includes line adapters
Ethernet adapter		
Video terminal		
Standard software		
Code management package		
X.25		
X.29		
C		
C library		
Text Editor		
Debugger support		
TCP/IP support		
SQL server		
Screen designer		
SQL editor		
SQL library		
TCP/IP application support		
SQL/C interface		
TCP/IP utilities		
Workstations with interfaces to server		Ten units with GUI interfaces
Monitors		Ten units
Ethernet Card		Ten units
Terminal Emulation		Two units
Extended keyboard		Four units
Workstation operating software		Multi-licence
Audio recording equipment		Eight units
Encryption box		Two units
Ethernet bridges		Three units
Printers		Ten units
Auto-dial modems		24 units
Cabinets and power supplies		

Sub-total
Travelling expenses
Accommodation expenses
Meetings and brainstorming

Grand total

In *Step 3* we identified the *project activities*, and the estimating baseline for the labour necessary to produce the deliverables. The following table is what we called *List 2,* containing the work breakdown structure (WBS). Each work package has four estimating components; Functional Specification, System Design, Code and Test and finally System Integration.

Number	Work package description	Functional Specification	System Design	Code and Test	System Integration
1000	*Initiation*				
1010	Induction				
1020	Planning				
1100	*Alarm Processing*				
1110	Messages				
1120	Filtering				
1130	Alarm treatment				
1140	Presentation				
1150	Storage				
1200	*Management Functions*				
1210	Data management				
1220	System management				
1300	*Statistical Functions*				
1400	*Front End Interface*				
1500	*Network interface*				
1510	Processing system interface				
1520	Management functions				
1530	Routing control				
1540	Presentation functions				
1550	Configuration functions				
1560	Security functions				
1600	*External Interfaces*				
1610	East regions interface				
1620	West regions interface				
1630	North regions interface				
1700	*System Control Functions*				
2000	User Acceptance				
3000	*Delivery and Site Installation*				
4000	*Site Acceptance*				
5000	*Documentation*				
5100	User guides				
5200	System reference guides				
5300	Technical documentation				
5400	Software manuals				
6000	*Training*				
6100	User training				
6200	System managers training				
7000	*Management*				
7100	Project management				
7200	Technical management				
7300	Integration management				
7400	Configuration management				

The team members used this table to produce their estimates. The project manager produced one top-down estimate for each super-work package (those packages in *italics*). The other three estimators produced four estimates (one for each phase: Functional

Specification, Design, Code and Test and Integration) for every work package. The resulting aggregated estimates (in person-days) were summarized in Table 3.1.

Table 3.1

Number	Work package	Estimator 1	Estimator 2	Estimator 3	Project manager	Consolidated estimate
1000	*Initiation*	20	30	15	50	45
1100	*Alarm Processing*	33	95	140	110	130
1200	*Management Functions*	18	70	60	40	50
1300	*Statistical Functions*	8	40	100	80	55
1400	*Front End Interface*	20	45	20	70	40
1500	*Network Interface*	80	120	130	80	90
1600	*External Interfaces*	25	100	170	120	110
1700	*System Control Functions*	30	30	20	80	35
2000	*User Acceptance*	20	40	25	60	55
3000	*Delivery and Site Installation*	35	20	10	15	15
4000	*Site Acceptance*	20	40	30	30	30
5000	*Documentation*	55	50	70	40	45
6000	*Training*	30	35	30	50	45
7000	*Management*	170	130	100	250	200

We consolidated the estimates in a meeting between the team and an independent consultant with an appropriate experience. When we discovered some large differences between the estimators we examined the assumptions they had made; in nearly all cases this gave us a satisfactory explanation for the discrepancies. In the one remaining case where we could not find an obvious reason other than a *difference of opinion*, the group made a decision which the project manager supported. The different opinions were recorded and presented in the formal review with line management.

SUMMARY OF ESTIMATING

1. No estimating method is 100 per cent certain. However, you estimate so that:

   • You can identify risks and uncertainties and plan for them.
   • You can learn from feedback and thus improve your estimating skills.
   • You can build a sense of realistic confidence for yourself, your client, your management and your team.

   Estimating is the first step towards team building and team motivation.

2. Plan your estimating by identifying with your team:

   • The scope
   • The production process

- All materials and expenses (Lists 1 and 2)
- Activities (WBS – List 2)
- Select your tools; use in combination with experience.

The accuracy of the end results will depend heavily upon the experience of the estimators.

3. To produce the estimates

- Use several different methods, and at least two estimators.
- Ensure that each estimator works independently.
- Consolidate via consensus.
- Produce lists of risks with associated costs.
- Check accuracy of estimates again, independently.
- Work iteratively if necessary to meet constraints.

4

PROJECT SET-UP

4.1 INTRODUCTION

By 'project set-up' we mean the things you do in order to create the optimum environment for your team and your project. This includes not only staffing, production processes, project tools and training but also the groundwork needed to build constructive relationships with your line manager and your client.

Sometimes you may be lucky enough to find that your project is part of an existing programme which already includes the key elements of a conducive environment; usually, however, project set-up is your direct responsibility. It is easy to overlook this phase when you are already under pressure, but failure to address it can result in conflicts and unpleasant surprises, which will cost much more of your time to sort out later.

Planning, estimating, project set-up and team building are activities which all take place within the same period. If you separate out these activities and consider them in isolation you can identify the most critical issues. This enables you to plan and use your time more effectively during the initial weeks of your project, and thus build a firm foundation for your project.

4.2 STAFFING PROBLEMS

A common source of frustration to project managers is the pressure to assign staff to projects long before project set-up is complete. Both your team members and your line manager may push you to allocate positions on the team at a time when you would rather keep your options open. If you have to take on staff early you may find you have team members hanging around with nothing to do, wanting attention from you at a time when you are especially busy. If you allocate positions on the team prematurely, you may regret your decisions later when you know your staff better and when changes would be met with resentment.

The needs of your team and your manager for some degree of certainty are understandable enough. If you have completed your plan and staffing profile you should be ready to resist pressure and to reply to their questions with answers such as 'I'm sorry, but we're not ready yet to take on any more staff. We will have opportunities for team members with your experience starting on this date . . .'

Recruit your core of key staff first. In particular, you need the people with the specialist technical and application knowledge, and those who will be helping you to manage the project. While your core team are helping with your plan they can also discuss with you the following questions:

- What is the production process?
- Which software and hardware tools will be most useful during the project?
- What training do we need?
- What can we do to ensure that all the team have a thorough understanding of what the users need?
- Which non-IT skills will we need on the project? Administrative support, help with public relations, accounting, legal, office management and logistics are examples of skills which can be important, especially on larger projects.

4.3 THE PRODUCTION PROCESS

The production process is the methodology which you plan to use. The range of formal methodologies on the market is now very wide: which should you choose? Some project managers strongly recommend System Development Methodology (SDM), the Waterfall model or some of the other methods recommended in the books we have included in the Further Reading at the end of this book. Each method has its advantages and disadvantages, and your choice will largely be a matter of personal preference. However, there are a number of criteria that can help you make a final decision. For instance, the methodology you choose should

- Be consistent with applicable standards
- Be easy to communicate, with simple, down-to earth terminology that your team, your client, management and other key players can all understand
- Include documentation as an integral part
- Build in user involvement throughout the project
- Provide for intermediate deliverables, to enable you to measure progress easily
- Include built-in feedback mechanisms, within the project and across projects, to facilitate learning and performance improvement.

Once you have selected your methodology the team should fine-tune it and you should organize any necessary training without delay. You must then ensure that everybody on your team is able to describe the process in a few sentences and within a few minutes. The production process is the route for your team to get to the target; if this route is not clear then they will lose their way. Be prepared to stop and explain, and to check understanding if you suspect that any team member is confused.

When your methodology is well understood and agreed within your team, start defining all the inputs and outputs at every stage in your production process. Each activity should appear as in Fig. 4.1.

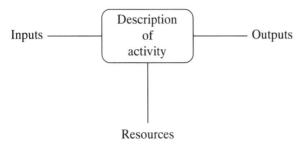

Figure 4.1   Presentation of project activities.

Ideally every activity in the project should be fully described, with the inputs, outputs and resources required. If you have a complete plan these descriptions will already exist as part of the plan or in one of the supporting documents.

4.4 THE PROJECT TOOLS

Tools can be used to reduce the time you and your team spend on some of the more boring or repetitive project tasks, and to free you all to use your creativity and energy where most appropriate. Your tool kit will be determined by the skills and working styles of your team members, so the team must identify for themselves the tools which they need. Don't be tempted to define these tools yourself, in isolation from your team; you will miss out on your colleagues' ideas and experience of the technologies. If you delegate the choice of tools to your technical staff, and let them have influence over their environment, the motivation and commitment of your team will invariably be higher.

In larger projects you should consider setting up a task force for planning and creating the support environment the team needs. Some projects place this activity within one of the standard project functions such as the integration team, the system management team or the configuration control and management team. If you dedicate a task force for this purpose you can ensure that the activity is not overlooked or dropped in favour of actions which can appear more urgent at the time.

A huge variety of tools exists. Computer systems often have standard tools of their own, workstations are equipped with powerful features of all kinds and personal computers come with planning packages, databases, and spreadsheets. If you use these tools sensibly they can make your life a lot easier. The following list gives a selection of the kinds of tools you could consider, based on our experience and that of our colleagues.

Development tools

The number and types of tools that are needed by any project will depend on your team and whether you have a standard development environment. If, for example, you have a project where Case Tools are available and well supported then you may simply be able to specify your additional needs and get them built by a dedicated support organization. Similarly, when projects are part of a programme then a team may well have been set up to develop tools and to support the development environment.

Test tools

These are often neglected or overlooked until the testing begins, and this may later put the team under strain. It is good discipline to consider these needs during project set-up. This will encourage the team to define test philosophies at an early stage in the project, and they will then be more aware of quality issues while they are working on the project. If you select your test tools early, you will often save valuable time towards the end of the project when every minute counts.

Test tools may vary from simple data generators to sophisticated programmable testers and simulators that can be initiated and left to run completely unattended. Most experienced system builders have the necessary knowledge to select from the various tools that are available in the marketplace.

Integration test tools are a crucial part of the test tool kit. Some development environments provide extensive test facilities that can be configured to suit the specific project needs. In other cases, the project team has to develop its own test tools from scratch.

Monitoring and control tools

These are the instruments needed to measure and monitor the status of their projects, and so they are the most important part of the project manager's tool kit. Experienced project managers generally have their own tried and tested tools, which they can adapt as needed. If you are new to project management you must first identify the types of tools you need, so you can recognize the right tool when you see it. The following is a list of the most common types of tools which are available off the shelf:

1. A tool for tracking the effort spent per activity in the project. A well-designed spreadsheet is usually all you need. In very large projects you may prefer to have a hierarchy of such tools, to monitor effort spending at different levels and in different areas in the project.
2. An action follow-up tool, preferably with an alarm facility to alert you when an action needs to be taken. The sophistication of the tool you need will depend on your management and delegation style. Again, a spreadsheet supported by an administrative procedure or a simple extension to a database in your workstation may be all you need. You may also want to consider one of the standard off-the-shelf electronic diaries with powerful functions.
3. A tool to track the overall project costs, with functions to structure the reporting information to meet not only your needs but also those of your management, your client and accounts. A project management planning and scheduling tool will often have standard features which may be enough for this purpose.
4. Documentation tools to enable the team to produce various kinds of standard documents. Your project may be required to comply with a standard template provided

by the organization for this purpose. Otherwise you can easily build such a tool using the standard facilities provided by some word-processing packages.

4.5 SEEING THE PROJECT THROUGH THE USERS' EYES

By this stage you are beginning to draw your team together, and you are getting a good idea of the methodology and tools you are going to use. You have hopefully given your core team a clear explanation of the business context for the project, and the plan has enabled you to specify your objectives. Before you all dive down into the implementation phase you need to help your team to get a deeper understanding of the purpose of your project by looking at it through the users' eyes. The case that follows shows how you can use some original ideas to help your team to realize what the project is really about.

> Our project to build a warehouse system had got off to a good start. The core team had worked on the functional specification and understood it well; we had a functional baseline that was properly documented and agreed with the users. We organized a series of group discussions to induct newcomers into the team. The first two sessions went well; the core team were good communicators, and the newcomers were enthusiastic.
>
> The basic requirements of the system were clear enough. The users had asked for printed reports and a suite of screens which would be available on a large number of stations scattered all over the warehouse. With the help of these reports and screens, the users would be able to load and unload their trolleys following specified instructions produced by the system. The users would then deliver the orders they had collected to specified addresses within the warehouse. So far, so good.
>
> The third group discussion was intended to help the new team members understand how the users would interact with the system and how the various functions would support their daily operation. And in this meeting we hit a problem.
>
> When we started discussing the performance and intensity of trolley traffic in the warehouse and the importance of optimizing this process our new team members became confused. A crucial part of our job on the project was to ensure that the empty trolleys would be stacked in an orderly way, while at the same time following the shortest route. The core team thought that this functionality was well described, but the newcomers had difficulties with the concept, which was unique to this particular client. They could not visualize it.
>
> Suddenly one team member had an idea: 'Suppose we actually ran the operation for a day or two ourselves to get a feel for it?' In retrospect this was a blinding flash of the obvious, but we were all excited – everyone thought it would be great to push trolleys around the warehouse for a couple of days.
>
> And so we did it. The advantages were enormous – we all had a common experience of the application, and we got to know each other. I'd recommend it to any project manager – it really helped us to understand what the user needed.

Site visits, presentations from the users and demonstrations are other examples of how you can help your team get a feel for what the users expect from you. Don't assume that your team has an accurate understanding of the users' needs. In the early days of the IT industry, computer systems were often built in complete isolation, and some project managers still have difficulty positioning the users in their projects. An understanding of the users' needs is a fundamental part of the common vision which will unite your team in moving towards your goal.

4.6 TRAINING

IT technology has evolved at a rate which is bewildering even to staff who are experienced and able. In nearly every project we will be faced with technologies which have either changed since we last worked with them or which are totally new to us – hence the need for training.

Unfortunately, the need for training in projects is often underestimated, and this can cause problems with both the project manager's budget and the staffing profile. Cutting costs in this area is false economy; if you have training requirements, try to train your team even if you have inherited a project without a training budget. Training contributes to team building and to motivation.

4.7 SETTING UP A CONSTRUCTIVE RELATIONSHIP WITH YOUR MANAGER

The nature of the relationship

Constructive relationships with your line manager and your client are an essential part of an effective working environment. Your aim when you start working with your line manager is to set up a relationship based on mutual trust and confidence – where you can get the job done and work together comfortably. The early experiences of working together set the framework either for success or, if you are unlucky, for increasing tension. As with so many aspects of project management, by investing effort at the start you can pre-empt problems later.

The relationship between the project manager and the line manager is a partnership based on mutual dependence. Both parties need each other in order to do a good job and to make progress in their careers.

A healthy relationship is based on realistic mutual expectations. We suggest that you, as the project manager, are entitled, for instance, to expect your line manager to:

- Organize the resources for you, and give you the authority levels to do your job
- Give you clear instructions and adequate briefing
- Mobilize support for your project in the wider organization, and at higher levels in your client organization
- Check that your understanding of your objectives is in line with the objectives set by your organization
- Offer you a reasonable amount of personal support.

Your line manager should also help you to understand and manage the broader context in which your project has been set: the main strategic, commercial and organizational issues, for instance, which have an influence both on your own and on the client's organization. We use a metaphor to explain this a different way. Think of your project as a black box. You as project manager are very familiar (hopefully) with the contents of the box, and spend most of your time inside it. Occasionally you can get so preoccupied with the contents of the box that you forget there is an outside world. Your manager must open the lid of the box, from time to time, to remind you to stick your head out and observe what is going on.

Looking at the relationship from the line manager's point of view, we suggest that the line manager can expect the project manager to:

- Supply reliable, accurate information about your part of the project as required
- Inform him or her early if you have problems which are outside your authority limits, or where you have insufficient experience and/or information
- Sort out other problems yourself, informing your manager as required
- Use the manager's time sensibly by coming with well-prepared arguments and possible solutions.

Neither of you is expected to be perfect. What you are aiming for is a reasonably good fit, as described in this example from a project manager talking about his manager:

> He's pretty good on the whole: loads of drive, some useful ideas. Occasionally he steps on my client's toes – I think he gets impatient when the client doesn't react as fast as he does. I have to keep reminding him to slow down.
>
> He says I'm a bit of a bureaucrat, and perhaps he's right – I like to have everything covered in writing. There have been a couple of times though when he's had cause to be grateful, since I had the documentation on file to cover his back. I suppose we're reasonably complementary.

Identify your manager's agenda

A good way to prepare for a constructive relationship is to think of your manager as an internal client, and to approach the relationship with the same professionalism as you show towards your external clients. This means that you need to be aware of your line manager's organizational and personal agenda. The following questions give you an idea of the sort of information you could collect:

1. What are your manager's organizational objectives for the next twelve months?
2. What are his or her Key Result Areas – the areas of the job which will have most impact on achieving the objectives?
3. What are the main pressures that your manager is under? What does he or she worry about?
4. What are your manager's personal objectives? What could he or she want to get out of your project?

Be prepared to adjust to your manager's style

You need to be flexible in adjusting to the preferred working style of your manager. This may seem rather unfair, but in reality we all have working styles which we tend to adopt regardless of who we are working with, and you will also expect your staff to adapt to your preferences. Good managers will adjust their style also to the strengths and weaknesses of their subordinates, but this requires a settling-down period where you can get used to working together.

You can save yourself time and aggravation by observing carefully how your manager operates in the first few weeks of your relationship. You can shorten the 'settling-in period' so that you are working smoothly together by the time any early problems emerge on the project. Try a few more questions, to help you to analyse your manager's working style:

1. What are the aspects of your manager's style that you find particularly helpful?
2. Which aspects are less helpful?
3. Which aspects of your working relationship are you pleased with? Are there any aspects that you would like to improve?

Typical aspects of working style which you need to identify are:

1. Decision-making methods: some managers are happy to delegate much of the day-to-day decision making, whereas others will tend to keep tighter control
2. Managing information: does your manager like information in writing or informally? In detail, or just the broad lines? In advance, or spontaneously? Focused, or more wide ranging and imaginative?

Agree explicitly with your manager how you are going to work together. Formal agreements such as terms of reference are also helpful, but often conflicts and disappointments arise from small misunderstandings and misinterpretations. Check, for instance:

• Which times of day are most convenient for you to come with questions and problems
• What sort of reporting your manager expects
• How much contact your manager wants with your team and your client
• Other aspects of your working relationship which you or your manager feel strongly about – including areas where you particularly want help and support.

Raising such issues openly at an early stage enables you to build trust.

If you are uncomfortable with some aspect of your manager's style, then try to analyse the problem in terms of differences in working styles rather than personalities. Suppose you are feeling frustrated because your manager never seems to be there in the office when you need to talk something through – and he has not returned your phone calls. A possible opening (when you do get hold of him!) would be: 'Can we talk about our contact time together? I've had some problems which I wanted to discuss, but I haven't been able to get hold of you.'

Working styles are neutral ground; other kinds of criticism (e.g. 'You're never there when I need you') can quickly deteriorate into personal attacks. Talk to your manager at an early stage, while the problem is still small and you have the excuse that you are still getting used to each other. The longer you put off discussing problems, the more difficult it will be to make changes.

4.8 SETTING UP A CONSTRUCTIVE RELATIONSHIP WITH YOUR CLIENT

The suggestions in the previous section are as applicable to your client as they are to your line manager, but there some additional points which need to be addressed separately. Your client's focus will be on the deliverables and the outcome from the project. The client's relationship with you will be short term, and he or she will see it as a means to an end; he or she does not share the responsibility of your line manager to develop you personally. Your client will be looking ahead to the output from the project and how that will help to achieve the broader, long-term organizational goals. Consequently many clients will worry most about the time scales and deadlines by which the project should be completed. Any developments which could threaten timely completion should be brought to your client's attention immediately, so that he or she can help in identifying or confirming appropriate courses of action.

What effect does your client's level of IT-related knowledge have on the relationship? If the client has expertise in this area, communication will be easier, and the client may take more of a direct interest in the technical issues on the project. Clients with less experience in IT may prefer to leave all the technical issues to you, in which case you should bear this in mind in your reporting.

Technically oriented project managers can sometimes be blind to the strengths of senior managers, both in their own line and in their client organization. Some project managers underestimate the help and support which can be provided by clients who have considerable experience in the broader aspects of management, even if they know little about IT. Finance managers, for instance, will often know a great deal about the strategic goals of the organization and can be very useful allies. Clients with general project management experience can offer sound advice with problems which are not purely technical. Assume that all senior managers will have expertise and experience which could be helpful to you.

SUMMARY OF PROJECT SET-UP

Planning, project set-up and team building are concurrent activities. By addressing each activity thoroughly you build a firm foundation for your project.

Staffing

- Use your staffing profile from your plan to resist pressure to take on staff early.
- Recruit your core first.

Production process/choice of methodology

- Select a methodology which is easy for everyone to understand.
- Ensure that the team are familiar with it.
- Define inputs and outputs for each activity.

Project tools

- Tools save your creativity for the most important tasks.
- Leave your team to choose their tool kit.
- Options include tools for development, testing, monitoring and control.

Seeing the project through the user's eyes

- Make sure that your team really understands what your user expects.

Setting up the relationship with your manager

- Work towards mutual trust and confidence.
- Check that you have realistic expectations. ⟵
- Identify your manager's agenda.
- Be prepared to adjust and discuss your style of working together.
- Sort out problems while they are small.

Setting up the relationship with your client

- Your client will focus on deliverables and deadlines.
- Inform early of any problems which could threaten deadlines.
- Assume that all managers have experience which can be of help.

5

TEAM BUILDING

5.1 WHY DO WE NEED TO BUILD TEAMS?

A group of senior project managers were discussing the critical project success factors. One of them said that project success can be attributed 90 per cent to having the right team and 10 per cent to luck.

The main organizational reason for building teams is to develop a sense of ownership in your staff. If you can break down the project into a number of clearly defined deliverables you can delegate each of them in turn to a person or a team of people who will take on the responsibility for producing the output required. Managerial gurus used to decree that a manager's span of control should be no larger than eight to ten staff, but many managers are currently managing teams of between ten and fifteen people. The better you are at delegating and training your staff, the larger the project you can manage.

Teams bring enjoyment as well as efficiency into the workplace. Some of the advantages of working in teams are that you can:

- Develop and learn from each other
- Solve problems by drawing on different resources and expertise
- Have a flexible resource with which to meet your milestones
- Create a small community of colleagues and friends who can offer you support and social contact.

Unfortunately, teams do not automatically bond and evolve; some project teams never truly develop synergy, where the 'whole is greater than the sum of the parts'. In a recent survey of nearly thirty projects, project managers described more than 70 per cent of typical difficulties as 'people problems'. This can be very frustrating to IT managers who are used to seeing technology as the answer to resolving their dilemmas. As yet, there is no automated tool for solving interpersonal tensions.

If you want synergy in your team, you will have to work for it: you will have to lead your team to success. The way you lead will depend partly on your personal style, but we have highlighted a number of issues which, as with planning and project set-up, you have to get right from the start:

- Select the team structure.
- Fit the people to the roles.
- Delegate clearly and effectively.
- Keep the team motivated.
- Make your meetings interesting.
- Set up a team 'culture' which is open and constructive.

Good teams can in time evolve into what we call *super-organisms*. Super-organisms have a life and identity of their own. They think and operate independently, they radiate energy, they have a sense of pride in their achievements. They also evolve and adapt with the changing world around them.

Super-organisms can produce extraordinary results – in terms not only of output but also of personal learning and growth. You can test this by thinking about teams you have known. Think of the *best* team you have ever worked in, and what you gained from the experience. We guess that along with technical knowledge and new relationships, you also increased in self-esteem – enabling you to tackle subsequent problems and 'bad patches' with more strength and skill. Your challenge as project manager is to provide that experience for your staff.

5.2 CHOOSING YOUR TEAM STRUCTURE

Your structure will depend on the purpose, size and complexity of your project. In small projects, several functions can be fulfilled by the same person; in larger ones you may assign several people to fulfil the same function. A common error is to underestimate the organizational support your project needs. Table 5.1 gives some examples of types of projects and the organizational support they require.

At one end of the project scale you have the small team, where technical tasks are delegated to individuals and the project manager does all the coordination. At the other end come the business programmes, which may be called projects but which are actually suites of projects serving one technical/business objective. These large projects are often set up like a business unit, with central support services such QA, PR, office management and even accounting provided by dedicated units that exist for the duration of the programme. Figure 5.1 is an example of this sort of project structure.

The programme manager shown in this diagram may be called the project manager or programme or project director.

The use of centralized support functions is a determining factor in the success of the project, according to a recent survey. Projects of up to a hundred people can usefully have seven or eight support staff, including, for instance, a quality manager, a technical

Table 5.1

Type of project	Organizational support required
Complex commercial environments involving unusual constructions and difficult deals.	Commercial and contractual management.
Difficult integration requirements internal within the project or with other external parties. This area is often overlooked.	Strong integration management supported by experienced technicians in all the relevant areas in the project, set up well before the integration is due to start.
Complex functionality.	Application specialists.
Many suppliers and subcontractors.	Suppliers management.
Complex administration needs.	Administrative support.
Very large projects.	Logistic management to plan and control movement of materials and equipment and office space.
Involvement of the public.	PR, market research and communication skills.

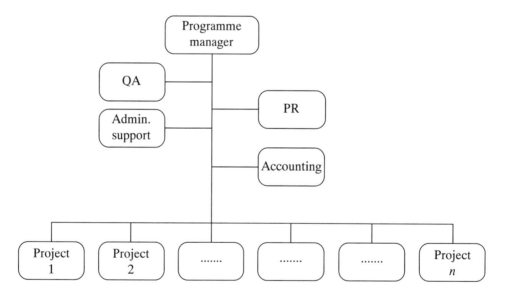

Figure 5.1 Programme organization.

manager, someone to organize the development environment, even a staff manager if you have a lot of people coming and going on the project.

The role of these functions must be made very clear to everyone on the project. You will need to explain their added value, their purpose, their authority levels and their relationship to the direct production staff. If you have a quality manager, is he or she authorized to reject a piece of work? Is your technical manager authorized to tell a team to go away and redesign something? Or are both these roles purely advisory, based on benefits of scale?

The project manager is responsible for ensuring that the internal organization is well defined with clear interfaces to the outside world and within the project organization itself. This is the case whether you are running a huge programme or just one of the smaller projects inside it. Every input into your project and every output from it should be clearly identified.

5.3 MATCHING THE PEOPLE TO THE PROJECT ROLES

Your team

By now, you should have your production process, your staffing profile and your description of the project organization, both for the current phase and for future phases. Your next step is to find the staff for the functions which you have carefully defined. Depending on where you work, you may have the authority to hire and fire; more usually your line manager will assign staff to you, leaving you perhaps some space to influence the process. It is your job to get the right resources for the job, so if you have some concerns about the quality of staff assigned to you should raise these with your manager at the start of the project.

Assess the strengths and weaknesses, experience and motivation of your staff. Keep an open mind; sometimes you may think you have found the perfect fit, but the team members think otherwise.

By the time we started recruiting the team, I felt I was well organized. I had defined the project organization and agreed it with the business unit director. We had drawn it in the form of an organogram, and printed it on good-quality paper – it looked like the chart of a well-established company organization. All we needed to do now was to fill in the blanks with some names, and that just seemed a formality.

The first few interviews we had were to staff the database team, and I had Steve clearly in mind for the team leader. He had several years' database experience and he had recently led a team of three people in a similar environment; he was the obvious candidate. When I offered him the position, though, I was surprised to see him hesitate – he said he needed time to think.

In the afternoon I interviewed another database analyst, who had two years' less experience than Steve. Carol was very interested in opportunities for team leadership later in the project. I said that was possible but we had to see how things developed first.

Later in the afternoon, I drove Steve and Carol in my car to the client's site. I listened with interest to the conversation between them. Steve said he enjoyed the technical side of a project; Carol was saying that she preferred the organizational side.

On our way back they both said they liked the look of the project site and the client environment, and were happy to take part in the project, but on one condition: they wanted to swap roles. Carol duly became the team leader and Steve took charge of the technical side. This partnership formed the basis of one of the strongest teams we had in the project.

We may be tempted to assume that everybody in our team would be pleased to be given a leadership position because that is 'the only way up'. In the case of Steve that assumption was wrong. Competent technicians want to do technical work and often have no qualms about reporting to somebody less technically experienced than themselves if this will give them the opportunity to do what they enjoy. Projects in IT often run into difficulties because we set up hierarchical organizations based solely on technical experience and competence. We ignore the personal qualities and preferences that play a major part in the way teams perform.

Assess your staff on the basis of both personal and technical input. The following list gives some examples of informal, non-technical roles which could be useful:

- *The ambassador* someone with good political skills, who understands how the organization functions as a whole: how decisions are made, who has most formal or informal influence, how to 'get things done around here'. One project manager cited a case where a team member who was weak technically was nonetheless a very valuable networker both in his own and in his client's organization.
- *The vision holder* someone who can keep the overview of the project in his or her head, but who can also dive down into details as necessary. Vision holders are essential on complex projects, because they can update and adjust the vision as the project progresses. Check that your vision holder has good communication skills, so that he or she can share his or her understanding with others in the team.
- *The implementers* these are staff who are solidly self-motivated, who enjoy translating plans into reality. They are the 'doers' in your team, and you are bound to need a number of them.
- *The super-star* the brain of the team, the technical whiz-kid who can be relied upon to find inventive solutions to problems.
- *The rapport builder* the person who provides the 'oil in the machine', by giving support, smoothing conflicts, building the relationships and the team spirit. Rapport builders will be prepared to fetch the pizzas when the team is working late, they will remember birthdays and they will enjoy organizing social events. Their contribution is sometimes underestimated; they are particularly useful on long-term projects, because they help to keep morale high.

5.4 YOUR ROLE – LEADING FROM THE MIDDLE

Here is how one senior manager described the role of the project manager:

> The most important thing is to have a clear vision of where the project is heading. Your job is to know the destination, and lead the team from A to B. Imagine you're taking them to the Promised Land; someone else can work out where to camp, how to get water, how to tend the sick and the injured. Your job is to get them there – nothing else matters.

Many successful project managers with a clear sense of vision will develop a leadership style which consists of 'leading from the middle', as this manager described:

> You should be in the centre of the team, building consensus and commitment. By leading from the middle you give space to others in your team to take responsibility and initiative. You can bring the others with you, moving in the right direction.

Leading from the middle enables you to create the super-organism team we were describing earlier. You are not hiding in the middle, of course, because your role is still to take responsibility for *everything to do with the project.* You will have to keep a sense of priorities, be able to make decisions in difficult circumstances, and to support and develop your staff. The following sections and subsequent chapters will cover the steps you should take to get to your destination.

5.5 DELEGATION

Once you have decided on your staff your next challenge is to delegate effectively to them. Unfortunately, this is sometimes harder in practice than on paper: staff may be unclear about what is expected of them, they may feel you intervene too little or interfere too much, and the balance between your workload and theirs may be inappropriate. You will at some time in your career undoubtedly have had a manager who made one of these mistakes with you.

In this section we will first look at the purpose of delegation, then address some of the problems and offer some guidelines for getting delegation right.

The purpose of delegation

Delegation enables you to achieve much more with your team than you could do on your own; it frees you to use your own time more effectively, by concentrating your energy on the areas which are critical to your job. Delegation enables you to develop your staff by offering them varied and challenging work; if your team members feel that they are expanding their knowledge and skills they will be more motivated and more productive. Effective delegation helps you and your staff to move further in your career progression.

The problems with delegation

If delegation is potentially so constructive, why are managers sometimes so reluctant to delegate? If you ask managers why they don't delegate more, you'll hear answers like the following:

'Delegation would be great – if I had the staff to delegate to!'
'Delegation's all very well in theory, but by the time I've organized the delegation I could have done the job myself.'
'I can't delegate this to my staff – it's too boring.'
'If I delegate it they'll make mistakes – and I'll get the blame from my boss.'
'I'm rushed off my feet at the moment – I'll do more delegating when I get the time to organize myself.'

If you press the manager further about her or his reluctance to delegate, sometimes you will hear different replies:

'To be honest, I'm reluctant to lose control – I like doing things my way.'

'I like doing the technical work, and I know I'm good at it, so I don't really want to give it up.'

'It's all very well, but suppose my team member turns out to be better at the job that I am – what happens to me?'

Do any of these look familiar? Before we start to examine them more closely, let's consider the consequences of insufficient delegation – starting with the sort of vicious circle which can emerge for the manager over time. If you overwork, after a while you will get tired and stressed. A common effect of stress is that you lose your ability to prioritize; this in turn eventually has a negative effect on your performance. Once you see the problems piling up, you may try to solve them by working harder – and the cycle starts again.

The team of such a boss will probably complain that they are understretched. If you have ever worked for a boss who has not delegated enough to his or her staff (or if you are currently working for such a boss!) you will probably recognize some of the following comments:

'I feel she doesn't trust me to do a good job.'

'He was very pleasant, but during all the time I worked for him (two years) I felt I learned very little – and I couldn't wait to be transferred.'

'We got fed up with hearing him say how busy he was, when we were doing the same old thing, day in, day out.'

Under-delegating can demotivate your staff – perhaps not in the short term, when they may be delighted to be getting home at a reasonable time in the evenings, but certainly in the long term, when they realize that:

- They are not developing.
- The project is not running as efficiently as it could.
- Overall performance may be suffering.
- The atmosphere in the team is deteriorating.

The irony is that the overworked manager may be seeing himself as the unsung, unappreciated hero, holding everything together – in the face of complaints from his partner and/or family as well as criticism from his team and his boss.

If you recognize at least some of these elements in yourself, and the way you work, what can you do about it? With delegation, as with motivation, much of your behaviour is determined by your underlying beliefs and attitudes – in this case in the key areas of trust and control.

Research has shown that many managers under-estimate what their staff can do. You can see this sometimes when a team member leaves one team, in which she has not performed well, and then positively flourishes in a team run by someone else: the difference lies in the way she has been managed. Now admittedly you have to be realistic here, but nonetheless, managers who have a *low level of trust* in others, and who therefore under-delegate, will probably make their staff under-perform.

The *need for control* is also strong in many managers. Often it has served them well in the past, driving them to produce work in small teams, for instance, which is of a high standard. In larger, perhaps more mature, teams, some staff may bitterly resent the very close supervision which such a manager may try to impose. Control and trust are here closely linked.

The need for control, and a reluctance to trust others to do a good job, will often prevent managers from acquiring and applying the relatively straightforward skills of planning, communicating, implementing and following through an effective piece of delegation. Quietly recognizing that your beliefs and attitudes in these key areas are blocking your own development, and possibly that of others, is the first step to improving your delegating skills.

What about the managers who go to the other extreme, and over-delegate? These managers confuse delegating with abdicating, or even dumping. Some may be unclear themselves about their goals, or expectations, or the authority levels which their staff need. Other managers will specify a task but fail to follow it through with enough supervision and support. When things inevitably go wrong, they fail to acknowledge their role and instead place the blame squarely on the team member.

Managers usually over-delegate because they don't fully understand the process of delegation. They don't realize that when you delegate, you still maintain responsibility for the end result. Indeed, outstanding delegators will often be quick to recognize their part in problems, but they will be generous in recognizing their staff's contribution when things go well.

Guidelines for delegation

Preparation   What should you delegate? Think about the purpose of your project, and your Key Results Areas: those parts of your job which contribute most to achieving your objectives. Sort out the tasks which are essential to your purpose and which only you are qualified to do (selecting the methodology, for instance, if your staff are less experienced). All the other tasks are ones which you could consider delegating.

Check that you don't retain the tasks which you *like*, in preference to those which are essential to your role and your purpose. It is very tempting to defer tackling the more difficult work (e.g. organizing an audit) in favour of the tasks which you know you can tackle really competently right now (e.g. writing a particular bit of code). The coding may be enjoyable, and it will make you feel good, but if you have someone in your team who can achieve the same result with it then coding (or even discussions about coding) would be an ineffective use of your time.

Your next step is to select the person to whom you will delegate the task. Less experienced managers often delegate solely by identifying available members in the team who have the necessary skills. This is a good starting point, but you may also need to think about the long-term implications. If Terry is a database expert who is also excellent at solving difficult technical problems, you may prefer to keep him available for a critical stage later in your project, and to train another member of the team in the meantime to manage the database. Delegation is an excellent opportunity for developing the skills of your staff and for giving them more varied work, so don't just give them the tasks they are already equipped to handle.

What if you have no-one to delegate to? This is a perception shared by many managers, but it is not always justified. The following story told by a project manager is a typical illustration of this point.

I had just set up the organization for a large project; the project was divided into a number of teams, including one large team of 15 staff. I decided to offer the team leader role to Rob, who had been managing a team of eight people very successfully and who was known to be ambitious.

When I told Rob about the opportunity he was clearly thrilled, and for the first few weeks I could see him working late every evening with great enthusiasm. After a month, however, his behaviour started to change; he looked tired, and sounded irritable. I was not surprised when one evening he stormed into my office, flung himself into a chair and demanded to talk.

'It's no good,' he said. 'This has got to change. Here are you, doing next to nothing because you've delegated all your work, while I have to work late every night just to get through my in-tray. You've got to help me out here – take on some of these tasks yourself.'

'What about your team?' I asked. 'You've got some very competent people there.'

'No way', he said. 'They're all far too inexperienced. I have to help them every step of the way.'

Rob was making the classic mistake of taking on everything himself. I pointed out that Veronique was quite capable of taking the responsibility for a large chunk of work, freeing him to do his essential tasks, He protested at first, but after we talked it through he agreed to give her a chance. To give Rob his credit, when she produced a good result he was delighted – and he now manages an even bigger project.

Note that Rob's suggestion was that his project manager should take back some of the tasks; in other words, Rob wanted to delegate up the line, not down. This is a common mistake, based presumably on the assumption that Rob's role was so difficult that only a more experienced manager could help. Often when managers go on holiday they try to persuade someone higher in the line to cover for them, instead of selecting and coaching someone in the team. Check that you delegate down, and organize yourself so that you can organize your team.

When you delegate, remember that you are not simply giving someone a task to perform; you are giving them a *result to achieve*. If you focus on results, you will give a clearer definition of what you want, you will be better able to measure the person's progress, and you will be able to allow your staff more freedom to carry out the task in the way they prefer. If you allow the team member to have more choice in determining how to achieve the result, she will also feel more responsibility for the success of the outcome.

A concept which is hard for some managers to grasp is that when you delegate, you retain responsibility for the outcome. Imagine that the square in Fig. 5.2 represents your job and all the tasks for which you are responsible. The shaded area represents the subset of your job (e.g. to design and code a part of the system) which you are passing on to Maria, a member of your team. The shaded area is Maria's responsibility, but it is also (still) yours. You must pass the task on to her, and monitor and support her, so that she has the best chance of achieving the result.

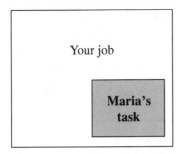

Figure 5.2 Scope of responsibility.

Your next step is to tailor the task, and your delegation style, to the person. First check the scope and the size of the task, then consider how much freedom you will give the person in deciding how to achieve the result. The criteria for your decision are the person's

- Expertise
- Experience
- Track record
- Confidence
- Motivation
- Desire to learn

and, generally, your 'gut feel' about the person and how far you trust them to do the job. Note that some people will have the knowledge and the experience, but not the confidence. You may have to give them more support, at least initially, than you think they really need. Others may have the confidence, but not necessarily the skill, and you may have to convince them of your need to monitor progress regularly.

Some managers use the same style for all their team members, regardless of individual needs; they may monitor all the team closely, for instance, or they may adopt a *laissez-faire* attitude to experienced staff and new joiners alike. This is bad managerial practice: you must adjust the amount of support and supervision to match the needs of each individual. You should also be building up the size and scope of the tasks you delegate, so that the team members can see themselves progressing.

The last, essential, part of your preparation is to identify the information the person will need from you. Remember, it's the result that counts. Bad managers will over-specify the means and under-specify the end. If you are unclear about your expectations but interfere in the methods that staff adopt, they will get confused and irritated. As a minimum, for each task you delegate, you must identify for yourself:

- The objective of the task
- The result you want the person to achieve (deliverables, etc.)
- The standards you expect him or her to follow
- The resources available (people, equipment, space, budget, etc.)
- Authority levels
- The milestones and deadlines
- The degree of freedom the person can have in choosing how to achieve the result.

Briefing   Make sure that you brief the person thoroughly when you delegate each task. Go through the list you have prepared and check that all your assumptions and expectations are explicit and understood. If you want to specify standards and methods which you want the other person to use, explain your reasons and check that the person agrees with them. Other points to cover are:

- How this particular task fits into the context of the project and the team member's personal goals
- How you want the person to make decisions (when should they consult you?)
- Training, coaching and support (when can they and should they come to you for help?)
- The degree to which you want to be involved
- What feedback you want, and when you want it.

If the person is less experienced, you may also want to suggest a possible approach and give any early coaching, so that the team member has got off to a good start. Let other people inside (and possibly outside) the team know that you have delegated this particular task to the person, to avoid misunderstandings and ensure that the person gets the necessary cooperation.

Once you have briefed the person and chosen your method of monitoring progress then you should let the team member get on with the task. Sometimes team members will keep coming to you with questions, because it is quicker to ask you for advice than it is to consult a book or another colleague. Beware: this is a subtle form of upwards delegation! Encourage them to sort out problems as far as possible for themselves, otherwise they really will absorb an unnecessary amount of your time.

5.6 MOTIVATING YOUR TEAM

What can you do to enable your team to work with energy, commitment and enjoyment? Many managers assume that the most powerful motivators are pay rises, promotion and job security, and they worry because in the current economic environment these are all in short supply. Although you may not be in a position to award bonuses, say, for good performance, there are still many straightforward actions which you can take on a day-to-day basis to keep motivation high on your project. To make these actions easier to remember, bear in mind that an *IDEAL* manager will:

*I*nform – about project vision and context, individual goals, organizational changes
*D*elegate – and also develop staff
*E*ncourage – via feedback, personal interest and opportunities for higher visibility
*A*ccept – that no-one is perfect, and you should focus on strengths
*L*isten – for early warning of problems, and to offer genuine support.

Inform (*I*deal)

If your staff don't know exactly what they are supposed to do, or why they are expected to do it, they won't work to the best of their capacity. This may seem obvious, but in practice it is easy to forget the value of information. Managers often assume that their staff will pick up information via some kind of office osmosis; the problem with this informal information is that it is often inaccurate and incomplete. You have to make time yourself to talk to your team regularly, and the following kinds of information are particularly important.

What's my role? Check that your team members fully understand how their work contributes to the project objectives, how it interfaces with that of colleagues, and how it will change and develop over time as the project progresses.

What's the purpose of the project? Everyone in the team, including new joiners and administrative staff, must know what the users expect, what the client requires, and how the project fits into the wider context of both the client's and their own organization. In small teams communication is relatively easy, particularly if you're sitting together in the same part of an open-plan office. In larger projects, staff can easily lose sight of the overview.

> A project manager decided to run a team-building day for his staff. His team was writing a large Functional Specification document, and each member was contributing part of the document. Morale was reasonably high, but the rate of production of output was a little disappointing, and the project manager thought that perhaps his team needed help with their writing skills.
>
> The trainer suggested that, logically, the day should start with a group definition of the objectives of the document – the purpose of the project. The project manager replied, a little impatiently, that this was really just a formality, and that this part of the programme would take, at most, an hour. In the event, it took the full morning for the team to come up with a satisfactory set of objectives. The project manager was startled – 'I thought it was obvious!'

An understanding of the strategic value of your project can also maintain your motivation if it starts to flag, as this project manager discovered:

> I was getting fed up with my four man project – it hadn't been easy working with the client, the work wasn't particularly interesting and the team members were getting on each others' nerves. I'd been managing the project for eight months but it felt like much longer.
>
> Then in a meeting of my Business Group my manager explained that 'my' project was strategically very significant for business development over the next two years. I couldn't believe my ears – he'd never mentioned that to me. It sounds stupid, but I suddenly felt really proud – all the aggravations now seemed minor and manageable in retrospect. My motivation rose, and so did that of my staff. We even got a follow-on project.

What's been happening recently? Keep your team *up to date* with any developments in the project: changes in emphasis, technical modifications, etc. Some managers start off the project with good intentions, but then let the information flow dry up when they come under pressure. Ironically, this is often when the team have the greatest need to be kept informed.

What's going on around here? Tell them about any *forthcoming changes in your own organization* at the earliest moment that you are allowed to do so: staff joining or leaving, reorganizations, changes in policy – anything which could affect them, even indirectly. Informing your team helps you to maintain trust and confidence; uncertainty causes stress. You have to use your judgement about information which is sensitive, or which could cause staff to worry unnecessarily – but the default option is that you let them know what is happening.

Delegate (I*D*eal)

We have covered this subject in the previous section but want to stress here how important it is for people to have tasks which stretch them. If team members feel that they are learning on your project they will be motivated. You will also be improving their prospects for future jobs.

Encourage (Id*E*al)

Motivation is based on sound self-esteem, as well as having the resources and the opportunity to demonstrate your capabilities. The word 'encourage' can sound a bit patronizing, but we mean it in the sense of showing interest, giving support and offering constructive feedback, so that your team members build a sense of realistic confidence.

Staff who are '*results-oriented*' will want to know how well they are performing. For such staff, feedback in the form both of praise and constructive criticism is a motivator. Managers who operate on the 'no news is good news' principle will leave their staff feeling uncertain, especially in the long term. It's all very well if your manager gives you a challenging task and tells you to get on with it – but how do you know if you are on the right track? Specific feedback confirms what you have done well and corrects what you have done wrong, so that you can see for yourself the progress you are making.

Giving feedback is a complex process, however, and it requires careful planning; see Chapter 6 for more detailed suggestions. Staff who are more interested in *relationships* may be especially sensitive to criticism, and often you can encourage them much more effectively by emphasizing what they have done well and by demonstrating personal interest. Tailor your feedback to the person.

A third form of encouragement is *political contact and visibility*. Suppose you have a young man on your team, Peter, who is clearly very ambitious. Feedback on performance and personal attention may both interest him, but what he really wants is access to the senior managers. Peter is motivated by the drive to exert influence, but he is too inexperienced as yet to be given the job of team leader. An example of a way to motivate the Peters of the world is to ask them to make a presentation to senior management. This gives them the opportunity to observe how managers behave, so they can model their style on that of their senior colleagues. Arranging for Peter to have direct contact with more experienced managers gives him the higher profile he aspires to – and unless you particularly enjoy making presentations, it will free you for more urgent and important tasks.

Encouragement comes in a number of forms, and as with delegation, your job is to tailor your style to meet your team member's needs. A helpful guideline is '*treat them all the same by treating them differently*'. The very fact that you adjust your approach for each person will show that you recognize that each person is unique.

Accept (Ide*A*l)

Accept your staff for who they are, including their strengths and weaknesses. Only in exceptional cases will you be able to reject staff or throw them off your project. On the whole, you will be expected to make the best of what you've got.

Effective managers seem to be particularly good at exploiting their team members' strengths, rather than getting irritated at their weaknesses.

In one project managers' workshop a very experienced manager was presented with a number of cases: examples of 'problem people' with whom the participants had to deal. One team leader was worried about a team member who would never deliver on time, another described a colleague who was always arguing with the standards, and so on. Each time the participant presented the problem, the manager would pause, think and ask 'OK – so how can you use that constructively?' His approach was entirely pragmatic: once you had identified the problem behaviour, you had to work out how you were going to cope with it. You could try coaching the team member to try to change the behaviour, but if that failed you simply had to find some way of working round it – by putting in extra contingency, or reducing the scope of the task or whatever. One thing was certain – there was no point in getting indignant.

Varying productivity levels are another typical worry for the project manager. Again the solution is often to plan to work with what you've got. One team member may be a super-star who completes twelve months' worth of work in four months; another may be doing his best but takes twelve months to finish what you had scheduled for four. As long as you know in advance what you can reasonably expect from your staff, you should be able to plan accordingly.

Personal strengths and weaknesses are often two sides of the same coin. You can't expect your staff to be perfect all-rounders – someone who is very creative, for instance, may be hopeless with details. A team member who has the intellectual drive and energy to challenge complacency can hardly be expected at the same time to be sensitive and diplomatic. Often we fail to see the qualities in colleagues that are complementary to our own; we may be very aware, however, of the areas where they don't match up to our own standards. If you focus too much on your team's weaknesses you may detract from some very valuable strengths.

John, a project manager, was lamenting the lack of drive and ambition in Boris, a young team member. He was discussing the problem with a friend. 'He ought to be ready to run a part of the project by now,' he said, 'but he doesn't seem very keen. Trouble is, he can't handle conflicts – he just backs off. He's a nice enough chap, but I really don't know what to do with him.' 'Can he get on well with his colleagues?' asked the friend. 'Oh, sure – everyone likes him. In fact, he's a lot more patient than I am.' 'How about putting him on the help desk then? We need someone with good interpersonal skills there.' 'That's an idea.' John replied. 'Why didn't I think of that myself?'

Accepting strengths and weaknesses does not imply that you should be passive with your staff – of course you should encourage them to develop and expand their skills. At times you will also have to confront inadequate results fairly but firmly. Realistically, though, we all have a number of underlying patterns of behaviour which can be difficult to change. Focusing on the negatives can sap people's confidence; building on existing strengths will often help them to improve their performance.

Listen (Idea*L*)

Listening demonstrates interest and respect: if a manager fails to listen attentively to her staff she will actively demotivate them. Many Europeans and native English speakers have been brought up to think that listening is essentially passive, and thus less useful than talking; consequently they don't develop their listening skills. They then miss out on a lot of important information, such as early indications of technical performance problems or hints about what motivates a key team member.

Other managers recognize the importance of listening but find that the quality of their listening deteriorates rapidly when they are under pressure. A number of techniques can help you to concentrate. They need to be practised in a 'live' situation if you really want to improve your skills, but here they are intended as a starting point or a reminder.

- Check how you are *sitting or standing*. Facing someone across a table, for instance, can put you into a confrontational position; sitting at right angles can make it easier for the other person to talk.
- *Show that you are listening*; nods, grunts, eye contact all demonstrate that you are paying attention and encourage the person to continue.
- *Listen to the end* of the sentence; if you interrupt, you may cut off important clues.
- Listen for *key words or phrases* which the other person emphasizes or repeats. This is an easy way to identify individual motivation profiles. Results-oriented staff will talk about performance, success or failure, improvement, goals, standards, getting things done, etc. Team members who are motivated by relationships will talk about other people, the team spirit or ambience, rapport, tensions or conflicts which could threaten the friendly atmosphere, and so on.
- Try to keep *an open mind*; often we filter out information which appears at first to be irrelevant (John, for instance, had screened out clues to Boris's interest in people, because this was not a pattern which interested him personally). You don't have to be a psychologist to find out what motivates people – you just have to concentrate on what they are saying.
- *Summarize.* This is the easiest way to improve your communication skills; it shows that you are listening, it helps you to concentrate and it enables you to check that you have understood.
- *Take your time.* Don't rush to solve a problem which you may not yet have fully understood. Allow pauses, and thinking time – both of you will need it. If you rush, you may find yourself thinking ahead of your next question while the person is still talking. Listen and concentrate, then pause to formulate your next remark. This tempo may seem slow, but it will enable you both to communicate much more effectively.
- *Say if you are too busy* – and make another appointment. Half-listening is often worse than nothing, and you have your rights too. Make sure that you keep the appointment, though – cancelling it a second time would send a very negative signal.

5.7 MANAGING MEETINGS AND SETTING UP THE CULTURE

Meetings have a critical effect on team building, because they are the occasions when all the group is together. If the meeting is well run, and progress is made, then the team gets an early sense of confidence in its own productivity; if the meeting lacks pace or control, then a team may disintegrate into a group of individuals. One of the tests of a good meeting is that the team members must feel more motivated at the end of the meeting than they did at the beginning. They should be clearer, for instance, on the direction the team is taking and the particular contribution they are expected to make. One of the tests of a good chairperson is that all the team meetings should be perceived as an effective use of the team members' time.

To make a team into a super-organism, you also need to observe and to shape the 'culture' which will quickly emerge in your group events. Experienced managers will stay on the alert for behaviours which, if left unchecked and uncommented, can quickly become covert norms and ground rules which are subsequently very difficult to change. If two senior members dominate the early meetings, for instance, you will find that the quieter team members will often remain hesitant later to voice their views. If sensitive issues are swept under the carpet in the first phase of the project, you can hardly expect your team to be open and direct with each other later on.

Think back to your schooldays for an easy analogy. The way the teacher interacted with the group during the first week usually set the pattern for the whole of the school year. Promoting a positive team culture is thought by many experts to be a key skill for leaders of small and big teams alike.

To make your meetings motivating you must be able to distinguish between the *task* (what you are working on) and the *process* (how you are working on it). An example of a *task* in a meeting could be checking and discussing a number of estimates submitted by the people present, in order to come to a joint decision. The *process* issues in the meeting would include the decision-making methods chosen, the amount of 'air space' given to individual contributors, the way you handle disagreements and so on. Managing both the task and the process in real time is very hard work, even for experienced facilitators: there is so much going on at the same time.

The solution is to prepare for all your meetings really thoroughly so that you can plan for as many eventualities as possible in advance. We will address some meetings with special objectives, such as monitoring progress, consensus building and conflict handling in subsequent chapters. The following guidelines offer a general framework for planning and running successful meetings.

Preparation

What's the purpose?   What's the meeting for? The purpose could be, for instance, to select a methodology which everyone in the team can understand and implement. You may also want to focus on the outcome – what do you want at the end of the meeting? Do you really want to have selected the final methodology or would you also be happy with a short list of options which you or the team could investigate further? What outcome would be a good result, considering the people present and the time available?

Who should be there?   Once you have defined the purpose, you can plan the attendees. If you want to make a decision in the meeting you must limit the number of those present, because otherwise there simply will not be enough time for each person to talk. Meetings for information dissemination can be larger.

Don't feel that you have to stick to a fixed list of attendees. Some topics may simply be irrelevant to certain team members, in which case they will get bored no matter how well you run the meeting. At other times you may want to invite outside resources to make a contribution. Perhaps some members can attend part of the meeting; you could agree to call them when you are ready, or let them leave after a particular point has been discussed. You have to be tactful here; on the one hand, you must be careful not to upset people by excluding them, and, on the other, your 'results-oriented' staff will appreciate your economical use of their time. Talk the matter through with your staff in advance to find out their views.

How long should it last? Ideally meetings should not last longer than an hour; two hours is probably a maximum. You can have longer events, of course, but they have to be carefully managed with planned breaks.

What agenda should you choose? Some meetings benefit greatly from the structure of a fixed agenda; you can cover a lot of minor points, and stop people from rambling. If you send out the agenda in advance you can help the other participants to prepare their thoughts in advance. The agenda will enable you to agree a timetable, and to structure the minutes of the meeting.

Occasionally a fixed agenda may be too inhibiting: if you want to promote creativity in problem solving, for instance, or allow for a free-ranging debate. In these cases a statement of objectives and a rough agreement about how you will spend your time may be all that is necessary. Work out in advance how much fixed structure would be appropriate.

Which practical arrangements should you make? Even well-prepared meetings can be ruined by prolonged exposure to rooms without windows or disappearing coffee trolleys. Check in advance that the facilities will be adequate; hourly breaks can help to keep the energy level high.

In the meeting

Start with alignment You must get everyone thinking in the same direction before you can make progress – whatever your chosen objective. Explain the purpose, and agree the procedures at the start of every meeting. Often in routine events (the Friday morning progress meeting, for example) the purpose gets blunted; people become hazy about why they are there. State a specific goal, to focus everyone's attention.

Visual aids support the alignment process. If you write key information such as the purpose or action points on a whiteboard or flipchart, or assign a 'scribe' to do this for you, then everyone in the meeting can use this as a reference point. Standing up to write can also give you more control over the group if you have a noisy meeting.

Alignment depends on joint understanding and a joint starting point. You may need to take action to bring part of the team up to date. If someone comes in late, for instance, help them to settle in by summarizing where you have got to so far. If you have colleagues whose native language differs from yours, start by speaking slowly, so they can 'tune in'. As in relay races, the pace at which you progress will depend on the speed of your slowest runner. If someone straggles behind, you will miss that person's contribution, and you may have to sort out misunderstandings later. A patient start will help you to reap rewards in terms of your outcome later.

Use a basic structure   Even if you are brainstorming, you will still need the framework of stating the purpose at the start and summarizing actions and conclusions at the end. Issue written minutes (you can delegate this) at the end of the meeting if you think people need a written record; take notes of actions yourself whatever happens.

Agree the structure explicitly at the start. If members then diverge from the agenda, you can draw their attention to it and help them to get back on track.

Check the ground rules   Audit the behaviours people use in the meeting; these will form the basis for the 'culture' we described at the start of this section. You will need to check your own behaviour, too. If you want punctuality as one of the ground rules, you should be careful about your own timekeeping. The easiest way to establish a constructive culture is by modelling it yourself. The following list gives examples of behaviours which are particularly important:

1. Are people listening to each other? Frequent interruptions may inhibit quieter members of the team, and cutting people off can be interpreted as a lack of respect. Point out to team members that they must treat each other's views seriously.
2. Is everyone included? Some people are happy to stay silent if they agree with what colleagues are saying; others will feel actively excluded if their opinion is never invited. Step in and ask less assertive team members for their views.
3. Are team members courteous to each other? Occasionally very technically oriented staff may be less sensitive to other colleagues' feelings. It's not much fun if your bright ideas are labelled 'ridiculous' by more aggressive colleagues. Remind team members to be constructive in criticizing each others' ideas – check Chapter 6 for more suggestions.
4. Are team members positive? If new ideas are constantly met with 'Yes, but' responses, then creativity will wither in your team. A useful guideline is that people should state what they like about an idea before they are entitled to attack it; that way you can build on each other's suggestions. Check too the use of language in the team; confirmed pessimists may harp on about 'problems' and 'difficulties', and in the long run this can make everyone feel depressed. Point out that 'problems' can be interesting 'challenges' too!

5.8 A CASE STUDY

Team building is not a single activity but a number of parallel processes which the project manager has to lead and direct. We conclude this chapter with an account of a meeting where a project manager is describing how he was working simultaneously on some of the key issues we have covered in this chapter:

- He was establishing the ground rules: the way the team would work together.
- He was setting up a team culture which was open and constructive.
- He was informing and consulting his team, so that they would be aligned.
- He was working with them to build a clear vision.

We were a new team of eight: three members had already worked with me on the Functional Specification for the project, but the others were fresh to the project and had come from sister companies. My task was to lead this team in the design phase of the project. The client had told us that for commercial reasons we would be under severe time pressure, so I was somewhat nervous. At least we all shared the same quality procedures and working practices, so I hoped that would give us a common language.

In our first meeting we decided to note down the key issues which we should be bearing in mind throughout the project in order to achieve the project objectives within the required time scales. We agreed a number of points. First, we would make sure that every potential candidate knew that the time scales were short and that this could cause potential problems. Second, we would also all do our best to carry out actions quickly and we would use every opportunity to save time. Third, system performance would be very challenging, so we would make sure that the whole team would be aware of this requirement at all times. We would improve performance wherever possible but not at the expense of losing time. Finally, we were all in this project because we agreed it was going to be exciting and because we would all learn a lot from the experience.

The meeting generated a lot of energy and emotion. It set the framework for our discussions over the next few weeks, and throughout the project the team worked to support the ground rules we had agreed. You could see this in day-to-day comments in memos and progress reports such as 'I have found a new way to do X which saved me two days last week'. There were similar suggestions from other team members in almost every project meeting.

I think a lot of our subsequent success can be attributed to that first meeting. We succeeded in making the whole team take responsibility from the start for meeting the time scales. The team members took their cue from each other, building on good ideas and implementing them fast. Together we created our vision – and together we achieved it.

SUMMARY OF TEAM BUILDING

1. The benefits of teams are that:
   - You can learn from each other.
   - You have a flexible pool of resources with which to tackle problems.
   - You set up a community of social support.
2. Select your team structure:
   - Check how much organizational support you will need.
   - Be explicit about roles, interfaces and authority levels.
3. Fit the people to the roles:
   - Keep an open mind.
   - Assess both technical and personal qualities.
   - Remember that your role is to keep the vision and 'lead from the middle'.
4. Delegate effectively:
   - Check the blocks: lack of trust, need for control.
   - Delegate to develop.
   - Prepare carefully.
   - Focus on results.
   - Brief thoroughly.

5. Motivate your team:
   *I*nform
   *D*elegate
   *E*ncourage
   *A*ccept
   *L*isten
6. Managing meetings – setting up the culture:
   - Members should be more motivated at end.
   - Manage task and process.
   - Prepare well.
   - Align at the start.
   - Check the ground rules.

6

STAYING ON TRACK

6.1 THE NEED FOR A MONITORING AND CONTROL SYSTEM

Once you have got the team functioning as a unit, you need to check that your monitoring and control system is working effectively. Monitoring the progress of a project is a highly complex undertaking. When you run a small team you can rely on daily checks with your staff to ensure that you are on track. When you are managing a project, you need to design and implement a coherent system to enable you to stay in control.

One colleague explained the monitoring and control process by comparing the project manager to a pilot:

> Running a project is like flying an aeroplane. You must know where you are going, and you need a powerful set of instruments to tell you where you are in relation to your planned route. More often than not you'll be slightly off target, so you'll have to take corrective action. Being passive is extremely dangerous: you've got to be fully in charge of that plane.

Another useful analogy is that of process control engineering. Projects, like other complex processes, undergo continual change. If a planned change is not properly controlled it sets up oscillations, which eventually destroy the process. Project engineers seek to control the process by moving their project successfully from one stable state to another.

The process control engineer aims to create stability at each state before moving on to the next. In Fig. 6.1 State A could be the start of the project, State B when the Functional Specification has been completed but the design phase has not yet begun, State C when the design has been completed, and so on. The lines in the diagram represent baselines, or milestones towards achieving the project objectives.

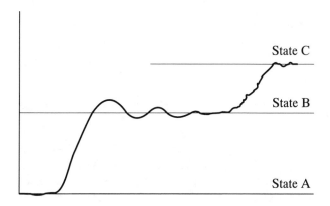

Figure 6.1   A stable process of state change – the Process Control Analogy.

The process engineer achieves progress through the states, usually with the help of an automated process control system, by defining 'set points' for the following state. As the product is moved towards the next state, measurements are taken of the product, and the results are compared with the set points the engineer has predefined. The system then decides on any corrective action needed.

The advantage of thinking about monitoring progress in terms of moving through a series of states or baselines, rather than along a continuum, is that you can secure each position before you move on. This enables you to stabilize progress, and gives you something to fall back on if you get into difficulties. You can also prove to the client and to your own management what you have achieved, and create a sense of confidence and security.

Unfortunately, as a project manager in IT you do not normally have the sophisticated measuring instruments of the pilot or the automated systems of the process engineer at your disposal – you have to design your own. In this chapter we will look first therefore at how to set up your monitoring and control system and how to organize your reporting. (You should already have decided on your overall approach to monitoring and reporting in your project plan, as described in Chapter 2.) We will then describe ways of monitoring the performance of your staff and offer guidelines for giving feedback – both to individuals and in review meetings. Finally we will cover action follow-up systems and the role of stocktaking sessions.

6.2 DESIGNING THE MONITORING AND CONTROL SYSTEM

Your first step is to select the variables which will give you the most useful data for keeping your project under control. Here we encounter some problems:

- The list of variables which impact the success of the project is very long.
- Some variables are notoriously difficult to measure (e.g. staff motivation and team spirit).
- Some are very expensive to measure.

Traditionally, we measure the following:

- Effort spent presented in labour units
- Project costs
- Quality
- People (we cover this subject in Sec. 6.5).

Effort monitoring will enable you to track the project time scales, and so it will be your starting point. You do not have to do all the effort monitoring yourself. You may choose to monitor the effort spent on every work package in the project or to monitor the higher-level work packages only. You can delegate lower-level work packages to team leaders or projects managers of subprojects who will aggregate the costs of these smaller work packages to report on the costs of their total subproject.

Project cost monitoring is a line management requirement, and it also enables you to have more flexibility in running your project. The effort spent represents only a part of your total project costs, and you will need to monitor all your costs so that you can make trade-offs. You can then decide how best to use your overall resources. You may opt, for instance, to spend part of your budget on a development machine rather than asking your team to expend more effort.

Quality monitoring is more complex than other variables. As we will see in Chapter 7 , 'quality' has many dimensions. You can also monitor quantitatively or qualitatively. Suppose you want to monitor maintainability of the system, for instance. You could devise quantitative measures of factors which affect maintainability, such as the length of a process or the number of interfaces in it. A qualitative approach would be to inspect the documentation and the structure of the code, both of which have a large impact on maintainability. If you address these dimensions in your quality plan for your project you will make everyone in your team more aware of their significance.

The quality of each work package should be monitored according to predefined quality criteria. You should also monitor the quality of the production process itself. Some projects choose to monitor the number of quality observations made per unit of work or the defects found in products which have been completed and have passed the quality checks. Statistical analysis of these measurements can provide a very useful insight into the overall quality of your production process.

6.3 REPORTING

Reporting is an important element of keeping the project on track. If you decide to take some corrective action you will usually need to involve other parties besides your own staff: management, the client, suppliers or perhaps some other party outside the project team. You must keep these parties informed of the status of the project to provide them with the background information for the actions they need to take.

Reporting also forces you to stand back and review the project for yourself. It gives you a regular opportunity to analyse your own progress – not just on a weekly basis, which gives you a 'worm's eye' view of the project but also monthly, where you will have to set your performance in a wider context. Big projects often need additional quarterly reviews to encourage you to look further into the future and think more strategically.

Think first when you report about your different sets of readers, their roles and their requirements, and structure your document accordingly. We will address written reports in more detail in Chapter 9, but the following is an overview of your main readers and what they expect from you.

The role of *supervisory and control functions*, both in your own and in your client's organization, is to check that people are doing their jobs correctly. They will expect you to answer the following questions:

- Which problems have you identified over the last reporting period?
- Which actions have you taken?
- What was the effect of your actions – have the problems been solved?
- Do you need any help from anyone else in tackling any remaining difficulties?
- What are your plans for the next reporting period?
- Which problems do you foresee?
- How will you tackle them?
- Will you require any additional help?

Reporting at this level is a cyclical process; you look back and review, look forward and plan and so on, so that you move forwards at a steady rate. Control functions will require a detailed picture from you, both of your problem areas and of your successes. If everything is going according to plan, you should tell them the good news. Going back to the process control analogy at the start of this chapter, they will want you to provide solid evidence that you are moving the project forward from your secured base at State A to your next baseline at State B. Your task is to reassure them that the project is fully under control. If you are running a large project, you will expect the same information from your team leaders.

Senior management will want the broad picture, including a longer-term perspective. They will not be interested in the details of what you have done and why. If you are running a large project, senior management will expect you to have the problems which are coming up over the next few months more or less under control: that is why they put you in charge. Some form of exception reporting might be helpful, but their key area of interest will be the problems which will be coming up in six months' time and which you may not have anticipated. As one senior project manager expressed it;

> Suppose you've fallen into two large holes over the last three months. Senior managers are not interested in hearing how you got out of the holes – they've delegated that to their controllers. They want to know if you're now standing back far enough to be able to survey the road ahead and check it for holes in advance. Reporting at this level makes you look up, look ahead and scan the horizon.

The ability to integrate the short-term detailed review with the longer-term strategic one is essential if you want to manage your project successfully. This is where your reporting links in with your understanding of the purpose and with your project vision. It helps you as project leader to distinguish between efficiency (doing the thing right) and effectiveness (doing the right thing). We will return to this theme in later chapters.

6.4 ACTIONS AND ACTION FOLLOW-UP

Part of your job is to ensure that all actions on the project are completed by you or by someone else. This can be a complex undertaking. During the lifetime of a project you will be interacting with a large number of people who must complete actions in order for you to achieve the project objectives.

Some kind of administrative support is essential. You may already have this if you are running a large project, otherwise you will have to set up your own system. The process of action follow-up can be defined as follows:

- Identify action.
- Define scope and time scale of action.
- Get commitment.
- Enter it into your system and follow up progress.
- Mark clearly the completed actions as closed.

Action follow-up systems vary from simple paper-based systems to very sophisticated databases with alarm and reminding facilities to help you to follow up the actions at preselected points in time. Many experienced managers rely on the word-processing packages and spreadsheets which are available on most networks these days. The type of system you would need would depend on the complexity of your project and on your own personal style. Some well-organized project managers can keep track of a complex array of actions using no more than a daily log book.

Summary

1. You need a monitoring and control system:
   - To help you identify, secure and move through a series of stable states
   - And thus to create confidence
2. Monitor effort, project costs (so you can make trade-offs), quality and people.
3. Reporting informs others so they can take action – and forces you to review the project from a number of perspectives:
   - Supervisory/control functions need the detailed picture.
   - Senior management need the long-term view.
4. You need both the short- and the long-term view in order to stay in control.
5. Organize your own system for action follow-up.

6.5 MONITORING THE PERFORMANCE OF YOUR STAFF

Monitoring the performance of *people* can be an emotive issue. Some managers will insist that it is necessary in order to ensure that staff 'do a decent job'. Others will feel that the very concept is patronizing.

Monitoring your staff's performance is an essential part of your responsibility towards both your team and your organization as a whole. Promotions and pay rises may well be based largely on your rating of your team members. Some project managers will feel uncomfortable at this thought, but if you dodge the issue, and avoid giving criticism, you are being unfair to your staff. They will only be disappointed later, and they will have been deprived of an early opportunity to make improvements.

The secret to effective monitoring is to use it as a motivator. Good monitoring provides a safety net for your staff, so that they don't have sleepless nights worrying about their work (and hopefully you won't either). Monitoring is an important source of feedback, intended to help staff to develop their skills. Of course, part of your job is measuring progress and, if necessary, taking corrective action. However, the emphasis should be not on tight constraints and punishment but on coaching, training and enabling the team to maintain high standards.

What's the best way to monitor your staff? If you read the following story, you can first test for yourself how you would handle the situation.

I'd been working on a fixed-price project which was running a bit behind. I asked for more resources and was given an older man, who had been working in the company for about a year. He seemed quite pleasant and his experience was comparable to mine. I asked around to get an idea of what his work was like but I couldn't get much information. I was pretty busy so once I'd briefed him I left him to get going by himself.

I'd assigned him a set of 10 report programs, with an original estimate of 100 days to do the lot. He'd been happy with the estimate. Now, however, he was 35 days into his work – and I suddenly realized that I hadn't seen any of the three report programs which should have been ready.

I had a quick chat with him, and he said he'd taken a bit longer than expected to get into the work, but he was confident he could deliver the 10 programs on time – he assured me I had no need to worry. I noticed that he was beginning to work late in the evenings, so the more I thought about it, the more nervous I became. I set up a more formal meeting with him to find out exactly what was going on.

How should the project manager handle this meeting? He should have followed up the programs earlier, of course. Experienced managers recommend monitoring every first program of a set, and certainly every first piece of work from a new team member. Now he'd realized his mistake. The two traps to avoid in the meeting are:

- *The interrogation* The project manager fires off a series of closed questions ('OK, where are the programs then? Why aren't they ready?') in a tense, confrontational atmosphere. Result: the team member becomes defensive and closes down – the manager makes no progress.
- *The soft approach* The project manager feels embarrassed that he has not intervened earlier; he is also reluctant to ask direct questions ('After all, the team member has the same experience as me'). The team member is able to satisfy the manager with some vague assurances; no concrete actions are agreed, and again no progress is made.

To manage the 'human' problem effectively you need to put yourself in the other person's place – in this case, in the place of the team member. If you were him, what would you need in order to give the full story?

The reality was that the team member had fallen seriously behind; he felt out of his depth technically, he was alarmed by the speed demonstrated by his younger colleagues, and he was hoping to catch up by working in the evenings, when no-one could see him. He needed both *technical help and some reassurance*. Initially in the meeting, he was evasive and tried hard to persuade the manager to leave him alone, because he felt that his pride and his reputation were at stake. The project manager had to strike a balance between getting at the truth and reassuring the team member that if he was honest about the facts, then it would be much easier for the manager to organize support and thus for the two to resolve the problem together. Some guidelines for a meeting such as this are as follows:

- *Set up a friendly climate* You want him to open up, not to close down defensively. Choose the time and location carefully; plan for no interruptions. Allow yourself and the other person some time to settle down – don't rush. Start by explaining the purpose of the meeting, e.g.
  'I've called the meeting because I'd like to hear how things are going, and how you're settling down in the team. I am a bit concerned that you may be having some problems, but if I know about them early we can work out together how to resolve them.'
- *Note his verbal and non-verbal reactions* By verbal we mean the words he uses; listen carefully for clues, as in the following:
  'It's going fine *on the whole*.'
  'It's all right *really*.'
  Pick up and reflect back these hesitations
  'You said 'on the whole' – which bits are you finding more difficult?'
  Non-verbal reactions include changes in facial expression, blushing, fidgeting, voice volume dropping or rising, shifts in the sitting position, etc. Be particularly alert to signs of stress. You may be tempted to press harder for an answer, but this may cause your team member to become defensive and shut up. Often it's better to slow the pace down and summarize, e.g.
  'Let me check if I understand you right – you say you haven't produced anything yet, but you're still confident you're on track – can we talk a bit more about that?'
- *Whatever happens, avoid blame* It's very tempting to say something like:
  'Why didn't you let me know earlier? I thought you had the experience to handle this!'
  Your job is to help him take responsibility for what has happened, in order to correct the situation. If you blame him, he may simply get stuck in defensive behaviour.
- *Don't get distracted by long stories or counter-attacks* Be prepared to interrupt a long monologue with a short summary, and a question to move him on, e.g.
  'Right, so I understand you took a few days to read through the documentation, and I'm sorry there was no-one around at that time to answer your questions. What extra information do you need exactly?'
  Some managers are reluctant to ask to *see* the programs which have been completed; they feel this may offend the other person. Beware of the '90 per cent complete' syndrome! The program is either ready or it isn't, and the team member must acknowledge this.
- *Check your use of questions* Use open questions at the start, to open up fields of information without constraining the scope of the answer. Examples of open questions are
  'How are you planning to move on from here?'

'What's your progress to date?'

Closed questions (which evoke 'yes' or 'no' as answers) are useful for clarification and for checking the facts:

'So you haven't actually produced anything yet?'

Again, check your non-verbal behaviour and avoid any hints of aggression, but don't be afraid to ask these questions. You have a right and a responsibility to know what is going on. Moreover, in practice, the team member felt a real sense of relief when the truth was out – he said he felt as if a heavy burden had been lifted from his shoulders, and he could then get the help he needed.

- *Help the other person to think the problem through* Suppose you have uncovered the scope of the problem, but the team member still protests that he can catch up and complete on time. You want to get him to realize for himself that his time estimates for completion are unrealistic. Use more open questions, e.g.

'What is your basis for thinking you can complete on time?'

'What do you think could go wrong?'

'What if this plan does not work out?'

- *Help him to come up with an action plan which you both believe in* If you impose an action plan the team member may not feel he is responsible for its success. Perversely, if more difficulties emerge later, he may even blame the manager for them ('The project manager made me do it this way – it's his problem!'). Ask questions such as:

'In the light of our discussion so far, how much time – realistically – do you think you will need now to complete the first program?'

'What do you plan to do first?'

If possible, ask the team member to summarize the actions agreed, and the time and date for the follow-up meeting. Make a written note for yourself. Try to end on a positive note, e.g.

'Right, we've covered a lot of ground and I think we've now got an approach that we both feel comfortable with. Let me know if you need any further help – otherwise I'll see you again next Monday.'

One final word of warning: resist the temptation now to check his work every day. Many managers will go from one extreme (not checking at all) to the other (checking at every opportunity) and this abrupt tightening of the reins could be counter-productive. Stick to the agreed action plan; you can always adjust it subsequently if necessary.

The frequency with which you monitor the work of your staff will vary widely according to the expertise, the confidence and the preferred working style of the individual. Some people like a very high degree of autonomy; if you monitor them too often they will interpret this as a sign that you don't trust them. Others prefer the reassurance of more frequent checks, and may feel unsupported if you don't talk to them regularly. Decide how you will monitor the work of each team member by:

- Asking what they prefer
- Explaining your needs
- Identifying an approach which will suit you both.

What about staff who are real specialists, or who are really very senior – should you still have to monitor their work? The answer is a definite yes. A senior consultant working on your project may not have the same sense of overall responsibility for the project as you have – after all, you're the manager, not her. Her priorities may be different, and this could cause her occasionally to slip her time scales.

Your technical specialist could also get out of his depth, for whatever reason, so you can't just abandon him to get on with things. Never leave things to chance; the longer you wait before you intervene, the harder it will be to get progress back on track, as can be seen from the story earlier in this section. If he insists that everything is under control, agree a meeting in about two or three weeks' time when he will produce the deliverable which he has promised. If in the meeting the deliverable is not 100 per cent complete, then intervene, using the guidelines we have described. You should also shorten the intervals between subsequent monitoring points.

Summary – Monitoring your staff

1. You are responsible both to your staff as individuals and to your organization for monitoring performance.
2. Use monitoring to intervene, support, train and achieve high standards.
3. With problem cases:
   - Avoid interrogations.
   - Be prepared to confront the '90 per cent complete' syndrome.
   - Put yourself in the other person's place – what does he or she need from you?
   - Prepare questions.
   - Pick up clues.
   - Don't blame.
   - Help the other person to think the problem through.
   - Agree an action plan and follow-up.
4. Adjust the frequency of monitoring to the individual – but monitor everyone, including senior staff.

6.6 GIVING FEEDBACK ON PERFORMANCE

He's a nice guy, and the project seems to be going OK, but he never really tells me how I'm doing. At first I was pleased – I assumed 'no news was good news' – but now I'm feeling unsettled because I don't know where I stand.

She's devastating with her criticism – red ink all over my work. I feel like I'm back at school.

Giving feedback on performance – both praise and criticism – is an integral part of the project manager's job, but it's a part that many managers feel unsure about. It requires planning, sensitivity and, sometimes, courage to do it properly. If you avoid giving criticism, as in the first example, the results-oriented staff (see Chapter 5) feel uncertain and their motivation will drop. If you take an authoritarian approach as in the second example, you may cause enormous resentment in your staff; you may hurt people's feelings and damage their self-esteem. The following are some suggestions for giving feedback so that

- The other person learns and develops.
- The relationship is at least maintained, and hopefully strengthened.
- The performance of the other person improves.

Prepare carefully

The golden rule of giving feedback is to *stick to the facts*: prepare a number of specific points which you can back up with evidence and a rationale. It's the vague, judgemental statements which are interpreted as personal attacks and which do damage.

> A young receptionist was working for a small systems house which had 20 staff. For three days running she had worked unpaid overtime, and her boyfriend was getting fed up with the disruption to their evenings. On the Thursday she had agreed to go out to an early film which he particularly wanted to see.
>
> To her dismay, at 5 o'clock a draft proposal landed on her desk for typing. She knew the proposal was important, so she set to work typing as much as she could. Her boyfriend arrived and was duly angry with her, but she continued on until finally the draft was finished.
>
> Next morning she found the draft back on her desk, with a message in large red letters. 'Irma, this is careless work – 43 mistakes!!' Not one of her colleagues could understand why she burst into tears. She handed in her notice shortly afterwards.

The word which caused the damage was 'careless'. It represented an attack on her personally; it implied that she had not done her best, whereas nothing could have been farther from the truth. The person who had written 'careless' had assumed, wrongly, that he could read her thoughts and feelings – something which most of us would find hard to do even with people who were very close to us. '43 mistakes' was a demonstrable fact, which she could agree with – no problem there. She left because her positive intentions had not been acknowledged.

Take the time to select *clear examples* of the work output or the work behaviour you want the person to change. When you are in the meeting, don't launch into personal attacks, e.g. 'Frances, this report is rubbish – I'm really disappointed in you'. Instead, focus on the specifics: 'I've got a comment on the introduction, Frances. I can't find the objectives clearly stated in the first few paragraphs.' The same rule applies to giving praise; if you are specific, then the other person knows exactly which behaviour was successful, and she can then repeat and build on the successful pattern in the future.

Concentrate on two or three items only

Sitting through a seemingly endless critique, no matter how well intentioned, would make most of us defensive, and when we become defensive, we don't learn. Some project managers feel very frustrated by this guideline and will protest: 'You mean that if the report really is rubbish, and there are ten pieces of criticism, that I'd have to spread it over three meetings? Wouldn't that be worse?' People are not machines; if you damage their self-esteem then you may cause much more serious problems in the future. Select the three messages which will best help the person to improve.

The report with the ten pieces of criticism raises other questions: for instance, was the delegation of this task adequately managed? As manager you share the responsibility for the errors made.

Give feedback as soon as possible after the event

Don't wait until someone's appraisal to give them feedback; they will have forgotten what was in their mind when they did a particular piece of work. Talk to them at the earliest opportunity.

Explain your rationale

Give your reasons – don't just tell someone that something is wrong. If the other person understands the reasoning behind your comment, he or she will learn more readily.

Give a balance of praise and criticism

Some managers will protest that since they learn only from criticism, not praise, their staff must be able to adopt the same approach. Others will say that their staff know what they're doing right, and don't need the manager to tell them.

A professional approach is to give both negative and positive feedback, so that the person receives a balanced evaluation of their work. Check your wording and your non-verbal behaviour, though; avoid the predictable format of 'The report is good on the whole – but...' where the listener will ignore the praise because the intonation of the 'but' warns him of trouble ahead! If necessary, separate out the good news and the bad, so that the other person really picks up both sets of messages, e.g. 'I thought Chapters 2 to 6 were well laid out; I liked the way you highlighted the main points, because I think that makes it very easy for the client to read. I've got some comments about the introduction, though.'

Check that the other person fully agrees with your evaluation

If she does, then you can ask her how she intends to change the piece of work and you can move into action planning. If she does not agree, you may waste time in unproductive argument. You have to go back to your rationale, and perhaps try to present your arguments in a different way so that she can accept them.

Occasionally you may be confronted with a counter-attack: 'That's all very well, but you told me to do it this way.'

Try to stay calm and open-minded – was there some aspect of the work which you did not make clear at the start? If so, you must acknowledge this: 'OK, I take the point – I should have given you the written standards at the start. Now, how can we correct this?' You would also need to agree the actions which you would take to avoid this sort of problem in the future.

Conclude with an action plan

Encourage the other person to set up an action plan. Provided she fully understands the reasoning behind the criticism, she should be able to see for herself what her next steps should be – and it is more motivating for her to correct the problem herself. You can offer a further coaching session if necessary; otherwise round off the interview on a positive note: 'Great – if you can make those corrections, then we'll be nicely on track.'

Sometimes your staff will need more help from you in the form of coaching and/or counselling. We cover these subjects in Chapter 8.

The alternative approach – when criticism is too risky

Sometimes the risks associated with giving criticism outweigh the benefits. Examples are if you are working with staff from other cultures where loss of face may be an issue, or if you criticize someone higher in the line who is sensitive about his position, or if you have a team member for whom relationships are extremely important and who may interpret your criticism as a sign that you do not like him.

The alternative approach consists of setting up the task so carefully that the team member (or manager!) has little chance of failure, and hence does not risk losing face. Suggestions are as follows:

- Take particular care when delegating up or down the line to agree objectives, standards and the outcome required.
- Encourage team members to submit drafts at an early stage, with the agreement that you can then discuss these together.
- Emphasize the successful parts of the person's work and be diplomatic about suggestions for changes. Most people in your 'high-risk' category will be quick to pick up your hints.
- If you feel sceptical about this approach, bear in mind that you can always move over to a harder approach later if necessary. If you start with criticism and upset someone, it will be very difficult subsequently to repair the damage!

Summary of giving feedback

The purpose of feedback is to confirm what the person is doing right, and to help him or her to improve in areas where performance is below standard. When you give feedback:

- Prepare carefully.
- Stick to the facts.
- Restrict criticism to about three points.
- Balance praise and criticism.
- Give feedback soon after the event.
- Check that the person agrees.
- Conclude with an action plan.

If criticism is too risky, maintain standards by careful delegation, asking for early drafts and stressing good points.

6.7 REVIEW MEETINGS

Review meetings must be constructive; people are particularly sensitive to criticism and potential loss of face in public. We have already offered guidelines to meetings in Chapter 5 and to giving feedback in Sec. 6.6 of this chapter. Additional suggestions are:

- Talk about *our* work, or *the* work, but not *his or her* work. Emphasize that you consider all work primarily as a team effort.
- Check the focus of the criticism; as one of our colleagues put it 'the review should not assess the designer's performance, but the performance of the design'.
- Check the level of the discussion; stay with the main points and don't get stuck in details.
- Prepare each meeting carefully, as though it were a unique occasion – don't get stuck in a routine which will bore both you and your team. Think to yourself 'What do I want to achieve in *this meeting*?' and make the specific purpose explicit to your attendees at the start.

6.8 STOCK TAKING

Occasionally even experienced and well-organized managers will get the uneasy feeling that they do not have the project completely under control. At such times you need to act quickly and decisively to work out where you are and where you are going. The best way to do that is to take stock – carefully, methodically, with the help of your team and possibly of some trusted 'outsiders' who can challenge your approach in a supportive way.

> The project had been running for over three months, and everyone had been working extremely hard. Just recently, though, I had been waking up at night, worrying about our performance.
>
> Every week I had been holding a progress meeting with each team leader, in which we would discuss the status of the active work packages and how the teams were performing against the plan. The weekly estimates for these work packages in all the teams were moving erratically. One week the estimates would go up by 20 per cent, the next week they would go down by 15 per cent, then they would go up by 10 per cent and so on.
>
> When I asked the team leaders to explain these fluctuations, they said they were caused by uncertainties in the interfaces between the teams. In some cases, work packages were also taking longer than at the start because people were getting tired – and they were wondering whether this could be an early symptom of demotivation.
>
> I called a general meeting to discuss ways of rising out of the spiral of lower productivity and falling morale. We considered the idea of holding general meetings for a whole week, and I took action to discuss this further with the team leaders. That evening, some of us decided to go for a drink together. After a few beers we came up with the idea of stocktaking. One of the team leaders was nominated to plan and run five stocktaking sessions over the following week. The objective was to identify all the risks in the project and to plan actions to deal with those risks. Eighteen of the thirty people working in the project would attend: in effect, we would stop the project for five days.

The big problem now was to convince the client and our line management to let us use up a whole week, when they knew only too well that our project had been under severe time pressure from day one. At that time we were nearly three months from finishing, and people outside the project were saying that we had no chance of achieving our overly ambitious plan.

With heart in mouth I went to the division director next morning, but to my relief he was fully in agreement with our plan. He said that he was worried too, and if we could finish only one week over the deadline he would be very pleased. The client was equally supportive. (When I think back to it I realize that this was a clever bit of delegation on their part. They had to accept a week's slip, but they left me still feeling fully committed to the original project schedule, and determined to regain control!)

We organized the stocktaking week as follows. There were four sessions, each lasting a total of four hours including presentations, discussions and brainstorming. Actions were identified, defined and assigned within the meeting. One person was responsible in each session for documenting the actions and the conclusions; these were used as the input for the following session. The final outcome was a list of 150 actions – some of which were simply to re-estimate work packages. We checked through the actions to make sure we could realistically implement them, then we made the list the basis of our new project plan for the following weeks.

The project administrator was charged with following up these actions reporting to the team on the status of the whole list. Within one week the motivation was noticeably higher and productivity had recovered. The estimates for the work packages stabilized, in line with the estimates we had made at the beginning of the project. I was sleeping better.

Five weeks after our week away, we met the first major milestone only a few days late. To our surprise and to everybody else's, we achieved the following milestone according to plan. We actually made up the time we had spent in our stocktaking sessions – and we had got back on track.

SUMMARY OF STAYING ON TRACK

1. A monitoring and control system helps you to move through a series of stable states.
2. Monitor effort, costs, people and quality.
3. Reporting informs others and forces you to maintain an overview of progress.
4. Organize your own action follow-up system.
5. Monitoring the performance of all your staff is a key responsibility.
6. Don't attack, but be prepared to confront and support through questions, helping the other person to think the problem through and making an action plan.
7. Give feedback which is specific and based on facts; balance praise and criticism.
8. Put more effort into careful delegation if criticism is too risky.
9. Prepare each review meeting carefully.
10. Use stocktaking sessions to act quickly if you need to get the project back on track.

7

THE FUNDAMENTALS OF QUALITY

7.1 INTRODUCTION

Project managers have divided views about quality. Some managers associate quality with sets of procedures which waste valuable time and interfere with their autonomy. Others will share our view that you need to control the quality of your products if you want to motivate your team and meet the expectations of your client.

The proper application of quality improves the visibility and measurability of progress in projects. The concepts of quality have been widely discussed over the last years, particularly now that the IT industry is facing challenges such as fierce competition, increased awareness on the part of users and clients, and the emergence of international standards and legislation such as consumer-protection Acts. Quality systems have proliferated, either designed from scratch or as upgrades intended to bring existing systems into line with the requirements of the International Standards Organization.

In this chapter we first explain the concepts of quality attributes, quality criteria and completion criteria. We discuss how carefully chosen procedures can enable you to keep track of quality without smothering you in unnecessary paperwork, and give some suggestions on how to set up your own project quality organization and quality system. We then address the general principles of quality planning. Finally, we describe how simple but effective quality systems can enable you to set up a genuine quality culture, through which you can achieve high performance standards in your team and satisfy the needs of your client.

7.2 THE QUALITY ATTRIBUTES

The concepts of quality attributes and quality procedures sometimes get confused, so we will start by clarifying what we mean by each of these terms. The *quality attributes* of any product are part of its inherent characteristics. Examples of IT system attributes are adequacy of documentation, performance, friendliness of the operator interface, maintainability and so on. *Quality procedures* are the working practices adopted to make the product and to check that its attributes are of the required level of quality.

Quality attributes are subjective. The individuals associated with your project will each have their own sets of attributes, based on their personal values and their particular role. Before you read any further, you may like to list for yourself the quality attributes which are most important for your current project.

The list of potential attributes is long, and different individuals will prioritize attributes in very different ways. If you think of the people working on a typical IT project, examples of the quality attributes chosen by different groups of people could be as follows:

- Users may be primarily interested in the operator interface. The quality attributes for them could be that the system is 'easy to use', or 'easy to modify in line with future needs'.
- System designers would probably focus on the internal details of the system, and their choice of quality attributes could be that the system is 'well designed', 'well structured', 'elegantly programmed' and so on.
- Senior line managers would almost certainly choose the classic attribute of 'on time and within budget, to customer specification' but we have also heard of managers who wanted the system to be 'a credit to our company'. Business managers in the client organization may emphasize economic attributes such as the system budget and the operational savings which the system can enable the client to achieve.
- Other attributes for an IT system will include 'well documented', 'easy to maintain', 'robust', 'high availability' and so on. You may be able to think of many more attributes yourself.

The problem with quality attributes is that they can be interpreted by different people in different ways. The person in the client organization who talks about wanting a system which is 'easy to use' will know what he or she means by that, but the systems designers and the project manager could interpret 'easy to use' quite differently. Programmers on one project used an arbitrarily chosen set of colours on screen displays for one client, thinking that this made the screen displays attractive and the interface 'easy to use'. Unfortunately, these colours had specific technical associations in the client's industry; a design which the programmers had assumed to be 'easy to use' was in fact very confusing for the client. Many systems have ended up disappointing users and clients alike because of such a difference in perception.

Another pitfall is the potential conflict about quality attributes which can emerge within the team. Because attributes are so closely associated with personal values, team members may feel that the project manager is asking them to 'betray their principles' if they feel they are being forced to produce something which is not perfectly elegant. The project manager needs some way of surfacing and reconciling the different perspectives on quality in order to meet the requirements of all the key parties associated with his or her project.

The solution to these problems is to translate the subjective *attributes*, which are often vague and woolly, into more specific and objectively defined *criteria*, so that you can create a 'common language' and a joint understanding of the quality expectations of all the key individuals associated with your project.

7.3 QUALITY CRITERIA

Quality criteria are the yardsticks or measures used to determine whether a product is up to the quality expectation. You need to define the quality *criteria* for each important *attribute*, so that you can build agreement between the maker of each product and the client or the user on the level of quality required.

You should define the quality criteria for products, subproducts and work packages during your quality planning. Ideally, each work package in the Work Breakdown Structure (WBS) would have its own quality criteria, quality procedure and completion criteria. To control the quality of the whole you must control the quality of the parts. This can be hard in practice, because it is sometimes impossible to define all the parameters for every work package at the beginning of the project. However, even if you are not able to do that at the beginning of your project you should check that these parameters are clear to the producer when he or she starts on the work package.

The following are some examples of quality criteria for work packages of different type, size and complexity.

Functional specification
- The document should be designed such that the system can be built in two phases. A minimum system should be built in the first phase and within 6 months. The rest of the system will be added in phase 2 of the project over a period of 6-12 months.
- The user will be one of the reviewers of the document. The language and style should allow for this requirement.
- Each defined functionality should cross-reference the user requirements it satisfies.

Computer system
- The system is to form the basis for five future systems.
- System availability should be no less than 99.8 per cent.

Consultancy report
- It should describe the advantages and disadvantages of the three alternatives.
- It should serve as the main input for the users to make the decision to proceed with the project.

Design of communication process
- It should handle a minimum of 500 messages per minute. (This criterion is also a requirement; this shows how difficult it is sometimes to distinguish between quality criteria and functional requirements.)
- It should comply with the error-handling standards and procedures.
- It should be able to recover from planned or unplanned system shutdowns in an orderly manner without the loss of any messages.

7.4 COMPLETION CRITERIA

Completion is one of the pillars of successful and effective project management. There is no such thing as a 95 per cent complete product – it either is complete or it is not. Completion is the discipline that helps to tidy up the mess left behind by colleagues with the '95 per cent complete' mentality. If you do not put effort into completion, you will find that unfinished actions pile up and eventually cause dissatisfaction and demotivation.

Completion is a stage beyond finishing, when:

- All the actions associated with an activity or a piece of work are closed.
- The producer has a sense of satisfaction and pride in the result.
- Another person has congratulated the producer on the achievement.

The project should be divided during the planning process into work packages resulting in a hierarchical structure that we call the Work Breakdown Structure. Each of these work packages should have its own quality and completion criteria.

Completion should be a clear visible point in the life-cycle of the product. It should be marked and celebrated however small the product or the associated celebration are. Signing off the product and briefly thanking the person are often all that is needed, but this acknowledgement is an important part of day-to-day motivation. One project manager described completion in the following way:

> Suppose you've just spent your whole Saturday clearing out the garage. You get to the end of the afternoon, and it looks great – the rubbish has gone, your tools are hung neatly on the wall, the floor's so clean you could eat off it. What you need now is someone to share your sense of achievement, so you call your partner and get her over to admire it with you.
>
> Completion is about sharing that sense of success. You need someone else to look at your product and say 'That's really good – you've worked hard.' Completion isn't about form filling – it's about recognition. When I sign off a certificate for a good piece of work, it's a pleasure to see the smile on the team member's face.

To make completion visible, you need some formal system for specifying work packages and allocating them within the team. A typical specification of work packages could be as shown in Fig. 7.1.

7.5 QUALITY PROCEDURES

Quality procedures are a crucial part of quality planning; they show you *how* you can achieve the quality criteria for your products and provide you with a series of steps to take. Quality forms and certificates provide the necessary written record that the procedures have been followed correctly.

Procedures are the most controversial side of quality application. The IT industry is full of quality theoreticians who move from project to project armed with dozens of slogans but with little or no understanding of the realities of the application of quality. Such theoreticians sometimes fall into the trap of defining tedious and difficult procedures with almost no feeling for those who have to use them. This causes resentment among project

Work package description:	A brief description of the objectives, scope and product(s) of the work package.
Effort required:	Estimated effort in person-days needed to finish the work.
Planned completion date:	dd.mm.yy
Quality criteria:	The definition of how you will determine whether the resulting products are of the required quality level.
Quality controllers:	The person or persons who will judge the quality of the product(s)
Completion criteria:	(For instance) • Product(s) have satisfied their quality criteria. • All quality actions and other actions are closed.
Signature of producer:	....
Signature of allocator:	....

Figure 7.1 Work specification form.

teams who are already suspicious of unnecessary bureaucracy and who far prefer the more creative and intellectually stimulating side of the job.

However, procedures act as a safety net: they provide your team with the secure feeling that someone else has checked their work, and that it fully meets the project requirements. Procedures can thus stimulate your team to produce their best work. Procedures also enable you with your team to achieve the correct balance between the team members' understandable need for high technical standards and the commercial constraints which are a key part of your responsibility for the project.

The challenge for the project manager is to devise or select procedures which are simple and effective, and to explain to the team members the benefits of working with them. When the producer has signed off a completed product, together with the allocator, the producer is demonstrating his or her conviction that the quality criteria have been satisfied. Procedures used in this way will encourage 'quality ownership' at all levels of the organization. The following story illustrates the point.

I'm currently running a project with a huge number of products. The client I'm working for doesn't have an established quality system or quality culture, so I wanted to find some way of controlling the quality of all these products quickly and efficiently.

I decided to tackle quality at the roots – at product level. Any unit of finished goods is defined as a product, with its own budget and time scales. Some of the products, such as specifications, are quite small, whereas other products are much larger – a help desk service, for instance. Each product has to have a work specification form, including the product description, the objectives which the product should achieve, the quality attributes and criteria, and the completion criteria. The form must also include the names of the quality controllers, who have to check and approve the product. We have also defined the prerequisites and risks for each product.

The system is beautifully simple. It forces each member of the team to think in terms of quality. At first, a couple of team members resisted filling in the forms but once they understood the advantages of having someone to cross-check their work, they started to relax. And it hasn't taken that long, either – in two months we've managed to turn the whole team round. They're all producing certificates now, and we're making visible progress.

In this example, we used the work specification form described in the previous section as our starting point. The process of filling in this form helped us to identify the quality controllers, the attributes and the quality criteria for each product. Equipped with this information we were able to devise simple quality procedures for these products.

Procedures play an important role in making the progress of projects and the quality of the products more visible and measurable. They also help the project team to communicate with one another more effectively, as demonstrated in the following story.

When I was asked to run this project I was told that about half the candidates for the project team would come from five separate sister companies from five different countries. However was I going to build a team out of such a variety of cultures and languages?

A few weeks later, however, when I was presenting the project plan and the quality plan to the team, I was encouraged to find that we had a very lively and useful discussion. All the team members were using the same technical terms and the same general vocabulary – they were actually communicating together fine. I realized later that this was because this particular company used the same quality system worldwide; although the nationalities of the team members were different, in this context the quality procedures enabled us literally to speak the same language.

Procedures can continue to have a function even after the project has ended. They can help you to identify errors while the products are being made, but you can also use the same procedures to measure and analyse defects in completed or even in working products. The purpose of such an analysis is to evaluate the effectiveness of the production process and to identify any possible weaknesses in it. The analysis could help you in turn to improve the working procedures.

7.6 THE PROJECT QUALITY ORGANIZATION

Before you set up a quality organization you first have to understand how projects relate to higher-level quality authorities. Some project managers can feel frustrated if they have to report on quality according to some predefined central procedures which they feel are distant from the realities of their project. This can be particularly difficult in organizations where quality application has not yet taken a stable form.

Organizations in our experience are often more flexible with their rule books than they initially appear to be. If your project is exceptional in some way such as in its size, complexity or staffing, you may be able to propose a different and more effective way of relating to the quality hierarchy in your own or your client organization. Higher management is very likely to view your proposal with pragmatic sympathy and understanding.

Flexibility of approach also applies within the project. Quality organizations often follow the project organizations very closely. We would like to challenge this tradition. You may find that a more effective quality organization can be formed which does not match the project organization hierarchy. We have seen many examples of project staff in the lowest management tiers playing very senior quality roles because of some specific expertise they have or because they possess some skills and work styles that qualify them for these roles.

To define your quality organization we propose that you start with a list of the products in the project. Define the quality roles you need per product; fill these roles in your project organization taking into consideration the products needs, the expertise of the individuals and their working styles. Your quality organization will be an integral part of the project organization (see Table 7.1).

Table 7.1

Product description	Quality controller(s)	Certification	Delivery approval
Product 1	Team leader of database team	Technical manager	Project manager
Product 2	Joe Bloggs – communication team	Team leader	Line manager

The quality controller is the person who has an adequate understanding of the internal details of the product and its quality criteria. *The certifier* is the person, within the project team, who has the responsibility for ensuring that the product is made and that it meets the quality criteria. The person who *approves the delivery* of the product has a delegated commercial and contractual responsibility for the product. This person is often the project manager or the line manager to whom the project reports.

The application of quality helps you to delegate work effectively within the team. Each work package will have the elements defined in the work specification (Fig. 7.1). The delegator or allocator then agrees specific objectives with the producer. You will thus have an effective mechanism for getting commitment from the delegator and the producer and for monitoring progress, quality and completion of the products.

7.7 QUALITY PLANNING

Quality planning is an integral part of project planning. Each product which is described in the scope of supply of the project will have associated quality expectations. Quality planning makes these expectations explicit and enables you to identify ways of achieving these expectations in a measurable and a controlled manner. A quality plan for any product must define:

- The quality attributes
- The quality criteria
- The completion criteria
- The quality procedures
- The quality organization

You may have a mature and well-developed quality system at your disposal that will help to produce quality plans and define the necessary quality procedures within them. If not, we hope that with the help of the general principles we have described you will be able to devise your own simple quality system for your project.

7.8 QUALITY SYSTEMS AND QUALITY CULTURES

A quality system is a set of standards, manuals and other advisory and guidance material such as working papers, reports and research papers. Projects are expected to comply with these systems or at least with a subset of them (the mandatory standards) depending on the project and the prevailing culture in the parent organization. Quality systems in the IT industry are increasingly being certified to ISO standards.

Quality systems are the basis for a quality culture. If the mandatory parts of the quality system are consistently imposed, people at all levels will get used to the principle of 'check and be checked'. The concept of quality control (checking of products) is based on the principle that the producer cannot reasonably be expected to detect all the flaws in his or her work because the producer is too close to the product. Individuals in organizations without a quality culture may regard any form of comment on their products as a personal attack; the inevitable consequence is that errors will go unspotted. Project managers who explain the benefits of quality control and introduce it sensitively will help their staff to see it as an opportunity to improve both their products and their own skills. Being open-minded to feedback is a crucial part of the quality culture.

The quality system also promotes debate inside the organization about the quality values of that organization. It provides a vocabulary for discussing the changing quality demands and expectations of the marketplace and it stimulates managers to select appropriate strategies for responding to these changes. A quality culture which constantly evolves is a sign that the organization is addressing and staying in touch with the inevitable changes in the market and in client expectations.

Some organizations do not have a quality system. If you have to run a project in such an organization, you will have to set up your own project-specific system. Don't rely solely on theory if you lack experience in this field. You can always ask for help from organizations which have practical experience in applying quality systems in a project similar to yours.

The following case study illustrates how a carefully chosen quality system can begin to promote a quality culture.

My task as project manager was to get over 500 computer systems connected to a central system via a national high-speed digital network. The systems were scattered over large geographical areas with hundreds of miles between them. Each system had to be modified and then tested to ensure that it complied with certain quality procedures, to check that there were no local system errors which could cause problems for the rest of the network and the central system.

We had a central team which was responsible for coordinating all the tests and for carrying out those tests which required special test facilities. Other tests were to be carried out by the organizations that owned the local systems. The central team also had to ensure that the tests were conducted according to the agreed standards. The whole system had to be fully tested and ready to go live within less than 12 months – it was what you could call a challenge!

The owners of the remote systems were not accustomed to quality procedures, but they were very keen to ensure that their part of the project was carried out to the highest standards. The question was – how to do it?

Our first task was to 'sell' the benefits of a quality approach in terms of improved work efficiency and so on. Most of the people in the local organizations responded with enthusiasm, and some even helped us to persuade those who were more doubtful.

Our discussion about the quality system was taking place during the project planning phase. A careful analysis of the various changes proposed in the 500 systems produced a list of up to 15 possible milestones. We defined the quality criteria to achieve these milestones and agreed them with the system owners.

Then we set up our quality organization, which needed to be simple and workable. Although we had over 500 systems, there were only 20 owner organizations which had to be directly involved in the procedures. We set up one person who would be the contact point for each organization, supported by two strong technicians who were responsible for getting the work done according to the agreed procedures. Now we had to pull the quality organization together with straightforward but effective procedures, which would enable us to achieve visibility, measurability and ownership of quality.

We designed some simple forms that could be transferred electronically to signal the completion of each step towards one of the milestones. We identified all the possible forms per system and per organization. With the help of databases and spreadsheets we were able to generate all the necessary forms for all the milestones for all the systems relatively easily, but there were still an awful lot of forms.

Our next step was to collate all the forms that each individual owner organization would need to send in response to the written and telephone requests from the central team, and put them in a separate file – one per organization. These files were indexed and organized with clear instructions so that each organization would know which form to send in response to any request.

Then we set up our 'quality campaign.' We invited all the key players in the owner organizations to take part in dedicated sessions to explain how the quality system would work. The message was very simple. As we handed over the file to the owner organization we said: *when this file is empty your work for all your systems will be complete!*

These sessions were very successful. Our simple procedures enabled us to keep track of the process, and the owner organizations could observe their files shrinking as the project moved on. Everyone throughout the project could understand the relevance of the procedures, and so the quality system functioned perfectly. In spite of the huge scale of the changes, each person knew exactly what to do. The result was satisfied clients all round and a very motivated team. And yes – the files were all empty when we hit our deadline!

SUMMARY OF THE FUNDAMENTALS OF QUALITY

1. Quality application is a management tool – to help you to control quality of products, make progress measurable and motivate your team.
2. Quality attributes are subjective – so make them objective by defining the quality criteria for each work package or product.
3. Completion criteria
   - Ensure that each work package meets the quality criteria.
   - Provide a sense of satisfaction.
4. Quality procedures
   - Show how you are going to achieve the quality criteria.
   - Should be simple and effective.
   - Should encourage 'quality ownership'.
5. Your project quality organization
   - Is independent of the project hierarchy.
   - Helps you to delegate effectively.
6. Quality planning
   - Pulls together all the principles of quality application.
   - Makes the users' expectations explicit.
7. Quality systems
   - Are the basis for a quality culture.
   - Help people get used to 'check and be checked'.
   - Provide a platform to debate the application of quality.

8

COACHING AND COUNSELLING

8.1 THE REASONS FOR COACHING AND COUNSELLING

Coaching and counselling are two additional ways of tackling performance problems and supporting your staff. We have described an approach in Chapter 6 for monitoring your staff and giving constructive feedback, and often this is enough in the short term to help your staff to progress. Occasionally, however, you may need to invest more time and energy and use a different approach, which will require extra thought and skill on your part.

We have distinguished between coaching and counselling, because they are used in different contexts to achieve different sorts of goals. The purpose of coaching is to enable your staff to gain new skills and knowledge in their working environment. Your role as coach is primarily to help the other person to set objectives, organize resources and monitor improvement. You also need to understand the different ways in which adults learn, and how to select the most appropriate method for each individual. The benefits to the project manager of this additional investment are that:

- Your staff will have broader skills, so you will have more resources if the project comes under pressure.
- Staff motivation will increase: team members will work more willingly if they feel they are learning.

We offer a framework for coaching in Sec. 8.2.

Counselling is useful when staff are upset or worried, and can't think through their problems clearly on their own. A project manager can use the counselling approach if team members are suffering, for instance, from stress caused by issues inside work and/or at home. Counselling addresses problems which are more personal in nature, and so the process is more ambiguous and open-ended. Your job as counsellor is not to solve the person's problems single-handed, because often you are not in a position to do so. You have to move out of your managerial role and act more as a sounding board to help your staff to think through a problem for themselves and identify their own appropriate course of action. The advantages of investing time and energy in counselling are that:

- You help individuals to manage their stress levels.
- You create a community where people can be more open and honest at work, and this will contribute to team spirit.

Because this is often a new field and an unfamiliar role for many managers, in Sec. 8.3 we give a number of detailed suggestions and examples.

We have separated out the two processes in order to emphasize the contrasting ways in which you can support your staff. In reality, the two processes will often overlap: in Sec. 8.4 we finish with a case study to show how in practice the project manager can integrate both counselling and coaching to offer sensitive, practical support and help staff to tackle problems, build skills and develop self-esteem.

8.2 COACHING

Coaching is about helping someone to learn. A course participant once described a cartoon in which a man was telling a friend of his that he had taught his dog, Johnny, to whistle. The friend, impressed, asked for a demonstration. The man replied that he'd only got as far as *teaching* Johnny – Johnny couldn't actually *do* it yet. Modern coaching focuses on making sure that Johnny really can whistle.

You can divide the coaching process into a number of steps; in each step you should work with the other person to:

1. Assess the current level of the person's skills, knowledge, etc.
2. Set realistic objectives for the new level of skills or knowledge that the person wants to attain.
3. Select an appropriate learning method.
4. Select opportunities at work to practise the new skills and apply the new knowledge.
5. Ensure that the person gets constructive feedback, so that you can both monitor progress.
6. Review the new level of skills: if you are both satisfied that you have achieved the objectives set in Step 2, then this coaching cycle has been completed. If you are not satisfied, then go back to Step 1 and start the cycle again.

We will illustrate the steps by working through a typical example.

Suppose one of your senior analyst programmers, Charles, is technically very competent but is as yet unable to give a clear, confident presentation to the client. He is sitting by your desk looking fed up and resentful, because he has had some negative feedback (again) from his colleagues in the team. He is the oldest and most senior person in the group, and he knows all the technical complexities of his part of the system, so he really is the logical choice as presenter; he tells you several times, however, that he hates doing it.

Step 1: Assess the current level

Your first priority is to motivate Charles to tackle the problem. Start by confirming the positive aspects of his presentation skills; examples could be that the overhead projector slides were well designed, and that the first part of the technical explanation came over clearly. On the negative side, the presentation overran by 15 minutes, Charles's style lacked energy, he talked to the screen rather than to the audience, and he reacted defensively to a couple of questions from the client.

Step 2: Set realistic objectives

Your task here is to lay down a framework of measurable goals, so you can both plan how to attain them. As manager, you can help Charles to place these in context. How important are his presentation skills for his performance on the project? For his career in general? You can also use your experience to help him to set objectives which are realistic. He doesn't need to be a charismatic speaker, but he must be able to stick to schedule and answer questions calmly and professionally.

Your framework can be based on different types of objectives:

- *Long-term objectives* What should Charles be able to do by the end of the project, in ten months' time?
- *Intermediate objectives* What will he have achieved at the end of the month, or after the current phase of the project has been completed? How will you both know he is making progress? Set milestones and agree deliverables.
- *Session objectives* What do you both want to achieve by the end of this session? What would make the next hour (or whatever) an effective use of your time?

The SMART acronym which we used in Chapter 2 can be helpful again in this context; objectives should be:

Specific: ⎫
Measurable: ⎬ so Charles can measure his own progress
Achievable: so he can build up confidence
Reasonable: so the objective fits in the context of the project and his career development
Time based: so he has some deadlines to work towards

When you want to develop your staff, you should also check that the objective is positively expressed, so that the person starts to get a vision in his head of what he is aiming towards. 'To stop getting into fights with the client' is a negatively expressed objective; 'To deal with questions calmly and constructively' is positively expressed. You can see the links with the quality approach described in Chapter 7 here – your coaching objectives can be expressed as quality criteria.

Step 3: Select an appropriate learning method

You can acquire new skills and knowledge by a variety of methods: you could read a book, or go on a course, or observe someone else, or talk the subject through with a colleague, or simply have a go and see what happens. There is no single approach which is inherently better than another; it all depends on what you want to learn, and what works best for you. Some people are very flexible learners, and they can benefit from almost any learning method. Most of us are not such good all-rounders, and we tend consciously or unconsciously to stick to one or two preferred approaches.

The common pitfall for managers is to assume that other people learn in the same way as they do. They choose their preferred method; if the other person happens to have the same preference then there will be no problem, but if he or she likes to learn in a different way, then the mismatch can make you both frustrated at the apparent lack of progress. (If you have felt exasperated trying to help a son or daughter with homework you will probably know what we mean.) You can use your time much more effectively if you identify at the start the learning approach which best suits the person you are coaching.

A helpful framework for doing this is the Adult Learning Styles model developed by Honey and Mumford (1992). They identify four main learning approaches: Activist, Reflector, Theorist and Pragmatist. We each use combinations of all four approaches, so when we talk about an 'Activist learner' we don't mean that the person only uses this approach: we mean that he or she tends to use this approach in preference to the others. We have used the original Honey and Mumford Learning Style descriptions as the basis for our own examples below.

Activists thrive on 'hands-on' experience, and are not afraid of taking risks. Team members who have a high preference for the Activist approach will get bored and impatient with lengthy explanations, so lectures and traditional training courses will usually be a waste of their time. Similarly, the subtleties of a supportive coaching style, based on a series of patient, carefully chosen questions, may be lost on them.

An ideal learning approach at work is to let Activists experiment in low-risk situations. If they want to acquire negotiating skills, for instance, let them conduct a small-scale negotiation and give them feedback. If you need to coach an Activist in presentation skills, you could suggest that he or she gives a short presentation to you on a piece of work they have just done. Give the person feedback and a few tips and then rerun the presentation.

Reflectors need time: they hate to be rushed. Unlike their Activist colleagues, they may dislike presentations, for instance, because of the need to react on the spot to questions which they may not have anticipated. The strength of Reflectors is their ability to think over past events and give a carefully considered response. You can best help Reflectors by starting with a thorough explanation of the subject area, and giving them plenty of opportunities to ask questions and review what they have learned. Only when they feel they really understand will they be confident enough to take action themselves.

Reflectors would feel very awkward in a high-pressure presentation skills course where participants had to go 'up front' and talk about something with very little time to prepare. If Charles had a preference for the Reflector learning approach, you could discuss a forthcoming presentation quietly with him well in advance of the actual event, and run through all the possible questions which he might be asked. (This is a time-consuming process, which you could delegate to someone else if necessary.) A few days before the presentation you could arrange to go through a dry run with him, leaving him a few days to integrate any constructive criticism and practise again if necessary.

Theorists pride themselves on their rigorous logic. They tend to learn best from well-planned coaching or training given by a recognized expert, and they will also be prepared to consult and learn from academic books. They will be impatient with 'quick and dirty' tips and techniques which are not supported by research. Similarly, any criticism for them must be backed up by a clear rationale.

Theorists, like Reflectors, will have the patience and the motivation to acquire a thorough understanding of the subject. Their weakness is a tendency to get lost in academic discussions and defer active experimentation and feedback. They are also uncomfortable in areas which are ambiguous (such as counselling) where they cannot depend on logic and have to deal with feelings. If Charles has a preference for the Theorist approach, you could send him on a course run by an expert. Set up a meeting for him when he returns to discuss what he has learned and how he will apply it to the project.

Pragmatists are motivated by relevance: they will put their best effort into learning if they know they will be able to apply it directly in their job in the near future (within a month, for instance). Their strength lies in action planning and implementation; their weakness can be a short-term, narrow focus. Staff with a high preference for the Pragmatist approach will get impatient with lengthy explanations and say to you in exasperation 'Just tell me what to *do* next Friday!'

Off-the-job training events are often not so suitable for them, because the material cannot be tailored exactly to meet their needs; Pragmatists will gain most therefore from on-the-job coaching, where you or another colleague can help them to prepare directly for an event coming up in the future. If Charles is a Pragmatist, you could point out to him that his next presentation is scheduled in a month's time, and give him some quick tips and guidelines to get him going. The dry run would again be helpful, with feedback and suggestions for improvement. Pragmatists will often be happy with something which is 80 per cent satisfactory, as long as they know they are working along the right lines.

Can you now make a tentative guess at the learning styles of your staff – and how about yourself? If people have very strong preferences you can often identify these by observation, or by asking them how they like to learn. The most accurate way to identify learning styles is to use Honey and Mumford's Learning Styles Questionnaire (consult the Further Reading for details).

Some combinations of learning style preferences between the coach and the team member can be particularly unfortunate. Imagine a Theorist manager droning on to an Activist, or a Pragmatist giving a Reflector a couple of tips and telling her then to 'get on with it'. If you are personally flexible enough to use any style you will have an enormous advantage when you coach your staff. If you are not such an all-rounder, you can at least be aware of the pitfalls and the options. Discuss with your team member his or her preferred way of learning, and select an approach together.

Step 4: Select opportunities at work

Plan occasions where your staff can apply new skills and knowledge, so that they can test their learning. If you send your team members on a course, try to find an early opportunity for them when they return to apply their learning. Otherwise good intentions can fade and they will forget the knowledge that they had acquired.

Step 5: Organize constructive feedback

Once you give them the correct opportunity, check that someone is also available to give comments on their performance. Make sure that whoever is giving the feedback knows which learning objectives were set in Step 2. The aim should be to confirm what the learner is doing right, and offer support and suggestions as needed if there are areas where the learner is still having difficulty. Look back to the guidelines to giving feedback in Chapter 6 if you want more reminders.

Step 6: Review

Round off the process with a review, even if it is only very short, to acknowledge and consolidate the progress which the team member has made. A couple of sentences to Charles, with constructive feedback, may be all that is needed. If he is still having problems, check that you or a colleague can help him further by reassessing his skills level, resetting objectives and cycling through the process once again.

You can see from this framework that your role as coach is to organize and facilitate the learning process of your staff. You don't have to be an expert in the subject matter to be effective. Sometimes you may enjoy acting as an expert resource, helping a Theorist learner, for instance, to understand the finer points of database design – providing you have the space in your schedule and that you genuinely think this is a sensible use of your time. Usually you will be coordinating other people to act as coaches: colleagues in the team, professional trainers, perhaps career advisors or mentors if you have them in your organization. Your main contribution is to help the other person to analyse, plan and practise until the team member has achieved his or her goals, and is hopefully ready to tackle the next challenge.

One last thought before we leave the subject of coaching: how are you managing your own learning and development? Continuous and effective acquisition of skills makes all of us more employable. You may want to consider the following:

- What new skills and knowledge could be most useful for your career over the next three years?
- Which learning methods work best for you?
- What resources (people, courses, etc.) are available in your own organization to help you?
- What actions could you take over the next week to start your own coaching programme?

Summary of coaching

Use the six-step approach with your staff:

1. Assess the current level of skills/knowledge.
2. Set objectives: long term, intermediate and per session (make them SMART, positively expressed, set quality criteria).
3. Select an appropriate learning method: check the preferred learning style:
   - Activist – hands-on experimentation

- Reflector – thorough preparation, plenty of time
- Theorist – logical explanation from recognized expert, courses
- Pragmatist – tips and techniques, relevance

4. Select opportunities at work so that the person can apply new skills and knowledge in the near future.
5. Organize constructive feedback: measure progress against the objectives agreed in Step 2.
6. Review: acknowledge progress, and, if necessary, start a new coaching cycle starting again at Step 1.

Apply the same approach to your own learning and development!

8.3 COUNSELLING

The role of the counsellor

Counselling brings you into the areas of your job where you have to accept that feelings and perceptions have as much impact on a person's performance as logic and rational argument. Some managers are uncomfortable with this idea, and they set up project cultures which are formal, distant, where people just get on with the technical part of the job and synergy is never fully developed. You may have worked in a team like this at some stage in your career, and on short-term projects such a team can be relatively successful.

In the long term, though, the chances are that one team member will inevitably bring a personal problem into the office. The following is a typical example:

> She came into the office looking terrible. She'd been working in my team for nearly a year – she was technically very good, but she was shy and we didn't know much about her home life. I could see something was wrong so I took her into my office . . . As soon as the door was shut she burst into tears, and said her boyfriend had left her that morning – they'd had a blazing row and he'd packed his bags. It took me some time to understand what she was saying, she was in such a state. I felt so sorry for her, but I was also very embarrassed – I mean, what could I do? I don't think I handled it very well . . . I just gave her the day off.

Staff who are left to fend for themselves may worry more than they work. In the longer term they may make more mistakes, get into more arguments, take more time off sick. One unhappy person will affect others in the team; if part of your super-organism is sick, the whole will suffer. Although you may feel reluctant to 'get involved' in people's personal lives, it is often the manager, on the spot, who is in the best position to help.

The difficulty is to know what kind of help to offer. In the example above you are highly unlikely to be in a position to 'do something' to sort the problem directly. You won't be able to bring back the boyfriend, or find a replacement, or offer an instant cure for broken hearts. You can tell someone how to run a spreadsheet but you can't tell them how to run their lives.

This frustrates many managers, who feel that they can only help properly if they can offer solutions. It is easy to understand why the project manager sent the team member home – he felt helpless at the sight of her distress. He ended up feeling guilty, however, because he knew that she would be returning to a lonely flat. Sometimes people need privacy, but usually they would welcome the opportunity to talk. Often we unconsciously isolate people who are upset; instead of alleviating their unhappiness, we exacerbate it.

Another common example of a counselling situation is the potential job move: less dramatic than the break-up of a relationship, but still the cause of sleepless nights. Suppose your project is coming to an end, and John, one of your 'super-stars', has received a number of suggestions for his next role. One suggestion is particularly attractive technically, but it involves relocating. He has two young children at school, and his wife has just started a job which she is very much enjoying. You note that he is looking tired, and is spending a fair amount of his time staring into space. Eventually John wanders over to your desk and asks if you can help him to make up his mind – should he accept the offer or not?

Various options are open to you at this stage, for instance:

- You could offer him advice, based on your own experience.
- You could give him information about future trends in the organization, and help him to put the job offer in context.
- You could suggest that he consults other colleagues for more advice and information.
- You could offer to talk to other managers on his behalf.

Any of these may be appropriate in certain circumstances, but they could also be more of a hindrance than a help. In each case you are taking over some of the responsibility from the team member – and ultimately, he must make his own decision. In some cultures managers will feel quite comfortable talking to a team member as though they were a friendly aunt or uncle addressing a young nephew, but in most English-speaking and Northern European countries such a tone would probably be interpreted as intrusive and patronizing. Your advice and information could be well intended, but irrelevant to the team member's particular situation.

Counselling is a different kind of help, based on listening rather than giving advice. This is the 'sounding-board' role we mentioned earlier. You probably have a friend, or colleague, or partner at home whom you can turn to when you have problems. They may not know anything about your business, but as you talk through your worries with them, unhurriedly and in confidence, you find yourself relaxing, opening up, and gradually able to look at things differently. Often after a session like this you can see for yourself which steps you should take; the other person doesn't have to tell you anything, they just have to support you.

If you think how you have felt when you have been trying to sort out problems, you'll probably recognize this 'see-saw' model (Fig. 8.1). When you become more upset, or angry, you can't think straight; as counsellor, your job is to help the person to express the emotions, discharge some of the tension and move gradually forward to establish options. Your task with John is to create an environment in which he can review the situation calmly for himself and then select the appropriate actions (Fig. 8.2).

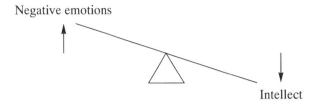

Figure 8.1 The effect of intense negative feelings on the intellect.

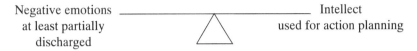

Figure 8.2 The effect of emotional release.

Setting up the session

When should you initiate a counselling session? If someone in your team is angry or upset, or wanders over to you like John, then the trigger is obvious. Occasionally you will need to set up the session yourself if you notice changes in the team member's behaviour and suspect that the person is suffering from undue stress. Examples of such changes are when the person:

- Starts coming in late or leaving early
- Is more withdrawn or irritable than usual
- Is making more mistakes
- Is having more problems in meeting deadlines
- Is reacting in extreme ways to situations which would not normally bother him or her.

These are all indications that you may need to talk in private with the person to identify the cause of the problem and a possible course of action. Be careful what you say to the person when you raise the possibility of a counselling session – avoid statements like 'You seem to be rather stressed lately', which can sound like an accusation. A better alternative is to say to the person quietly and in private that you have noticed some changes and would like to talk.

Changes in behaviour could be caused by problems at home, or at work, or a combination of both. Personal changes all bring pressure with them; we expect events such as bereavement, divorce and financial worries to stress staff, but even pleasurable events such as getting married or having a baby cause disruptions to familiar routines. If a team member is going through a personal change at the same time as the project comes under pressure, life can suddenly seem very difficult.

Before you talk to your staff you also need to think whether the person might be under additional pressure at work because of some aspect of your managerial style or your organization of the team. We talk more about stress management in Chapter 10, but typical examples of work-related stress which you may have to deal with in counselling situations are:

- Worries about job security
- Conflicts with colleagues
- Unclear definitions of roles and responsibilities
- Work overload/underload
- Inadequate skills/ training for the job
- Environmental factors such as heating, lighting, poorly designed offices
- Inadequate resources
- Inadequate information about procedures, economic status of organization, etc.
- Lack of influence over decisions which affect the person
- Frequent organizational changes.

Even experienced managers may find that they have unintentionally put their staff under undue stress, and at least with work-related problems it can be easier to identify a course of action which will relieve the pressure.

Whatever the problem, your team members must be able to trust you to keep the matter confidential, and they must feel secure that their job prospects will not be jeopardized if they 'open up' to you. Occasionally this will put you in an awkward position, and you will have conflicting loyalties. Suppose a subordinate tells you that she's unhappy, but also that she's found another job. Do you owe it to the company to inform your manager? If you begin to hear information that could put you in a difficult situation, interrupt the other person and make this clear to her, and, if necessary, suggest that she talks to a different counsellor.

Other situations where you should not counsel are if there are legal implications or if the person requires specialized help – if you suspect someone has a drinking problem, for instance. In these cases you will need to consult someone else whom you trust and who has the necessary expertise. Usually, however, you will be dealing with day-to-day problems which do not require special experience and where the support offered by ordinary counselling will be all that is needed.

A framework for a counselling session

This framework is only a suggestion, because to counsel effectively you have to be genuine and you have to use your own experience and intuition. A framework is a starting point, however, and we will take the case described earlier of John's potential job move to use as an example.

Once you have identified the problem, check that you have enough time available to concentrate on the person in a private setting, free from interruptions. A rushed interview may be worse than nothing, so if you have some other, urgent, task you must either delegate the counselling or delegate the task. Tell the person how much time you have available, so they know what to expect.

Your first task is to set up a climate where the other person feels free to open up and talk. This is not as straightforward as it seems. The degree to which a person will talk to you depends very much on the extent to which they trust you. You will promote trust by being non-judgemental; any expressions of disapproval may inhibit the person's communication with you.

Managers often make the mistake of interrupting too much, or jumping to conclusions, or thinking ahead to solutions, rather than listening to understand the problem itself. You may find it hard to concentrate when people seem to be rambling, or when their explanation seems incomplete or simply unclear. Bear in mind that if the problem were straightforward the other person would already have sorted it out for himself. It is because John is feeling confused that he has asked to talk to you.

Two helpful guidelines are to *keep asking questions* and to *summarize regularly*. Think of the interview as progressing through three stages:

- Stage 1 – Check that you both understand the problem fully
- Stage 2 – Explore the options
- Stage 3 – Agree the next steps.

Stage 1 – Check that you both understand the problem fully   Let John talk, concentrate on his story and clarify only when necessary. Show you are listening by checking back occasionally: 'So if I've understood you right, what you are saying is . . .'

After you check back the other person will often modify or add to your summary. This is a good sign; you may be moving on a level, getting past the symptoms to a deeper exploration of the problem.

Listen for the feelings as well as the facts; this is the essence of good counselling! Managers often take a 'flight path' away from emotions and into the more familiar realm of detailed factual information. In John's case, don't be tempted to ask for lots of details about the job offer, and thus to lose track of the issues which are really causing him to worry. Try to put yourself in his place. If you have been through a similar experience yourself, you may want to tell him that 'you have been there yourself'.

Expressing feelings helps you to deal with them. John may find it difficult to describe his emotions clearly, but you can try to do that for him by summarizing your understanding: 'So you're feeling really torn – you were excited at being offered the team leader role, but you're worried that your wife could resent you if she's unable to find a new job?'

This is obviously a sensitive area, so check back whether your version is correct. Once he agrees that you have fully understood all the complexities of the problem, you can both move on to the next stage.

Stage 2 – Explore the options   Here you help John to explore alternatives and weigh up the advantages and disadvantages. 'What if . . . ?' questions can encourage him to try out different courses of action. 'What if you took Carol out for a day to look at the new location?' Other possible questions are:

'What's the part of the problem that is worrying you most?'
'What options do you think other people would consider if they were in your situation?'
'What is the worst/best thing that could happen?'
'Suppose you could sort out one part of the problem (e.g. Carol could find an equivalent job in the new location). Would you feel happy at moving then?'
'Suppose you followed one particular course of action (e.g. you decided not to put the happiness of the family at risk and hence not to move). How do you think you would feel in one or two years' time?'

Remember not to push John for a decision – the more important the dilemma, the more time he will need. If you can help him to identify two or three options which he can think about further at his leisure, you may already have given him considerable support.

Stage 3 – Agree the next steps Because counselling is not a tidy process it can be difficult to find a smooth way of bringing the interview to a conclusion. Often the best approach is to summarize where you have got to in the discussion, and ask the other person how they want to progress. John may feel that he is clear enough now in his own mind to go away, talk matters through again with his family and come to a decision in his own time. Alternatively, you may both agree to take on certain actions, or he may simply say that he would like to talk to you again later. In either case you need to decide how you will review progress in a follow-up meeting.

Counselling when people are distressed

What about the case of the young woman at the start of the section – how can you best help her? Often all you can do is to let her talk, and show that you understand how she is feeling. Then focus on the day ahead of her with simple questions such as: 'How can we best help you now?' 'How do you want to spend the day?'

Some people may prefer to stay working in the office, so the best help you can offer is to keep them busy; at other times they may ask for time to make phone calls or sort practical arrangements. You may also want to agree with them whether they would like you to tell the other members of the team what has happened, or whether they would prefer to keep the matter private.

After the session, carry on working as though nothing has happened, but keep a check on the person to make sure that he or she looks reasonably all right. Be prepared to initiate another interview if you spot further warning signs.

Counselling is a low-key affair, where your contribution is to offer quiet, confidential support. You may not receive any thanks for the time you spend, because part of the skill of counselling is to enable people to find their own solutions. Nonetheless, as the last story illustrates, this sort of support can be immensely helpful when people are confronted with some of the more frightening aspects of everyday life, and you will have developed a deeper relationship which can lead to a more satisfying working environment.

When he put the phone down, he looked grey. I asked him if anything was wrong, and he said he'd had a bit of a shock – he'd had 'a difficult conversation' with his doctor. 'I hope it's nothing too serious,' I said. To my horror he replied that actually it was. He clearly needed someone he could talk to. The thought that went through my head was 'Oh no – what should I say now?' I just bashed on, asking questions, and it actually went OK. I was probably the right person for him to talk to. Some months later, after he'd come out of hospital and had returned to work part-time, I was surprised when he said how helpful I'd been. That talk had been a safety valve – he'd been better able to tell his family the news, and he'd really appreciated the support. It's funny how a bit of counselling can make such a difference.

Summary of counselling

- Counselling supports staff when they have personal problems which are affecting their performance at work.

- Your role is to act as a *sounding board* – to help your staff to find their own solutions. Avoid giving advice. What works for you may not work for them.
- Set up a session if staff come to you or if you notice changes in their behaviour.
- Don't counsel if there are legal implications, conflicts of interest, or if the person needs a specialist – consult other resources.
- Concentrate on the problem by *listening, asking questions and summarizing*.

A possible framework is to

1. Check that you both understand the problem fully
2. Explore the options
3. Agree the next steps

then let the person make his or her decision at his or her own pace.

- When people are distressed, listen, show that you understand, ask them what they need to get through the day
- Keep information confidential – carry on as normal, but check progress.

8.4 INTEGRATING COUNSELLING AND COACHING

Often staff will come to you initially very upset about something, and you will use counselling techniques to identify the problem and help them to calm down. Once they are able to think and express themselves more clearly, the more structured coaching techniques can help your staff to develop the skills they need in order to solve the problem and move forward. The following case illustrates this integrated approach.

I'd asked two of my junior team leaders to handle an important meeting with the client and some external contacts. We all knew it could be a tricky occasion because of some underlying political issues, but we had discussed it in advance and they left my office at 10 o'clock full of smiles and confidence.

Two hours later they came back in a flat panic. The meeting had been a disaster, they had made complete fools of themselves in front of the client, if they'd had two sharp swords they would have fallen on them and so on. I've never seen the two of them in such a state – they were so upset I couldn't really work out what had been going on. I listened and let them talk, then suggested we should all have a break over lunch and then have another go at the problem. We went off to the canteen where they picked at their food and we talked resolutely about last night's football, and after coffee they trudged back to the office.

It took me an hour or so of solid counselling to get the full story. The situation wasn't as bad as they'd first thought, though they had indeed made some mistakes. The external people had attacked them in front of the client, criticizing them for areas of the project for which my staff had not been fully responsible. Neither of the team leaders was experienced enough to think quickly on his feet, so they'd both responded with counter-attacks, and that had started a downwards spiral. They felt ashamed of their performance.

Once they realized that I understood their position they were able to put the whole thing into proportion. Their mistakes were regrettable, but understandable. The next step was to take fast corrective action, and to make sure that they would know next time exactly how to handle the situation. I agreed to go and explain the situation to the client, and also to coach them so they could redeem their reputations in the meeting which was scheduled for two days later.

I asked them how they wanted to prepare for the meeting, and they said they wanted to discuss everything in detail. We stayed until 11 o'clock that night and the next. I explained to them how they should handle conflicts, and got them to practise responding to all the possible attacks. Finally we drafted an agenda and I told them to go home and get a good night's rest.

The meeting went fine, though I must say I couldn't quite concentrate on my work while they were away. Their faces said it all when they finally emerged through the door – they looked extremely relieved!

Coaching and counselling are underpinned by a good command of influencing and conflict-handling skills, which we will cover in the next chapter.

9

INFLUENCING AND CONFLICT HANDLING

9.1 THE BENEFITS OF DEVELOPING YOUR INFLUENCING SKILLS

This chapter is an opportunity for you to focus on the advanced communication skills which are an integral part of your day-to-day work. Influencing skills enable you to build sound relationships with your manager, your client and your team so that you can get things done through other people. The whole process of project management from the early stages of building support for your plan through the subsequent stages of delegating, monitoring performance, coaching, motivating and counselling involves influencing in one form or another.

Conflict handling is closely related to influencing. If you are a good influencer, you will use conflict constructively to promote openness and debate, and you will be able to pre-empt many of the interpersonal clashes which can cause stress. You will also be able to handle the conflicts of interest which are an inevitable result of the complexity of projects, by reconciling as far as possible the needs of the individuals involved and thus enabling the project to progress.

Some project managers are nonetheless uncomfortable about the idea of 'influencing consciously'. There are two main areas of concern:

- 'I don't want to manipulate my staff – that's dishonest.'
- 'Good ideas should sell themselves – do I really have to go to all that work to package them?'

These are important objections which prevent some managers from developing their skills in this area, so we will address each of them in turn.

The key difference between influencing and manipulation is in the underlying intention of the person carrying out the process. *Manipulating* is based on a win–lose outcome: the manipulator gets what he or she wants, and if the other person suffers in the process then that's too bad. Suppose, for example, that a project manager needs a team member to take on a very dull, long piece of work, such as programming a hundred reports. A manipulative approach would be to pretend that the work was more interesting than it was, or to imply that the person's performance would be rewarded by senior management when this was unlikely, or to apply emotional pressure ('I thought I could count on you – don't tell me you're going to let me down').

Manipulation will sometimes work, but in reputable organizations it won't be supported overall because of the cost it entails in trust and the damage to long-term relationships. Once manipulators have been exposed, they lose power and credibility.

Influencing is based on the belief that you are working not only in your personal interest but also genuinely in the interest of your team members, your project and your organization. You are aiming for some kind of win–win outcome, as far as that is feasible. With the boring reports there is no win–win to the team member personally in the short term, but in the long term he is contributing to a successful project with the genuine possibility of more challenging work at a later stage. A more honest project manager might therefore bundle all the dull tasks together and share them out as fairly as possible among the team members. She would be open with her team member. ('I'm sorry about this Fred, but it has to be done, so let's all do our best to get it out of the way as quickly and efficiently as possible. We can then get on to the more interesting stuff.')

Influencing is a more overt process; it leaves the choices open to the other party, who can decide (within reason) whether to cooperate or not. It would be naive, however, to think that good influencing just depends on personal integrity. You also need careful planning and a mastery of advanced communication skills, and this brings us on to the second objection.

Is all that effort spent on 'packaging' ideas in reports, meetings and presentations really necessary? Or is it some kind of indulgence towards the readers or the audience, who should be intelligent enough to pick out the key points for themselves?

Other people have their own worries, needs and pressures, which will be taking up their energy and their time. Good communicators will show their respect for these pressures by presenting ideas in a form which is easy to absorb, and which demonstrates how the ideas will also meet the readers' or the audience's needs. This sort of conversion requires effort; it's not enough just to say or write what comes into your head. A senior manager sitting at her desk with a pile of papers gave the following example:

Take progress reports – they're an opportunity to use your influence with the line to build up a constructive relationship from the start.

Some project managers don't realize this, and think of the reports as a chore imposed for the sake of bureaucracy. Their view is that while the project is running OK, the line should stay away. Their reports will either be too long, with a mass of irrelevant information, or so scanty that we get no real idea of what is going on. And while the project seems to be under control, that may indeed not matter. When the project hits problems however, it takes us time – and costs us unnecessary effort – to pick up the threads and work out how best to intervene.

Contrast that with a project manager who knows something about influencing. You can see from his early reports that he's taken the trouble to present the information we need in a form that is easy to read. Reports like this give me a warm feeling – and if such a project manager needs help, I'll jump. The good influencers get the fast responses.

We can summarize the benefits of developing your influencing skills as follows:

- You build short- and long-term cooperation, based on genuine trust.
- You make it easier for people to assimilate your ideas, so they will help you more readily.
- You pre-empt unnecessary stress.
- You can use influencing skills as a basis for reconciling conflicts.

Section 9.2 offers guidelines for influencing and conflict handling, with an example of how you can use a structured approach to build support for an idea. In Sec. 9.3 we will describe how to apply the guidelines in small meetings, if you want to resolve a problem with your client or your manager, for instance. We will then offer some suggestions in Secs 9.4 and 9.5 for influencing using presentations and reports and finally in Sec. 9.6 we will look at how to use conflict constructively in consensus-building meetings.

9.2 GUIDELINES FOR INFLUENCING AND CONFLICT HANDLING

Some general principles

These principles of influencing and conflict handling may well look familiar to you, but they are so often forgotten in the heat of the moment that we have included them here as a reminder.

Whatever the context you are working in, you will have to address the *needs and interests* of the individuals present. It follows that:

- Influencing is always easier 'one to one', because you have to work only on a single set of needs at a time.
- Influencing is more effective in face-to-face meetings, because you can get direct feedback which enables you to modify your approach as necessary.

Project managers often ask how they should influence a number of people in a meeting. The larger the number of people present, the harder it will be for you to tailor your message to meet the different needs, and so the more preparation time you will need. Even if you have prepared carefully you may still find it difficult to keep track of all the different agendas, let alone control them once you are in the meeting itself.

Experienced influencers will often solve this problem by lobbying key individuals before a meeting, to find out their views and try to influence them on a one-to-one basis before they come into the public arena, where they may be less prepared to be flexible. A phone call or a short meeting with the person may be all that is needed. At the very least, you will have a better idea of the objections to expect, and hence you will be able to prepare some answers. We come back to the subject of meetings at the end of the chapter.

Some managers are not so comfortable talking to people they don't know well, and they may prefer to put their ideas in writing. The problem with the written medium is that it is much less persuasive than face-to-face contact, because of the lack of continuous feedback.

Compare a report with a presentation; in both cases you are influencing 'one to many', but at least in the presentation you can monitor whether individuals are listening to you, and adjust your style if necessary. Once you have submitted your report, you have no further direct contact with the reader while he is going through your material. Most members of an audience are too polite to walk out or fall asleep, but your reader can put your report aside or file it in the wastepaper basket in complete privacy. Never assume therefore that your report or your email message has been read. Cross-check and follow up with phone calls and meetings, to see if there are any further questions you need to answer.

An added problem in conflict situations is that the written word can easily be misinterpreted, and a memo or a report can be passed around to other colleagues with the offending sentences highlighted, thus fuelling the conflict further. Whatever the situation, talk through important documents with your readers and/or submit drafts for discussion wherever possible.

Conflict situations require more preparation than influencing situations, because they tend to be more confused and emotional. The difference between a conflict and an influencing situation is often a question of perception and interpretation. The more you see the needs and objectives of the individuals concerned as overlapping, the more you will see the success of the meeting as depending on good communication, and hence primarily influencing. The more you see the different needs as opposing, the more likely you will be to label the situation as a potential conflict. You may become tense, and hence less rational, as a result.

The key to conflict handling is to deal with the emotions first, using some of the suggestions in Chapter 8 if necessary, so you can put the situation into perspective. You can then plan how you will influence the other parties involved and build cooperation. We will illustrate this further in one of the conflict-handling cases in Sec. 9.3, but first we will describe in more detail how you can use a structured approach for putting across good ideas effectively.

A structured approach for influencing and conflict handling

The following story describes what can go wrong when someone tries to sell an idea without sufficient preparation, and how you can use a structured approach to get back on track.

Peter was a consultant who wanted to persuade his business manager to invest in a new network to link the two existing offices owned by his company with a third, recent, acquisition. He firmly believed that this network would enhance both his team's performance and that of his organization as a whole. Peter agreed with his project manager that as he had a little time to spare, he would research the different options, and recommend one which offered the best contribution, in his view, to the company's technical performance. He set about writing an informal proposal, and became so absorbed in his research that he carried on working on it in his own time. Finally he submitted the proposal, feeling fully confident that his recommendation would get the business manager's approval.

The days and weeks passed, with no response. Peter caught sight of Rob, the business manager, in the office car park, and took the opportunity to ask him for a reaction. Rob was much calmer and quieter than Peter. He paused for a moment and his response was friendly but firm – he had no time right now to consider such proposals.

Peter stormed into the office of Caroline, his project manager, and complained loudly to her about the conservatism of senior staff. Caroline waited for him to cool down. She knew Rob well, and she and Rob respected each other. She then asked to see the proposal. It was ten pages long, and the first page was already full of technical detail. She put away her work and suggested they should have a coffee together.

'What do you think will concern Rob most?' she asked. Peter eventually came up with a list of criteria, including return on investment, compliance with the current drive for costs savings, and being able to justify his decision to his manager. 'What sort of information will he be looking for?' she continued. The consultant frowned. 'More numbers, less technical stuff I suppose.' 'And how about the length of the report?' 'The shorter the better, as he's so busy', Peter conceded. 'OK, I've got the message – I'll rewrite it'.

Together they redrafted the report. The final version was two pages only, and it started with an outline of the benefits, expressed in terms of return on investment. Technical detail was kept to a minimum. This time Rob was more interested, and he agreed to give Peter a 15-minute appointment, during which they could talk through the proposal together.

Peter failed at first to interest Rob in his proposal, but with Caroline's help he managed to get a second chance. If you want to influence someone to adopt one of your good ideas, you can avoid the pitfalls which Peter fell into with his first version of the proposal by going through the following steps.

1. Set your objectives: what do you want to achieve?
2. Put yourself in the other person's place: what does he or she need?
3. Identify the overlap between your needs and those of the other person (if there is no overlap, change your strategy).
4. Formulate the benefits of your proposal: what will the other person get out of it?
5. Package your ideas in a way which will attract the other person's attention.

This approach will help you to be more effective at influencing in any situation: a meeting, a presentation or a report.

We will get back to the story to illustrate each of these steps in more detail. Peter is now at the stage of planning his meeting with Rob, and this time he is going to think through his influencing strategy much more carefully.

1. Set your objectives   The meeting is for Peter a means to an end. His end objective is to get Rob's agreement to implement the network. The objective for the meeting is to get Rob to consider Peter's proposal more seriously. Peter formulates the objective for the meeting as follows: 'By the end of the meeting, we will have had a productive and friendly discussion, and Rob will say that he is prepared to think seriously about my proposal.'

2. Put yourself in the other person's place   This is one of those suggestions which seems so obvious and yet many managers, like Peter, omit this step in practice.

We are often reluctant to put ourselves in the other person's place if the other person seems very different to us. Peter saw Rob as 'commercial' rather than 'technical'. Other barriers are if we don't like the other person much, or feel that the other person doesn't really respect us. In these circumstances an influencing situation can slide into a potential conflict, where both sides only see the differences between them rather than the things they have in common. This preparation step enables you to remain constructive. You can use a number of techniques to remind you to complete this step. You could talk it through with a colleague, as Peter did with Caroline, or sit at your desk and make a list of the other person's concerns.

Your initial list could, of course, be wrong, so you will often need a meeting with the other person to check that you have identified the other person's needs accurately. Use the time to ask questions and to listen to the other person's answers. Many managers think of influencing as talking, and spend the whole meeting restating their arguments. If the arguments are based on faulty assumptions, then the managers are sabotaging their own success. Peter should use the first half of the meeting primarily to check Rob's concerns.

3. Identify the overlap   The overlap between the two sets of needs is the basis for getting the other person's attention and cooperation. Both Peter and Rob want to improve the company's technical performance; Peter's challenge is to convince Rob that this is possible within Rob's budgetary constraints.

Occasionally you will discover that there is no real overlap between the two sets of needs: at this point you have to drop or modify your original influencing plan. You may decide to choose a different person to influence, or go for a less ambitious objective, or wait until circumstances are more favourable. Managers with a reputation for being trustworthy can occasionally ask for favours on a 'goodwill' basis ('If you can help me with this problem then I'll help you if you get into difficulties later').

If you 'desk check' the feasibility of your influencing strategy you can spare yourself failures which could have a negative effect on your credibility within your organization, and which could cause you disappointment and stress. You can also use your time and energy more productively on influencing projects which will have a better chance of success.

4. Identify the benefit   The benefit makes the overlap explicit to the other person. Some managers are good at identifying the overlap in needs, but they then assume that this is obvious to the other person. In practice, if you state the benefit clearly and concisely at the start of a meeting you will, at the very least, remind the other person why he is making time for you. If you state the benefit clearly you also demonstrate to the other person that you have thought carefully about his situation and respect his objectives.

In his meeting with Rob, Peter should put the benefit early in his introduction, for instance: 'Thank you for giving me the time to talk through my proposal with you, Rob. I think this particular solution will offer an excellent improvement in the communication between the offices, for a very reasonable price.'

5. Adjust your communication style to attract the other person's attention   The more you adjust the presentation of your ideas to the preferred working style of the person you want to influence, the better the response. The exception to the rule is if you are genuinely a recognized expert with very high personal credibility. In that case other people will adjust to you.

How far you go in packaging your ideas, and the time you invest in doing so, will largely depend on

- How important the particular objective is to you
- How much personal credibility and power you have in this particular context
- The amount of resistance you anticipate.

Your aim when you adjust your style is to *match the other person's patterns* and expectations as far as possible. Peter's second version of the proposal got a much better response from Rob because he had made it shorter, addressed Rob's concerns at the start and used Rob's language (return on investment, cost savings, profit, etc.) Some straightforward techniques which could help Peter in his meeting with Rob are as follows.

Peter should *establish cooperation at the start* by giving his initial statement of the benefit, then cross-checking the manager's needs explicitly, using open questions, letting Rob talk, summarizing to show that he has listened and understood.

Rob is a quiet speaker, Peter talks much faster. Differences in non-verbal patterns can make communication hard work. Peter should try to *adjust the way he speaks* by slowing down his pace to match Rob's calmer way of speaking. This will help Rob to feel less rushed and more relaxed.

Peter may be tempted to jump in with an explanation of all his ideas right at the start. A better approach is to *pace* the meeting carefully, by checking at each stage that Rob is in agreement, before he moves on to present his proposal in detail.

Towards the end of the 15 minutes Peter should *reposition his proposal carefully* in the context of the business manager's concerns, fine-tuning the benefit in the light of what he has learned during the meeting. He could say, for instance,

> I appreciate that we need to be aware of the current pressure on costs and investment. However, this new network will not only enable our team to work more quickly and to reach our deadlines, it will also improve communication between other teams which are located in different offices.

Peter could also say explicitly that he has talked the proposal through extensively with Caroline, the project manager – knowing that the business manager respects her judgement.

Common sense? Certainly – but have a look round your office, and note how many good ideas get lost because people fail to prepare and present properly. A little desk-checking and patience can produce rewarding results.

We will offer more suggestions for packaging ideas in the sections on presentations and reports. First we will take this framework a little further by explaining how you can use it as a basis for handling one-to-one conflicts.

9.3 CONFLICT HANDLING IN ONE-TO-ONE MEETINGS

Some conflicts can blow up quite unexpectedly.

> Heena walked into the meeting with her client feeling positively cheerful. The client was a rather distant, older man, who in the past had made her rather nervous, but she was integration manager on a large project, and her team had worked so hard that they were actually ahead of schedule. He must be pleased with her by now.

The client indeed congratulated her, but then he went on to present her with an unexpected development. The test machine, which was planned to arrive in seven weeks' time, was actually going to be delivered the following week. 'So, good news from our side, too,' he said. 'We want you to move the system acceptance forward.'

Heena's mind raced. 'I don't think that's possible,' she replied. She could feel her face flushing. 'My two most experienced team members are going on holiday next week.' She dared not add that a third had a new baby in the family, and certainly wouldn't be prepared to work weekends. The client's face darkened. 'You'll have to make it possible,' he snapped. 'When I said you've got to move acceptance forward, I meant it.'

What should she do next? Heena is at a critical point in the interview. Both she and her client are stating their positions: she says she can't move acceptance forward, he says she has to do so. Positions can easily become entrenched, particularly if they are both getting angry.

Different people react in different ways to this sort of pressure. One project manager might give in, only to find herself confronted by angry team members refusing to work overtime. Another might refuse to budge in the meeting, and then get told off by her own manager when the client rings up and complains that she has been too inflexible. The solution is to take a deep breath, and change direction, using the influencing framework as your guide.

'Can I think for a moment?' Heena asked. 'It's just that your request has taken me by surprise, and my team really are quite tired. Couldn't we carry on with the current schedule and let the machine wait?' Her voice trailed off as the client looked about to explode. She tried again. 'Could you explain to me please why you need the integration moved forward – why is this all so urgent?'

The client sighed, and sat back. 'It's my manager,' he said at last. 'He wants to have an article about the system in the next edition of our client newsletter, and that gives us very little time. He's already made arrangements for a photographer and a demonstration of the system next month. I'm under a lot of pressure.'

It is usually pressure of some kind which makes a normally reasonable person act unreasonably. Your task as project manager is to ask *why* – to identify the needs which underlie the statement of the position. Once Heena has identified her client's needs, she can move on to explore options in order to find the overlap: the solution which in this example will enable Heena to meet her obligations to her staff and the client to meet his obligation to his manager. Perhaps Heena can bring in additional staff, for instance, if the client can make more budget available and if she is prepared to put in extra hours herself to train them.

Another way of reducing the pressure on the client is for Heena to ask him what his most *urgent* needs are. Suppose he needs to get a clear commitment from her before a meeting with his manager at the end of the afternoon. She could agree to try to contact her manager immediately, to talk through the possible options and check what was feasible.

Once you have set up a spirit of cooperation ('How can we best solve this together?') you can attack the problem, not each other. When you are both less tense, you will be much more resourceful.

A different type of conflict is the sort which builds up slowly over a period of time, until the person gets really depressed and resentful.

Franklin had been working for a few months for Joanne, a successful project manager with a reputation for bringing in projects on time and in budget. Franklin was fairly new to management and he'd started running his small team with a great deal of enthusiasm.

Gradually, however, his enthusiasm had waned. Joanne kept intervening with his team members to check how they were getting on. 'I might as well not be here,' he told a colleague one evening. 'She does all my monitoring for me. Even if I tell her I've got it all under control she doesn't believe me. I've tried to talk to her but she just sweeps my comments aside. I don't know why I bother.'

The friend thought a drink in the local bar was called for. 'What's upsetting you most?' he asked when they were comfortably installed. 'It's the fact that she doesn't trust me,' Franklin replied.

The perceptions of individuals involved in a conflict are often strongly coloured by their feelings, rather than facts. What may start off as a difference in working styles can soon appear to be much more serious ('She doesn't trust me') and a vicious circle can quickly emerge. Franklin gets more withdrawn because he feels he can't communicate with Joanne, so Joanne loses more confidence in him and checks again with his staff to make sure everything is in control, and so on.

Talking the situation through with a friend enables you to get a more accurate definition of the problem. 'She keeps intervening with my staff' is a fact; 'She doesn't trust me' is an interpretation, or assumption. Once you have separated out the facts you can use the influencing approach to plan how to improve the relationship and solve the problem. The key step, as always, is to try to identify Joanne's needs – in this case, she presumably wants to be sure that the project is really in control. Franklin's next challenge is to get her attention to the problem, check that they both understand each other's needs, and work together to find a solution. Franklin could try the following:

- *Get Joanne to take the problem seriously*. He could say: 'Joanne, could we make some time in the meeting today to discuss how we are working together? There's something I feel very strongly about.'
- *Describe the problem in neutral terms*, e.g. 'I know it's very important for us to stay on track, and I have been checking on progress in my team every day. It's difficult for me though if you come and check directly with my team yourself.'
- *Check that he has understood Joanne's needs correctly*: 'Can you explain to me how you see the situation?'

Once he is sure that he has understood her viewpoint, he should *summarize their joint definition* of the problem:

So what we're saying is that this part of the project is critical, and you were aware that I was new to the job so you were trying to give me a safety net. I'd rather do the checking myself, but you say you need clearer evidence from me that I'm in control. How can I do that?'

The final step for Franklin is to explore options, then agree actions and follow up, and perhaps celebrate with the friend who had helped him in the first place.

We will move on now to consider influencing in one-to-many situations, in presentations, reports and larger meetings.

9.4 PRESENTATIONS

Preparation

When you prepare a presentation, what is your first step? Many managers will reply 'I work out my message' or 'I think about the structure'. Beware: this is often where presentations start to go wrong.

You can only identify your message, or choose a suitable structure, if you have gone through the first two steps of the influencing framework. *What do I want to achieve?* and *What do they need to know?* Many presentations fail not because of the quality of the overhead slides, or even the style of the presenter, but because the speaker never really identified the overlap between what he or she wanted to achieve and what the audience wanted to hear.

Check how you formulate your objectives. Often presenters confuse an objective with a brief description of the content: 'The purpose of this presentation is to give an overview of the current technical options for local area networks.' A better formulation would be: 'The purpose of this presentation is to present to you the different options, with their advantages and disadvantages, *so you can choose the option* which best meets your requirements.'

You can get a better overview of the different needs in the audience by plotting them with other key information on a matrix:

Name	Needs	Level	Role/function	Problem areas

Clashes between needs can be a clue that you need to organize yourself differently. Perhaps you should restrict the audience for your presentation, for instance, or replace the presentation with an informal meeting, or lobby key individuals as suggested earlier.

Your next step is to identify the overlap between your objective and their needs. Here you may encounter some problems straightaway. What if you are stuck, for some reason, with a mixed audience of technical experts and non-technical managers? How can you formulate objectives and a structure to meet different sets of needs during the same event? A faulty strategy is to 'go for the middle ground'; if you are unlucky with the distribution, you can end up boring everyone. A better approach, if you cannot give two separate presentations, is to split your presentation into sections explicitly aimed at the different types of listeners. In a conference on X.400 some years ago, the speaker opened with two discrete objectives:

> To give managers who are new to the area an understanding of current applications, benefits and pitfalls; to give the experts in the audience an update on the results of the recent leading edge projects and the newest developments

and he structured his talk accordingly.

Your definition of objectives and needs form the basis for your structure and your selection of content. Each time you get stuck on issues such as 'Should I put this in or not?' you should go back to your basis and check whether the particular idea is relevant to the needs of your audience or readers, and whether it will help you to reach your objective. On the whole, we tend to overload presentations with information – so 'if in doubt, leave it out!'

The benefit of your presentation should answer the question 'Why should you all listen to me?' If you have got a good statement of the benefit, this will make both you and the audience feel confident that the presentation will be a success. Consider putting it on an overhead slide, and showing it within the first 2 minutes so that you get off to a strong start.

Next, think about how you will maintain audience interest. Attention is typically highest at the start of any sequence of communication. In a 20-minute presentation, attention will be highest during the first 5 minutes, then it will drop down to a 'trough' or lowest point between 10 and 15 minutes. If the presenter announces that she is coming to the conclusion, attention will rise again for the last few minutes.

The total length of a presentation also affects the level of attention. Most people will listen to a 5-minute presentation, but you have to be a really good presenter to maintain interest for more than 25 minutes. Attention also depends on the relevance of the subject and the quality of delivery, of course, but, on the whole, you should assume that *20 minutes is the maximum* you can realistically keep your audience alert. If you know you are not a good presenter, you can make your life and that of the audience much easier with a 10-minute presentation, consisting of a few carefully selected points, followed by questions.

Try to put your main points at a stage in the presentation when you know attention will be highest. A good approach is to make your most important point first, supported by subsidiary points, and expanded in your conclusion. Of course, this depends on the situation and your audience, but if you build up to your key point about two-thirds of the way through, then your audience may be in the attention 'trough' and they will miss what you are saying.

Make a sketch of your schedule. Suppose you are planning a 15-minute presentation, for instance, then your schedule may look like this:

Introduction	3 minutes
Idea A	4 minutes
Idea B	3 minutes
Idea C	3 minutes
Conclusion	2 minutes

If you know you have a tendency to run over time, you may want to restrict Idea A to 3 minutes, and keep 1 minute as contingency. A rehearsal will also be essential for you, to help you practise sticking to schedule.

Allow about 2 minutes to get any idea across coherently. A good introduction, where you introduce yourself and give your objective, the benefit and an overview of your content and schedule will take at least 2 minutes to present, and is essential as a starting point for your audience. Conclusions which take less than 2 minutes will appear rushed and unconvincing. This leaves you space to present only three or four ideas, so you must select your material rigorously according to audience needs and your objective. If you only have a few points, it will be much easier for you to remember your structure, and easier for the audience to remember your message.

Allow roughly 2 minutes per slide, so that your audience can absorb your message. Restrict text to about six lines, and check that the lettering is large enough to be easily visible. Prefer key words and phrases to complete sentences, because with key words your audience will have to listen to your explanation. Use simple diagrams and pictures wherever possible.

Flipcharts and whiteboards are visual aids which encourage audience participation. Use thick pens, write letters at least 5 centimetres high, and express ideas in the words of the contributor wherever possible.

For important presentations, you may want to submit a draft of your objective, your benefit and your schedule to the key person who has asked for your presentation. This enables you to check whether you are on track before you start making slides and getting into detailed preparation, and it checks the commitment and support of your potential audience.

'On-stage' techniques for more impact

If you have correctly identified the benefit and structured your presentation to meet the needs of the audience, you will already have a good chance of achieving your objective. You should also be feeling realistically confident; thorough preparation helps you to overcome nerves.

Many managers ask for tips and techniques to help them to have more impact, given that in presentations you have such high visibility and can feel very exposed. Each presenter should develop the style which feels right for him or her, so the suggestions in this section are intended very much as options rather than as rules or guidelines. Select the points which fit best with your personal style; the main thing is to feel comfortable and to be yourself.

'What should I do with my hands?' is a common question. One answer is to check your feet. At the start, stand facing the audience, with your weight evenly distributed. Don't worry too much about your arms, because as long as you have a stable base, your hands will tend to sort themselves out. Take up this stance whenever you feel under pressure – with difficult questions, for instance, and at the end.

If you like to walk around, try to move only forwards and backwards, avoiding sideways movement. If you move nearer towards the audience, you will increase impact; if you move back behind a desk for the conclusion, you convey formality and order. Sideways movement tends to distract. Rehearse in front of a mirror to find out what feels natural for you.

Try to look at your audience as much as possible. In European and native English-speaking cultures, eye contact conveys confidence and sincerity. If you find eye contact difficult, then at least look at key members of the audience when you are making your most important points. Make sure that you don't look too long at any one individual, because prolonged eye contact can make people feel uncomfortable; move from person to person.

Similarly, aim to face the audience throughout. Avoid turning your back to point on a screen; you will lose contact with the audience, and you will not be able to monitor their reactions.

Take care with jokes in presentations. By their very nature they are risky, and a story intended to amuse can end up causing offence. If humour is not normally part of your personal style, stick to a well-planned professional approach.

Should you take questions during your presentation or at the end? Questions give you useful feedback, so in general you should take questions as you go. If individuals ask for detailed information, however, which may not be relevant for others in the audience, you must be firm about moving on. Tell the audience at the start whether or not they can interrupt you. If you want to restrict questions until the end, double-check that your material, structure and sequence are carefully tailored to meet audience needs.

What if you don't have the answer to a question? The best policy is to be honest and say that you don't know. Perhaps others in the audience can help you with their experience, or perhaps you can contact a colleague later and pass on the answer subsequently to the person who asked the question.

With complex questions, start by clarifying ('Can I just check that I have understood you right?'). This also gives you time to think. Often you can at least answer part of a question, and that might be enough to satisfy the person who asked you.

If your mind goes blank and you can't think of your next point, try simply summarizing the points you have covered so far. Don't apologize. A summary nearly always reminds you (and the audience) of your original structure and gets you back on track.

Schedule a practice run with colleagues before you give important presentations to make sure that you have not missed any important points. Allow yourself enough time to integrate constructive criticism, and, if necessary, dry run again so that you feel fully confident. In the event itself, don't worry if you make the odd slip. As long as you have delivered what you have promised, your presentation will have every chance of being rated a success.

9.5 PLANNING AND WRITING REPORTS

Your preparation for a report will be exactly the same as for a presentation in terms of identifying the overlap and the benefit. If your report is destined for readers with different needs, you can divide it into different sections and provide careful 'sign posting' in your introduction so that each reader can quickly turn to the sections which are most relevant for him or for her. If we take a user guide as an example:

Section 2 is a summary, which gives an overview of the system.
Section 3 is a more detailed description of each command available.
Section 4 is intended for readers who want to make modifications to the system.

If we now look at the packaging of your reports, you'll see that there are a number of options open to you which can help you to motivate your readers to keep reading. The first step is to check the layout of your reports very carefully Make sure that your key ideas are near the beginning, in a summary of conclusions, for instance, so that you have the best possible chance that the reader will actually digest your information.

Some simple techniques can help you to develop a more readable style, for instance:

- Restrict paragraph length to a maximum of seven or eight lines. Readers tend to skip the middle sentences of longer paragraphs.
- Restrict sentence length to a maximum of two and a half lines. If you are not too good at grammar, or if are writing in a foreign language, this will encourage you to use simple structures which are easier for the reader as well. If you like using varied punctuation, then use semi-colons instead of the occasional full stop, to increase 'flow' (see the next sentence if you would like an example).
- Put your main idea in the first line of your paragraph wherever possible; use the rest of the paragraph to expand on the initial idea. The reader can then decide quickly whether he or she wants to read all the paragraph or just the key idea.
- Check the three words at the start of each paragraph – they should catch the reader's attention. If you use 'strong openers' consistently, the reader can scan the left-hand margin of your text to select what is most relevant.

Test your completed page by folding over the right-hand edge to touch the line marked B (Fig. 9.1).

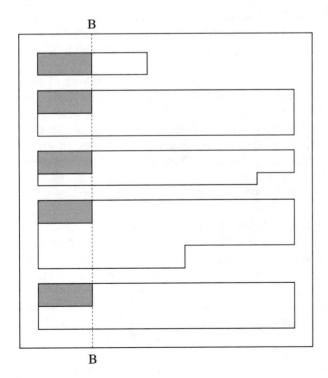

Figure 9.1 Test for readability.

Give your text to a colleague to test: can she still pick up the clues to your main ideas, just by reading the openers? If she opens out the page, can she identify the main points accurately after a 30-second scan?

Another advantage of developing a more readable style is that you can check your own material more efficiently. (There are few things more frustrating than reading your own work and realizing that you are confusing yourself!) You will also be able to produce reports more quickly, because you will feel confident that you are writing clearly.

9.6 INFLUENCING AND CONFLICT HANDLING IN CONSENSUS-BUILDING MEETINGS

The purpose of consensus building is to:

- Integrate different viewpoints, experience and expertise in order to make decisions of the highest possible quality
- Get the full commitment of everyone in the meeting to the decisions which will have the greatest impact on the project.

Managers who 'lead from the middle' will work more through consensus than those who 'lead from the front', because careful use of consensus helps to develop teams into 'super-organisms'.

Consensus building requires a great deal of skill. You need all the techniques which we have already covered in this chapter, and, of course, you are managing a group of people with a wide range of views, interests, expertise and needs. Badly managed meetings can quickly degenerate into personal attacks or long, rambling events with no discernible results.

Your first step is to decide which decisions in your team are important enough to merit the consensus-building approach, and who should be involved in the process. Consensus can be tiring and time consuming to achieve even if you manage the process well, so you should use it only when you truly require the participation, contribution and commitment of those present. Examples of such decisions are consolidating major estimates, all the key planning decisions and the fundamental design decisions. These are worth the extra effort. If people agree, and are seen to agree to these key decisions, then each individual will work conscientiously to support the decision outside the meetings and over a long period of time.

Some managers confuse consensus building with majority decisions, and when they get under time pressure they resort to voting. This is dangerous, because it sets up 'winners and losers'; what you gain in speed you lose in long-term commitment. Voting and other forms of majority decision making are only appropriate for decisions which are less important.

With experience you can speed up the process of reaching consensus. Super-organism teams will often learn from your example and use consensus very effectively in smaller meetings to maintain a high level of commitment throughout the project.

To run a consensus meeting successfully you should think carefully about your role. You may well have experience and expertise of your own which you will want to bring into the team. However, your main contribution will be to integrate the expertise of the individuals in the group and thus achieve some degree of synergy (the '2 + 2 = 5' effect). Remember that you must manage both

- The *task* (the decision to be made) and
- The *process* (the way in which the group is working).

If you sense that the group is getting stuck, and going round in circles, then you should ask yourself the *process* questions:

- What is going on?
- How effectively are we working together?

and, if necessary, call a break so that you can assess for yourself where you have got to and how you can progress.

Further suggestions for running this type of meeting are as follows:

1. State the *objective* of the meeting clearly at the start, e.g. 'The purpose of our meeting is to consolidate our estimates and form a joint view'.
2. Establish your *procedures* – explain how the meeting will run, how you will tackle the problem, e.g. 'Each estimator will present his estimate and explain how he arrived at his conclusions. When he has finished, the other members of the team can ask for clarification. After we have heard from everyone, we will start the consolidation process.'
3. Explain also how you intend to take the major *decisions*, e.g. 'I'd like us to reach consensus on as many points as possible. If at the end of the meeting we still disagree on something, then I will take a decision on it myself.'
4. Check right at the start that everyone *agrees with these procedures*. If someone has a better suggestion, modify the procedures and summarize what has been agreed.
5. Ensure that everyone *listens* – don't allow interruptions when one estimator is presenting his or her case. Later if the debate gets lively you may decide to work more informally, but keep checking that people are not talking over each other and cutting each other off in mid-sentence.
6. *Encourage the quieter members* of the group to participate – don't let the more vocal members dominate the discussion.
7. *Clarification questions* must be genuine requests for explanation – not politely formulated attacks. Set a good example yourself by formulating your questions carefully, e.g. 'I agree with your first point, but I can't quite follow the reasoning behind the second calculation Could you explain it to me again?'
8. Keep the emphasis of the meeting on *rational arguments*, information and checking assumptions; if people take up positions ask for the reasons behind the position.
9. *Acknowledge constructive behaviour.* Because meetings are public arenas, some people are very sensitive to 'loss of face'. If there's a debate which can't be resolved by rational argument, and at a given moment you want to make a majority decision and move on, then thank the minority for their cooperation. Give them the opportunity to start off the discussion on the next point, so that they stay involved in the meeting.

10. Consider using a *flipchart or whiteboard* to summarize conclusions. This also moves the debate away from the people and on to a neutral space where team members can review the argument in a more detached frame of mind.

11. Stress areas of *agreement* as you go – and show the team that they are making progress, e.g. 'Right, we have all reached consensus on the first three points – that's very helpful. Now let's tackle point four again – can we talk through the assumptions again?'

12. *Thank* everyone at the end for their contribution, and tell them what the next step in the process will be.

SUMMARY OF INFLUENCING AND CONFLICT HANDLING

1. Influencing
   - Works genuinely towards a realistic 'win–win' outcome
   - Helps others to assimilate your good ideas
   - Is the basis for effective conflict handling
   - Is always easier on a 'one-to-one' basis
2. A structured approach for influencing and conflict handling is to
   - Set objectives
   - Put yourself in the other person's place
   - Identify the overlap in needs and interests
   - Formulate the benefits
   - Package your ideas to attract attention
3. Conflict handling one to one
   - Ask why? Identify the needs behind the position
   - Talk through your emotions first with a trusted colleague, to clear your mind
   - Describe the problem in neutral terms
4. Presentations
   - Start with your objective and the audience's needs
   - Check your schedule
   - Do a dry run for confidence
   - Prepare well, then be yourself
5. Reports
   - Prepare as for presentations – your objective, readers' needs
   - Check the layout
   - Use a readable style
6. Consensus-building meetings
   - Use when you need the full support of all present to a decision
   - Ask – how effectively are we working together?
   - Establish procedures
   - Remember to thank team members for constructive contributions

---

MANAGING YOURSELF

10.1 INTRODUCTION

This chapter is for you, personally. So far in this book we have talked a lot about how you can help other people; here we talk about how you can help yourself. The topics we have chosen have been raised by project managers on our workshops as areas of common concern:

- How to manage your time
- How to manage your stress level so you can stay healthy and effective in your job and at home

The tips and techniques in all these areas which work for you can be usefully passed on to your staff via coaching, but our main focus here is you and your needs.

The more senior you are in an organization, the more you are expected to manage yourself. You may be lucky enough to have a manager who offers you a great deal of support – or you may have a manager who is very busy, or less interested in people, or who simply expects that you would prefer to sort out your own problems yourself. Some managers have not come into contact with the ideas on counselling, so you could be providing more support to your staff than you are getting from your own manager. This may leave you at times feeling isolated and vulnerable.

In this chapter we provide some tools, information and suggestions to help you to manage yourself. This is also an area where there are some good books available to provide further ideas. We have drawn on some of these sources in this chapter, and you can find the references in the Further Reading.

10.2 MANAGING YOUR TIME

Two common problems for managers are, first, the tendency over a period of time to get overwhelmed by the burden of day-to-day tasks:

> Helen rang up on the morning of the course. She sounded edgy. 'Sorry,' she said. 'The stuff on time management looks really useful, but I'm just too busy to attend. I know it sounds stupid, but I'm rushed off my feet – let me know when you run another one'

and, second, the nagging suspicion that you are not using your time as effectively as you could:

> When my partner asks me what I did today, I don't know what to answer . . . I've been busy, all right, but what have I actually achieved?

Time management depends on a clear understanding of your goals and priorities, supported by a competent system of personal organization. In this section we first give a range of suggestions to help you to prioritize and distinguish between working efficiently (doing the thing right) and working effectively (doing the right thing). The later sections offer ideas for improving your personal organization, by keeping daily action lists, making time free to concentrate, dealing with requests for help and organizing your incoming mail.

Prioritizing

The first and most important step towards prioritizing effectively is to make some time and space for yourself to think. If you are currently feeling overwhelmed, this is, of course, counter-intuitive – like Helen, you just want to get back to work and 'get things done'. The question remains: are you doing the *right* things?

Managers who feel themselves beginning to get stressed by their workload will find it helpful to talk through their priorities with someone who will act as a sounding board for them. The other person helps you to stick to the process, and can reassure you that this really is a good use of your time. If you just want to check that you are on track with your priorities then initially a quiet undisturbed half-hour may be all you need.

Start by going back to the *purpose* of your project. What is it for? Who is paying for it? What do they expect? Why is it running? When you are setting up the project you cannot imagine losing sight of the purpose; when you are half-way through and sorting out the inevitable problems, it is easy to lose sight of the end goal.

Once you have reminded yourself of all the important aspects of the purpose, you can select from a number of tools and techniques to help you to prioritize further.

Some managers prioritize by identifying their *Key Result Areas*: those activities which will have most impact on achieving your objectives. Try the challenge of Pareto's principle, which suggests that 20 per cent of your activities will typically yield 80 per cent of the results – and conversely, the remaining 80 per cent yields only 20 per cent of the results. What is the 20 per cent of your work that is critical to your success?

Another, related, technique is to distinguish for yourself between

- *Proactive tasks* – which contribute to your Key Results Areas and should be planned ahead and

- *Reactive tasks* – which crop up unexpectedly.

Reactive tasks include requests for help, routine paperwork and so on. Some organizations expect you to be particularly flexible with reactive tasks. The problem for managers is that time spent on reactive tasks means that less time is available for the more important proactive ones. Achieving a balance between the two sets of expectations is not always easy.

You can check for yourself whether the balance between reactive and proactive tasks is appropriate by keeping a time log. Time logs require discipline, but they often provide surprising insights into how we *actually* spend our time at work. A suggested format is as follows:

Time (in 15-minute blocks)	Activity	Your comments on effectiveness	Suggestions for improvement

Keep a piece of paper for your time log with you throughout the day and update as you go. Try to stick to the small blocks of 15 minutes and to keep the log with you for a week because you need detailed information in order to spot patterns. You could give yourself a treat when you complete it – logs, like diets, require quite a bit of self-discipline. You will notice, though, that virtue is often its own reward, because the simple act of recording your use of time will tend to make you more effective in your use of it as you progress through the week.

The log will give you answers to some key time management questions, for instance:

- How much of your time did you spend on proactive tasks in your Key Results Areas?
- How much reactive time did you need in the week which you recorded?
- How did this affect your Key Result Areas?
- How much contingency time would you need, realistically, to schedule for reactive tasks in a typical week?
- How satisfied are you with the way you spent your time?

If you are not happy with the balance between reactive and proactive time you may decide to:

- Show your log to your manager and discuss some suggestions for improving the distribution
- Revisit your delegation patterns – can you assign some tasks to team members? Would they need any coaching or training for this?

Urgency ↑	B Very urgent, not so important DELEGATE?	A Very important, very urgent DO!
	D Not so urgent, not so important POSTPONE	C Very important, not so urgent PLAN!
	LEAVE	**Importance** →

Figure 10.1 Prioritizing tasks.

Another tool for sorting out tasks quickly on a daily or weekly basis is the matrix in Fig. 10.1. The matrix distinguishes between *urgent* and *important* tasks. If you are not aware of the difference, the risk for the busy project manager is that urgent but less important tasks can distract you from the important tasks which require your full attention. Some examples of activities sorted according to the matrix categories are as follows.

A activities – very important, very urgent

Example Your client has made an important complaint and you need to check with your staff what has happened. One of your key team members has told you that he has just received a job offer from a competitor.

These activities are top priority, and if they impact your Key Results Areas you will probably have to tackle them yourself.

B activities – very urgent, not so important

Example Your time sheet is due in today. You need to arrange a meeting with your client before she goes on holiday at the end of the week. You must phone the travel agent to book a flight to London.

You have several options here. Some B tasks can be delegated, such as the phone call, or batched together to save time. Tasks which you cannot delegate should be scheduled for a specific time, depending on your deadline: find a quiet office, shut yourself away with the relevant paperwork and complete the time sheet.

C activities – very important, not so urgent

Example You need to plan two performance appraisals for your staff. You want to set up a coaching and development plan for yourself, and your first step is to make an appointment to discuss it with your manager.

C activities are the test of good time management – poor time managers will never get round to completing them. The problem is that because C tasks are not urgent, they are often put to the bottom of the list; because they are important, however, neglected C activities may become A activities. The staff who don't get their appraisals, for instance, may start to get demotivated and look for jobs elsewhere.

Hard-working managers often put the C activities which are in their personal interest at the bottom of their list, to their own long-term disadvantage. C activities also tend to be broad in scope, so that busy managers feel they don't know where to start. The only thing they are sure about is that they have not enough time to complete their C activities right now.

The solution is to plan your C activities, so that even if you are currently very busy you can at least make a start on them. Take your diary and block out some space over the next few weeks. Break large tasks into smaller chunks which are more manageable. Check that your filing and paperwork are efficient, so you can easily pick up the task and know what the next step is. Allow yourself 'warm-up' and 'cool-down' times, as these are usually tasks that need peak concentration.

D activities – not so urgent or important

Example   You have received an invitation to attend a conference, and a memo asking you for feedback on the services of in-house automation.

Some paperwork which starts as a D activity may end up in the B box, especially if other people in your organization regard it as more important. Tasks such as the feedback may turn out to be more significant than you had assumed. If you cannot delegate your D activities, try getting them out of the way when you are waiting for a meeting, or a plane, or when you are too tired to tackle anything more demanding. Activities at the bottom-left of the matrix in Fig. 10.1 may be so trivial that they are best left undone.

When you are under extreme time pressure, list the main tasks to be completed and simply check each task against the following questions suggested by Dr David Cormack [1986]:

1. Must it be done?
2. Must it be done by me?
3. Must it be done now?

If you answer 'yes' to all three questions then move on to the next:

4. How much time do I have?

If you are in the middle of a crisis, try focusing on the time available rather than on the tasks:

5. How can I use the next 3 (or whatever) hours most effectively?

Improve your personal organization

Make a daily action list   Once you have prioritized the incoming demands, you can move on to your action list. If you put your list in a hardback day book you will also have a record of actions undertaken, which you can use later if necessary.

Some managers make their action lists first thing in the morning; others prefer to do them at the end of the day, before they leave. Some tips for effective lists are as follows.

- Be realistic; you will feel better if you complete five out of five actions on your list than if you are over-ambitious in your planning and only manage to complete five out of ten. Your action list should help you to motivate yourself.
- Cross off completed actions as you go, so that you can see what you have achieved. If you complete actions in addition to those on your list, add them at the bottom, so you have a record of your effectiveness and can feel good about yourself. Uncompleted actions should be reassessed when you prioritize again for the list for the following day.
- Identify for yourself the times when you have most mental energy and when you have least. If you know that you are at your most creative early in the morning, then try to maximize your use of that peak time – for your Key Result Areas, ideally. If you know you have a trough on Wednesday afternoons, put your less demanding activities, if possible, in that slot.
- Check that you leave enough contingency time for unexpected reactive tasks – otherwise your list could make you feel stressed.
- Review your lists and your use of time at the end of the week. Can you now say that you have made the most effective use of your time? If so, congratulate yourself!

Organize time for peak concentration Some activities require a period of uninterrupted time, where you can settle down comfortably to work with maximum concentration, preferably for at least an hour or so. Design work, planning, report writing are all examples. With these tasks, in order to make progress you need to settle into a state of 'flow', where time passes without your noticing, and where you will often produce your best-quality work. To reach this state, however, you first need a period of immersion, of about 15 minutes. If you are interrupted during this period, for instance by a phone call, your concentration is disturbed and you have to start all over again.

The difficulty in most offices is to balance the need for uninterrupted 'flow' time against the need for your availability to others, and it is a problem, of course, not just for you but for all your staff.

To promote and protect flow hours requires planning and clear agreements with your team. In some open-plan offices there is an unwritten code that if a colleague does not look up from her desk as you pass by, she is trying to concentrate – interrupt only if it's really urgent. Or perhaps you can designate certain small rooms which are shared between you and your team for the tasks which require peak concentration. Depending on the conventions of your organization, you may be able to schedule one particular hour where people are asked not to interrupt you except in case of emergencies. Perhaps you could also let people outside the team know of this arrangement, so that they defer non-urgent phone calls to times which are more convenient for you.

Whatever method you decide to adopt, try to schedule peak concentration time for yourself during working hours. So many diligent managers accept a high level of interruptions during the day on the basis that 'they do their thinking at home'. This eats into your leisure and family time and can cause problems in the long run.

Refusing requests Some managers find it very difficult to say 'no' to requests. A large proportion of their work will then inevitably be reactive, and unless this is really part of their job description, other Key Result Areas may suffer. Helpfulness is expected at work, along with some flexibility, but if you recognize that you find it inherently difficult to refuse requests, you may need to review some more of the underlying beliefs which so often shape behaviour unconsciously. Examples of beliefs which may stop you saying 'no' are:

'I'm the only one who can do it'
'It's my job – I can't ask anyone else'
'I don't want to upset them'
'It would look rude'
'They wouldn't ask me again'
'I want people to think I can cope with everything – I don't want to seem inadequate' and so on.

If you can recognize some of these in yourself, challenge their relevance to your current situation. Is it really your job to answer every incoming query? How does that contribute to your Key Result Areas? Would you really appear inadequate if you refused one request on the grounds that you were particularly busy at the time? Will the other person really take your refusal personally?

Some managers lack the 'formats' for refusing requests politely. Others end up making excuses. This may trigger more pressure from the person making the request, with the result that the manager gives in – and subsequently asks herself 'How did I let myself get manipulated *again*?' You can say 'no' without offending others in a number of ways, for instance:

- Select a more convenient time: 'I'm sorry, I'm so busy that I can't help right now – but next week things get easier. Would that be any use to you?'
- Suggest another resource: 'I can't help, but perhaps I know someone else who may be able to answer some of your queries.'
- Offer partial help: 'I haven't the time to help you with all of this, but if I do this piece could you manage the rest?'
- Swap tasks: 'I'd be happy to help, but I'm very short of time. If I help you with this, could you take over another task for me?'
- Ask for more notice – next time: 'I can't help this time, but if you let me know a little more in advance next time round, I may be able to help you then.'
- Refuse firmly but pleasantly: 'This week I really haven't any time – but please feel free to ask again another time.'

The solution is to support the person but refuse the request. (If you would like more suggestions on assertive behaviour, consult Cormack (1986) and O'Brien (1992) in the Further Reading.)

Dealing with incoming mail What does your desk look like, right now? If you're confronted by piles of papers and an overflowing in-tray, then here are some suggestions which will help you to be more organized. We will tackle the in-tray first.

Classify incoming mail, at a time of day that is convenient to you. Incoming phone calls may be difficult to ignore; incoming mail should not interrupt your work, unless you are waiting for some urgent letter. One useful method is to sort mail into one of four categories according to the AIRS system (see Cormack, 1986):

A – Action
I – Information
R – Reading material
S – Scrap

Action material is dealt with during your usual prioritizing process. Urgent material will be handled on the same day. The problem comes when managers want to postpone action until another date, but when the day comes they have lost the relevant papers.

If you do not want to deal with something immediately, but want to put it where you can find it and deal with it on another day, put it into an expanding file marked 'pending'. Do not use a 'heap' system – that makes you lose time sifting through. Set up your expanding file in date order, according to the date on which you plan to deal with this particular action. This sort of file is often called a 'bring-forward' file, and you can mark the pockets according to months of the year or, if you are very busy, days of the week. If you file consistently and check the file regularly, this system will keep you organized – and it requires relatively little effort.

Similarly, some *information* needs to be read on the same day; some can be left in a specific place on your desk for a time later in the afternoon, when you are too tired to tackle anything too demanding. Information which is background for subsequent action can be added to the documents in your 'pending' file.

Reading material can go into a special folder that you work through, for instance, during waiting time. If you are travelling around for meetings, take the folder with you.

Junk mail to *scrap* may include material which has been copied to you but which is irrelevant to your needs. Many organizations are now using electronic mail systems, which save paper but do not always save time. Senders have easy access to automatic mailing lists. If they are not disciplined enough to check that the lists are really appropriate, then memos will propagate themselves on screens throughout the office.

If you get inundated with electronic mail take a minute to analyse the sources. Check the difference between mail which is currently addressed to you – where the sender assumes that you will take action – and mail which is simply copied to you, where the sender should assume that this will take lower priority, as background reading. Is your name on the right list? Should your name be deleted from any list? Talk to the sender to save yourself time.

Summary of time management

1. Prioritize – Be effective, not just efficient
   - Review your objectives
   - Check your Key Result Areas
   - Separate proactive from reactive tasks
   - Keep a log to audit your current use of time
   - Separate important tasks from urgent ones
2. Check your personal organization
   - Make daily action lists

- Plan your 'flow' time
- Be prepared to say 'no'
- Sort out your incoming mail

10.3 STRESS MANAGEMENT

Poor time management is one common cause of work-related stress. Other causes, as described in Chapter 8, can be home and family problems. Until a few years ago, staff who talked of stress were often considered to be inadequate in some way. Now we recognize that stress-related problems lower morale and productivity, and that absenteeism due to stress is a costly business for organizations and governments alike. In this section we consider:

- What is meant by stress
- The relationship between stress and performance
- How to recognize when stress is a problem for you
- Strategies for handling stress effectively.

What is stress?

The concept of stress is complex and often not fully understood. Stress, in terms of pressure, can be positive as well as negative; you will recognize that much of your best work is produced when you know you have to rise to a challenge. The adrenaline produced by stress at the start of a presentation, for instance, can make you more alert and responsive. The stress of an upcoming deadline can work wonders for productivity. In these examples the level of stress is just right for you to perform at your best.

Stress works against us if we feel unable to meet the demands placed upon us. These demands can come from any source: on a bad day, the project manager may feel under pressure both at home and at work. Interestingly, we also suffer if we feel 'under-stressed' and work does not provide enough challenge; in this case we feel we are able to meet far more pressure than we are currently facing. Boredom appears to be as bad for our health as overload.

Stress is therefore about the balance in our lives between pressure and our ability to cope. A useful definition from Jane Cranwell-Ward (1990) is: 'Stress is the physiological and psychological reaction which occurs when people perceive an imbalance between the level of demand placed upon them, and their capability to meet those demands.'

The relationship between performance and pressure can be represented as in Fig. 10.2. Each person's experience of stress is unique, and each person will react to a given situation differently. A crisis on the project could be stimulating for one person and put him in the Peak Performance Zone, it could be threatening to another team member and put him under too much pressure so he moves into the 'burn-out' zone, and conceivably someone who 'had seen it all before' could be bored and in the 'rust-out' zone. Because stress is about balance, your experience of stress is also constantly changing and dynamic.

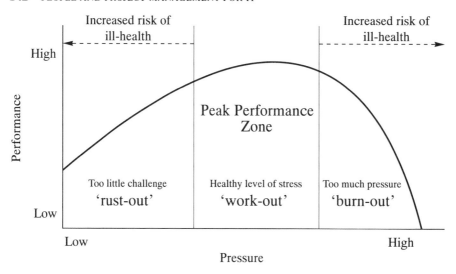

Figure 10.2   The relationship between performance and pressure.

The art of stress management is to stay as much as possible within your Peak Performance Zone, and help your team to do the same. This requires you to recognize in yourself and others the signs of too much or too little stress. Unfortunately, many busy managers filter out the danger signs that they are moving into the 'burn-out' zone. A brief experience of excess stress may do you no harm if you can recover with a break or a good holiday; prolonged exposure could leave you exhausted.

The following is one project manager's description of how he suddenly found himself in the 'burn-out' zone.

> I'd always thought of myself as being pretty good at coping with pressure. I was running a large and difficult project, but on the whole I was enjoying the challenge and the project was going well. The problems started when an old friend from university days rang me up because of serious family problems: his wife had left with his children, and he was absolutely distraught. I did my best over the next few weeks to offer him support, but the situation got worse. The wife started ringing up too – the whole thing became very emotional and difficult, and I found myself caught in the middle. Before I knew it, I was waking up in the middle of the night worrying – soon their problems occupied all my thoughts outside work.
>
>   I started to feel very tired, but I put that down to the long hours on the project. Then suddenly something very frightening happened. I was in the middle of an important meeting, and had stood up to answer the client's questions with a short presentation. As I was speaking, the room seemed to go darker around me, and I could hear my own voice drifting away . . . I grasped a chair to support myself, but then the room blackened completely and I collapsed.
>
>   The following week I saw my doctor, and he arranged for me to have some tests in hospital. I carried on working in the meantime, and the friend carried on ringing, sometimes late at night. I collapsed again. It began to affect my confidence – I couldn't understand what was happening to me. My family and team were all very supportive, but also very concerned.

I had the tests, and went to the doctor again for the results. 'There's nothing obviously physically wrong with you,' he said. 'It must be excess stress.'

How can you recognize whether your stress level is healthy or not?

The first step towards stress management is to learn to recognize for yourself whether stress is working for you or against you. The following is a list from project managers of signs that they were comfortably in the Peak Performance Zone.

Examples of indicators that you are in the Peak Performance Zone - you are working at your best
Physical indicators
- I sleep well – have a good energy level at work and at home.
- I can enjoy my leisure time even after a busy day.
- I feel physically fit, can perform well in sports, etc.
- I'm generally healthy and resistant to colds, etc.
- My appetite is good, and I eat healthily – I'm able to stay off junk food, cigarettes and excess alcohol.

Intellectual indicators
- My concentration level is good.
- I'm creative – lots of good ideas.
- I'm decisive, and the quality of my decisions is high.
- I'm able to prioritize – I can hold the overview in my head and dive down into details as necessary.

Emotional indicators
- I'm happy! and emotionally stable.
- I'm much more responsive to others – I can pick up signs that something is wrong and respond appropriately.
- I can keep things in proportion – don't get so wound up.
- I'm able to be patient: if I come home and the family needs my attention, I've got the emotional energy for them.

The other indicators which are very useful are the early-warning signs. The following is a checklist of example indicators from other project managers; make a note of the ones you recognize. Some physical indicators could be straightforward symptoms of illness, so check first with your doctor. If the doctor cannot find any obvious medical explanation, as with the project manager who collapsed, then the physical problem may be due to stress.

Examples of warning signs – indicators that you may be understressed or overstressed
Physical indicators
- Disturbances in sleeping patterns – I wake up feeling tired.
- I eat more or less than usual.
- I reach for the alcohol/the cigarettes/I stuff myself with junk food.
- I get headaches/problems with digestion/backache/little things like spots or mouth ulcers.
- I seem to go down with every cold that is around.

Intellectual indicators
- I have real difficulty concentrating – my head feels like it's filled with cotton wool.
- I'm indecisive – can't even make up my mind about trivial things.
- I can't prioritize – start taking a 'worm's eye' view of things.
- I work harder but not smarter – feel like the kids' hamster going round on his little wheel and getting nowhere.

Emotional indicators
- I get impatient and irritable.
- If I get home and the children make a noise I just explode.
- I brood – can't switch off from work when I get home.
- I lose my sense of humour, and don't feel like socializing. I'm too tired to listen to other people's problems.

Once you have picked up some warning signs you will need to take corrective action. The following section gives you a range of suggestions for dealing effectively with stress; you can also test yourself to see which strategies you use most effectively.

10.4 EFFECTIVE STRATEGIES FOR COPING WITH STRESS

The following strategies can help you to stay in the Peak Performance Zone.

Confront problems directly

For instance, if you feel overworked, or underworked, do you confront the problem by going directly to the source and talking to your line manager? Or do you have a tendency to tackle the problem only indirectly, by complaining to colleagues, or by battling on until your family get fed up with your long hours? Other indirect and less effective strategies are to pretend the problem does not exist, or blame others, or blame your organization ('The trouble with senior management is that they never . . .'). Direct confrontation gets results, though it requires courage and planning.

Put problems into perspective

One senior project manager who used this strategy effectively expressed it this way:

> Some junior staff get scared by the complexities of the project and the sorts of difficulties we have to resolve. Once you've run a few projects, you can put things into perspective – you don't panic, or get depressed, you just get down to tackling the problems because you know they aren't as disastrous as they may appear. That way you stay calm, the staff have more confidence and you get more done.

This successful project manager was able to leave his problems at work and relax in the evening. Are you able to do this too?

Give support

Counselling is essential for the stress management of your staff; it also helps your stress level, because counselling enables you to pick up problems early so that you do not get burdened by them later when they may have become more serious. A more open atmosphere in your team, where people can be honest about their fears and worries, will raise trust and make the team more rewarding also for you to work in. How comfortable and confident do you feel about your ability to give support?

Receive support

Having your own network of friends, family and colleagues with whom you can share your problems and successes is one of the most important stress-management strategies. Check that you are not dependent on just one person, such as your partner at home, for support. Valuable though this support may be, if you go through a bad patch you may be putting quite a strain on the relationship which is most important to you.

Some managers who give support quite readily feel much more awkward about receiving it – how about you?

Exercise regularly

Energetic exercise can help to burn off some of the fats and sugar released as part of the stress response and enables you to relax better afterwards. Choose something you enjoy, so that you can exercise at least twice a week, and again there are many specialist books to give you ideas. Make sure that you exercise sensibly. Many managers have suddenly felt inspired to take up running, without adequate equipment or preparation, and suffered afterwards with sports injuries that knocked them out of action.

With both diet and exercise, you are aiming for a life-style which offers long-term benefits. If you are not fit enough to tackle squash, tennis and jogging, consider the gentler sports such as walking, cycling, golf, swimming and yoga, all of which can be practised and enjoyed for years. What exercise is right for you? Do you exercise regularly?

Allow yourself to relax

Strategies in this category enable you to get your 'rest and recuperation' system going. Activities can be anything from a hot bath, stroking a pet, meditation and yoga, music, good company, a brisk walk – whatever works for you. Any absorbing hobby such as gardening, dancing, singing in a choir that gets thoughts of work out of your head will help you to unwind. Breathing and relaxation exercises can be very helpful, and sometimes you can fit in a simple breathing exercise quietly in your office – consult the Further Reading for ideas.

Some managers get too caught up in their work and forget that there is life outside the office; others, such as parents of young children sometimes feel they have no time for outside interests. The key is to be aware that relaxation is essential: it's no luxury, and you should not feel guilty about it! What outside interests do you enjoy? How do you typically wind down outside work?

Eat a healthy diet

A healthy diet means that you take care of your body. Current thinking emphasizes the importance of cutting down on fats and eating more fruit and vegetables, and specialist books and articles are widely available for more detailed guidance.

Restrict your use of alcohol

Current recommendations for alcohol are to restrict your drinking to a maximum of 21 units (bar measures) per week for men and 14 for women, spread over the week, though these recommendations may change as a result of further research. How good are you at looking after yourself with what you eat and drink?

How many of these strategies do you use successfully? Which additional strategies could you consider trying?

This is how the project manager from the earlier story recovered from his collapse and returned to his Peak Performance Zone.

I went home and told my wife that the tests were clear. At first, of course, she was just very relieved; then we started discussing the stress problem. 'It's your friend,' she said. 'You've done all you can for him – now you've got to look after yourself.' The next time he rang I told him this had to stop – I'd still be his friend, but the phone calls weren't getting him anywhere and he had to get some professional help. He tried again a couple of times but then the calls stopped.

I also talked to the doctor about my running. He understood my reluctance to give it up – he was a runner himself. 'Try shorter runs,' he suggested 'Just as good for your health. You can't expect to work at your current pace and do long-distance running as well – it's just too much.' Finally I delegated a bit more of my work so I could come home earlier without my briefcase – the children were delighted, and I had some time to relax in the evenings.

The result? Well, I've started an even bigger project now, I feel great and I've had no more health problems. But I take my stress level much more seriously.

Summary of stress management

1. Stress can work for and against you.
2. Aim to stay in the Peak Performance Zone.
3. Monitor your health by identifying your physical, intellectual and emotional indicators.
4. Use a range of strategies:
   - Confront problems directly
   - Put problems into perspective
   - Give support
   - Receive support
   - Take regular exercise
   - Allow yourself to relax
   - Eat a healthy diet
   - Restrict your use of alcohol

11

MANAGING COMMON RISKS

11.1 INTRODUCTION

Projects commonly get into difficulties because time scales are too short, the users expected something different, or performance is inadequate. This chapter gives you some ideas on how to manage these risks.

11.2 THE DELIVERY PROCESS

Delivery to the user is the ultimate objective of any project. This should be planned as a process, right from the start of your project, so that if you come under pressure towards the end of your project you will have your tools and approaches already in place to help you.

The key to a successful delivery lies also in the quality of your relationship with your users. We have emphasized throughout this book the importance of involving your users actively at every major stage of the project. Managers who exclude the users on the basis, for instance, that 'they won't understand what is going on' may find themselves isolated and stressed towards the end of the project when user requirements may have to be renegotiated under time pressure. If you have established sound cooperation and a basis of trust with your users at the start, then any problems you encounter later can be addressed with the users' collaboration and help. You can be realistically confident that together you will find a satisfactory solution.

You should have identified and understood your users' expectations from the start, and have worked actively with the users to ensure that those expectations are realistic and feasible within the technical and commercial constraints of your project. You should also have formulated the expectations together in a language which all parties can fully understand. This is what we mean by 'managing users' expectations'. It gives you a basis on which, if necessary, you can jointly prioritize further, using the Minimum System approach, for instance, as described later.

This chapter addresses how to manage risks such as last-minute time pressure or performance in the context of a constructive user/producer relationship. We show how the Minimum System approach, prototyping and benchmarking are not just technical tools but also managerial ones which can help you to verify that your understanding of your users' needs is still accurate. We will not address the technical aspects of these tools, which are covered in detail in the relevant technical literature. We will use the tools here as examples of how to work with your users throughout your project to check that you are on track. Delivery is then not just an end point but the logical culmination of a successful partnership which both parties can celebrate.

11.3 COPING WITH PROJECT TIME PRESSURE – THE MINIMUM SYSTEM

What can you do when you come under time pressure? One possibility is to employ additional resources to increase the production capacity of the team. Unfortunately, in the majority of cases pressures come at the end of projects when the skills required are very specific to the project itself and therefore are difficult to find outside the project team. Another obstacle in employing additional resources is that activities at the end of a project are usually resource bound: the activity cannot be split any further to divide it among more people.

Another way of coping with time pressure is to get agreement to build the Minimum System that the users need and postpone the non-time-critical system components to a later date. The Minimum System meets only the most crucial needs of the users, and if you have planned well this option can keep all parties reasonably happy. You need, however, to be aware of both its potential and its risks and you should integrate the Minimum System concept into production methodology at the beginning of the project. If you are forced to adopt the technique at a later stage in the project, then the inconvenience to the users and the associated consequences may be more disruptive than the project delays which you are trying to avoid. We will now look at this option in more detail.

Validating and prioritizing the requirements is an important point in any project and therefore should be made a visible milestone to the users and the team. It is also the first step in recognizing the Minimum System.

Agree with the users the relative importance and urgency of their needs during the process of validating the requirements. This is not always straightforward. The first answer from the users may well be 'All requirements are equally important and very urgent'. Such a response is the result of real fears and concerns which you must understand and handle. It is natural for the users to assume that requirements that would come at the bottom of the priority list would be delayed whatever happens. In return, you need to assure them that the project plans to build the total project within agreed time scales. You must support your claims with concrete commitments such as existing commercial statements within the contract or outside it. Highlight the benefits of the approach and explain that the emergency scenario would only be adopted if it became absolutely necessary. You must also demonstrate realistically that the postponed functionality would be delivered 'not long' after the planned date in the worst case.

Prioritizing the system requirements is only the first step on the way to adopting the Minimum System strategy. At every stage in the production process you must make new decisions along the lines of what to leave out and what the consequences are. You may choose to exclude some system components early such as during the design stage or even earlier. Similar decisions may be made at later stages.

Reviewing plans and priorities at the end of the design stage is advisable regardless of whether you want the Minimum System or not. Your assessment of the project costs and time scales is a lot more accurate at that point than at the initial specification stage. After the design stage you may be confronted with postponing other system components. As well as verifying such decisions with the users and senior management you need to document clearly the deviations from the existing designs. As you go further into the production process new decisions to postpone other system components will carry with them increasingly higher overheads to keep the project documentation in step with the real system baseline. However, decisions to drop some system components during the closing stages such as system integration may also become necessary because time pressures are more likely to become noticeable then than at the early stages.

When we produced the Functional Specification we established what the Minimum System was. The main system functions were prioritized with the users and then marked as 1, 2 or 3. Priority 1 functions defined the Minimum System and priorities 2 and 3 were functions we could drop in favour of achieving the project time scales. Where choices were possible we would consider dropping 3 first before 2.

Throughout the project we had dropped functions at different stages until we reached the integration stage. We had an absolute deadline for bringing the system live because two other systems which were being developed by two other parties were dependent on our delivery – any delays we hit would be commercially unacceptable to the client. The users fully sympathized with our Minimum System strategy as they knew that we were under severe time pressure at their request and that the option of delaying the delivery date was not acceptable.

When we started the system integration it was reasonably stable and we thought we were in a good position to meet the time scales. Then we did our performance test, and that confirmed our worst fears. We had made many performance measurements at various points during the building process. We had identified potential performance bottlenecks where we would only just achieve the targets.

We estimated that database and other system tuning would deal with those bottlenecks but it would take several weeks to achieve – and we did not have the time available. The only alternative was to remove the offending parts until the system performance was improved. This was agreed and implemented within a few days. The required performance was achieved and the system went live.

The parts that were postponed were added later in several steps. We tuned the system further with each step until the total functionality was implemented and we had achieved the required performance.

11.4 PROTOTYPING

Prototyping is sometimes used as an alternative to specifying the system functions and is well established in the system-building industry. The main purpose of this section is to present prototyping as a means to help project managers to improve communication with the users.

Prototyping and specifying functionality are not mutually exclusive; they can be combined very effectively to research and articulate the users' needs. Where the users are uncertain about their exact needs, prototypes can be built so that the users can experiment with the available options. The large number of prototyping tools which run on wide ranges of hardware have made this process much easier. Such tools have introduced concepts like rapid development and rapid prototyping.

The operator interface is an obvious candidate for prototyping. If you are building a large number of screens, for example, it would be more effective and more user friendly to build samples of each type of screen first so that you can review them with the users. Management Information Systems or System Reports can also be built interactively with the users.

One problem you may encounter with prototyping, however, is that the users are not always easily identified and contacted. Some projects have many and different types of users. In the case of public service systems, for instance, you cannot easily contact a representative sample of the public. These projects often resort to market surveys and research programmes as a means of communication with the users. If you are involved in such a project you may very well have formed a team of market researchers and communication specialists to carry out this task for you.

Cynics may say that a good specification need not be supported by prototyping. Proper specification will indeed often be sufficient. However, if you can offer the users examples of what the project plans to deliver we believe that this will enhance the value of the specification, especially where the product is repeated many times. If the development environment is available, this approach can be particularly valuable both during and after the specification.

11.5 BENCHMARKING

Your project may be using software and hardware products that have off-the-shelf models; these offer good starting points for benchmarking your system. In most cases, however, you may have concerns about your system performance but you will have no system models to help you, and you will have to build your own system models if you want to benchmark.

In some major projects, system benchmarking is identified as part of the contractual agreements with the users. One of the first project deliverables is the system model which is tuned and modified as the project team gains more understanding of the system and its relationship to the system model. A dedicated team may be formed to carry out the system modelling and benchmarking tasks. System measurements provided by benchmarking can have a significant impact on the direction of the project, its organization and the commercial agreements between the system builder and the users. These measurements must therefore be planned and executed carefully.

Performance concerns are common not only in the major projects but also in smaller ones which do not have the dedicated resources and expertise to produce full and complete system models. The project managers of these smaller projects are faced with the difficult decision of how much to invest and how far to go along the way of system modelling and benchmarking.

Performance was identified as a major risk in the project. The system had to be based on the house standard database product. The supplier of the database product had planned to release a new, vastly improved version of the product which we estimated would cope with the required performance. We agreed to start the development on that basis, but we knew that the risk of not having the new version on time would have very serious consequences for the time scales. And we were aware that we had a considerable performance problem.

As part of the specification phase, we planned to benchmark the system to get a feeling for the magnitude of the risk. The model we used was, of course, very simple, built using the existing database but with the new requirement of the increased user transactions per minute. The results were alarming. We knew then that without the new version of the database product we would have to build a complex piece of software to cope with the required performance.

When we finished the design, we had a better understanding of the internal working of the system, and we were able to build a more representative system model. The new performance measurements confirmed our worst fears. At the end of the detailed design we were able to pinpoint the performance bottlenecks in the system; we could then use our newly improved model to experiment with system-tuning ideas.

We concluded that if the database supplier did not come up with the goods, we still had a fighting chance of achieving the performance but only if we delayed those parts of the system with some of the performance bottlenecks to a later date. We suggested to the users that we should postpone some items, and they agreed to our proposal.

This was a very significant development in the project. We had all been feeling under a black cloud – now the cloud lifted and we set to work with renewed optimism and enthusiasm within the project team. This new surge of motivation enabled us to think more creatively. This was just as well, because, sure enough, the database supplier did not deliver on time. Our project team started a parallel development which provided the answers that achieved the required system performance.

Benchmarking in this story was used to manage a risk that could have caused the project to fail. The turning point in the project happened when the benchmarking process provided hope and guidance to work towards the final solution.

SUMMARY OF MANAGING COMMON RISKS

1. Three common problems are
   - Time scales too short
   - Users expected something different
   - Performance is inadequate

2. The delivery process
   - Plan from the start of the project
   - Involve the users from the start in order to build a constructive relationship
3. The minimum system
   - Meet only the users' most crucial needs
   - Validate the requirements with the users
   - Review priorities at the end of the design stage
4. Prototyping
   - Use in combination with specifying functionality
   - Prototyping brings you close to the user
5. Benchmarking
   - Off-the-shelf models of products provide a starting point
   - You may have to build your own benchmarking tools with the users' help

12

THE FINISHING TOUCHES

12.1 INTRODUCTION

We have included this chapter because experience shows that the finishing touches in projects are often the most difficult. Many managers underestimate the problems they will encounter at this stage. Also, these activities take place at the end of the project when the team is tired and looking forward to doing something else, and the other people associated with the project have turned their attention to other more interesting matters such as new projects. It is not surprising that even the healthiest of projects run into some problems during this stage.

To help you to avoid some of the pitfalls we look first at integrating the parts, involving the users and the importance of maintaining momentum. We then consider how to deliver the system, set up the operations organization, and organize training, support and maintenance.

12.2 INTEGRATING THE PARTS

The engineering world has been successful at integrating components made by different teams into a working whole – for example, in cars, bridges, oil platforms and many other complex systems. Unfortunately, integration in IT is often not so successful.

Most experienced project managers can recall at least one project which came under severe pressure at the end because the integration had taken longer than planned. These project managers have then learned to assess the risks associated with integration, and to plan to deal with them before they turn into problems.

Most project managers start with some functional baseline or an overall system design. They then allocate the various parts of the system to different team members who go ahead and build their respective parts independently of each other. Splitting the system in this manner is unavoidable, but it brings with it the risk of misunderstandings and differences in interpretation; the bigger the team, the bigger this risk will be.

The solution is to plan the integration as part of the project planning, and the more complex the system is, the more important it is to plan the integration early in the project. That is why we have covered integration in the early chapters on planning and project set-up (Chapters 2 and 4).

It is also essential to involve the users during this process. System integration is often seen as an internal activity on the project, carried out in isolation from the outside world including the users. One reason for working this way is that the contractual agreements may dictate this approach. Another reason for working in isolation is that when the system components are thrown together for the first time the system will be unstable, and you may not want to worry the users unduly.

It is also good project management discipline to ensure that each phase of the project is clearly completed and a new project baseline is defined before the next phase can formally start.

We suggest, however, that you will gain enormous benefits from involving the users right the way through the integration. The best approach is to overlap the integration phase and the user acceptance phase, keeping in mind the formal boundaries between the two phases as proposed by the Waterfall model for system development.

Evolutionary system development methods tend to take this idea much further by building a much greater degree of overlap between project phases and by actively involving the user throughout the system development life-cycle. Whether you prefer to follow the Waterfall model or some evolutionary development method or a mix of the two, your success will depend on satisfying two requirements. First, the users must be sufficiently involved so that you don't surprise them at the end when you deliver the products. Second, you must have clear decision points in the development process, to ensure that you have clear, visible and formally recognizable progress in the project.

The users can be involved throughout at appropriate points in the integration: when the user interface is first integrated, for example. The first benefit of this approach is that the users' ideas and suggestions will enrich those of the project team. Second, the users themselves will become more attached to the resulting products because they are made in front of their eyes. A third benefit is the understanding that the users gain of the building process. Frequent and uncontrolled changes appear very high on the list of major project risks. The increased understanding between project team and users will help you to discuss the impact of potential functional changes in a cooperative atmosphere and to manage expectations more easily.

If your project has a contractual construction which does not allow for this kind of open interaction with the users, it would still be a good idea to consider ways of getting them involved within the limitations you have. The minimum you should do is to ensure that the users' acceptance criteria are part of the integration testing. If the users are dissatisfied with anything, you can then find out as soon as possible and give yourself the time to deal with the problem.

12.3 MAINTAINING THE MOMENTUM

Projects enjoy a lot of attention at the beginning because they have high priority on the management agenda. In the middle stages they continue to be carefully nurtured because of the very high 'burn rate' of money and resources. At the end, when the project starts tailing off, it begins to fade into insignificance in people's minds, particularly if the project has been going well. Unfortunately, projects need much more attention during this final stage because:

- The team will be getting tired and will be losing interest.
- Projects that progress well during the start and middle stages may suffer from complacency at the end.
- There is more pressure on resources when new and more urgent projects compete for them.
- The team members will be under pressure to leave the project, as more tempting opportunities and new challenges present themselves to them.
- There is often more emphasis on time scales during the closing stages of the project, putting the team (often a small integration team) under severe pressure to work long hours.

The following is a story told by an integration manager.

We had just completed the coding and testing in our team when the project manager was taken away to start up another project. I was asked to take over the project, and my manager explained that this was a straightforward task – merely an integration activity. The other two teams had nearly finished and I was available. I didn't worry about the responsibility because I had been the integration manager of my previous project, and that had gone smoothly.

It took me a couple of weeks to get used to the reporting system and so on. The previous project manager gave me some help but he was getting increasingly busy with his new project. Finally I was in a position to understand what the other two teams were doing. My first impression was not very encouraging.

Total system integration was due to start but all the objects that were being built by these teams were unstable. Significant changes were being made almost daily, because the test team kept discovering errors. By then I was really worried. The previous project manager had left, so I decided to start the overall system integration using a small team of the strongest team members we had at the time. I hoped that we would be able to sort out the last few errors during the integration.

When we first put the whole system together I was appalled. I knew it was going to be bad but I hadn't realized it would be that bad. The system failed every test case we had for the integration. Most of the problems were occurring in the parts built by team members who had already left. The team got frustrated because of all the extra time they had to spend investigating these problems and resolving them.

We tried to get some of the team members who had left the project to come back and help us, but this was almost impossible. Many of the problems we encountered needed days to resolve. We finally decided to cut our losses and rewrite the worst parts of the software. By then we were running more than two months behind, and rewriting those parts cost us a few weeks more. The system was delivered to the users over three months late.

It was a bad time for all of us, made worse by the realization that these problems could have been avoided if integration had been properly planned at an early stage. And at the time I felt very isolated – it felt as though nobody was listening to us.

If the project does not get the attention it deserves during these closing stages the team can get demotivated. The project can enter into a downward spiral of lower productivity and plummeting morale while the outside world thinks that all is well.

12.4 DELIVERY OF THE PRODUCT

When you plan to deliver the product remember first, that the end user is the real user and second, that addressing the needs of the end user is essential for the success of the project. If you involve the users in your project as early as possible they will help you to do your job better.

If you are making a one-off product and you are lucky enough to have the users as part of your project, you will be able to check at every step of the process how well the product addresses the real needs.

You must verify that your understanding of the requirements is the same as the users' understanding, whether or not the user has been part of the requirements definition. The users will formulate their requirements in business or operational terms, which you must translate into technical design terms.

Start by bringing the user acceptance as early as possible in the integration. One way of enhancing the translation step is to produce an acceptance test specification as early as possible in the process. Although it is usual to produce the final version of this document towards the end of the project, you can still start thinking about it early. The main purpose of this document is to lay down the users' acceptance criteria of the system. It should do this in a way that clearly relates to the user requirements specification.

The users themselves should play an active and visible role in the production of the Acceptance Test Specification document. More importantly, the document must be checked and agreed by the users before it is finally issued. If the users have been excluded from the production of the Acceptance Test Specification, it is the task of the project manager to find legitimate and commercially acceptable ways to get the users involved and to seek their approval during the process.

We have underlined the importance of involving the users throughout this activity. The system acceptance runs a parallel path with integration. It too should involve the users from start to finish.

12.5 THE BIG DAY

Handing over a product with a smile is the most important single point in the project. This point may occur at the end of the project, in the middle or at the start of another project for the team, depending on how the project fits in the business programme.

Some users choose to take delivery of the system at the bay of the factory following the Factory Acceptance Test (FAT). Other users prefer to accept the system only when it is fully integrated into the operation. The exact choice depends on the users' organization and on the role they play during the manufacturing process of the system. Whatever option the users choose, it is the professional responsibility of the project team to ensure that the system satisfies the users' needs.

We can now review the steps that lead up to this big day. At the start of the project the team would have produced an Acceptance Test Specification together with the users. The document would have been based on the requirement or technical specification depending on the project initial baseline. The test document would have been modified several times as the project progressed through its various phases of specification, design, coding, testing and finally the integration phase. The users would have been involved directly or indirectly in the production and modification of this test document.

The system integration would have been initiated with the integration planning as part of the specification phase. Prototyping would have been used to check that the team had the right interpretation of the requirements. This would have been particularly important when the team was building system components which required close interaction with the users such as the operator interface, or where the users' application or operational experience was crucial.

System performance would have been closely monitored by benchmarking the system at various phases of the project. During the integration phase, system performance would have been measured using real operational data wherever possible and under representative operational conditions. Performance concerns would have been documented and, where mutually beneficial, discussed with the users.

System components that were either unstable or that contributed towards the deterioration of the performance of the system would have been clearly identified and the team would have assessed the possibility of postponing each of these components to a later date. Where the project was under severe time pressure, the team would have considered the possibility of delivering the system in steps to avoid business difficulties that could be caused by project delays.

Throughout the project, the project manager would have identified the Minimum System that would meet the most important and pressing users' needs. The functions that fell outside this Minimum System would have either been postponed or put on a 'hit list' with different priorities. These functions on the 'hit list' would also be postponed if necessary during the final stages of the project. A system release plan to reintroduce the functions to be postponed would have been agreed with the users.

Imagine now that the team is at the point of delivering the Minimum System, the total system, or any variation in between. The Acceptance Test Specification would have defined the acceptance criteria which may be met partly or completely.

Strictly speaking, the users can refuse to take any delivery until the full requirements are met in every detail and with no deviations. In reality, users have practical needs to be addressed by the system, even if it does not comply with every detail. That is why users usually take pragmatic, fair and reasonable decisions during the system acceptance of the system. Experienced users and experienced system buyers contribute in an active way to finding ways out of sticky situations during this phase of the project and without compromising the overall quality of the products. They do that in the belief that system builders have vested interests in making sure that the users walk away satisfied. The project manager's job is to ensure that all parties are aware of this at all times.

Finally we come to the point of delivering the product to the users. This point should be seen as a reinforcement of the partnership that was created at the beginning of the project. The next chapter will look at how to plan for this momentous occasion. We present below one project manager's account of his personal experiences in the weeks leading up to the celebration.

The last six months were difficult for the project team because of the time pressure we were under. To make matters worse, we were working overtime right in the middle of the school summer holiday period. Six days a week and well over 10 hours per day was the norm for everybody in the project.

We had predicted this work peak well in advance and planned to deal with the side effects in every way we could. One measure was to ensure that holidays would not be cancelled in the last-minute panics. We planned our holidays well in advance but made sure that all the functions in the project would continue to be supported at all times.

My holiday fell at the end of the period overlapping the acceptance testing and delivery to the users. The main integration milestone which represented the go/no-go decision for the acceptance testing fell only a few days before I was due to leave. To my relief we achieved the milestone and this made us all feel more confident that we would achieve the delivery milestone as well. However, every remaining activity was on the critical path so we had no room for any delays anywhere in the project.

I promised my family to forget about work while I was on holiday – they had seen very little of me over the last few months. I soon realized that this was not an easy promise to keep – I was longing to phone the team to find out how they were doing. Every day I would go through the rehearsal of what I would say if I called, then I'd walk to a telephone and just manage to stop myself at the last moment. This went on for the two weeks I was away.

I arrived back home on Sunday – a normal working day for most of the team. Within half an hour I was in the project area, but it was empty. My mind raced – this could mean one of two things. Either we had made it, in which case the team would be enjoying their Sunday, or we hadn't, in which case the pressure would be off. If we had failed to meet the milestone this would be a great disappointment and an embarrassment for both the users and the team. The users had organized an open day and had invited both local and national public figures; the main event of the day was to be a demonstration of the system.

I looked around for a while in the project area hoping to pick up any clues of what had actually happened but without any success. I wondered whether to call the integration manager who was running the show during my absence but I hesitated for a while. Then something occurred to me.

The integration manager was a compulsive documentor and a doodler. He would have recorded in his log book the main events of the previous two weeks. Perhaps the log book was not locked away with the rest of the project documentation. I was lucky; it was in the first drawer I opened. Frantically I turned over the pages – then I noticed a folded piece of paper. It was a memo to the team and to the others who were close to the project. The first sentence read: 'You are invited to join us for a glass of champagne.'

12.6 SETTING UP THE OPERATIONS ORGANIZATION

Projects are temporary organizations with specific limited objectives that should be achieved within defined time scales. The products they produce, however, fit into existing organizations and often have far-reaching consequences for the way these organizations run their operations. This raises a fundamental question regarding the role of project managers. Do you throw the products you build 'over the wall' and assume that somebody else will pick them up, or do you stay with your products until they are fully integrated into the organization for which they were intended?

Project managers should accept their part in managing the organizational change during which their products can be effectively integrated into the user organization and can thus serve their intended business purpose. Your job is not complete until your products have achieved the business objectives for which the project was set up. Even if the contract sets limits on your involvement at the delivery point to the user, you must facilitate the hand-over process. One possible approach is to consider the post-delivery activities as another project with the objective of integrating the system or the products into the users' organization or community. Whichever way you choose, you have to bear in mind that you may be handing over your product to people whose working styles and working needs could be very different from what you expect.

The first version of the system had just been completed and delivered to the users. The service provided by our products covered the whole country and involved several millions of potential customers. It was scheduled to be launched within two months.

A hardware-support organization existed, but the people in it had no experience of the hardware platform of the new system. We chose a task force of two users and five project members to set up the production organization and environment.

The task force set up the environment, but to our disappointment and slight bewilderment, the people in the operations and support organization were not settling down – in fact, they seemed anxious and stressed. Six weeks into the activity an audit was conducted by experienced operators of similar systems, and they were able to spot the root of the problem. They concluded that the operations procedures and environment were more suitable for a project than for a permanent production organization. Projects allow people a great deal of discretion. This approach was confusing for the staff in the hardware support organization, who needed much more explicit instructions to help them to understand what they had to do.

The task force rethought its approach and made the procedures considerably more detailed. Just to check, we had another audit just before the launch of the service. The conclusions were much more positive.

Most projects produce a single product. When you integrate this product into the user organization and set up the production environment, you need to remember that the people in the new environment will have very different backgrounds from your team members and you will have to set up a different type of procedure which can be followed successfully in a fixed routine. Examples of such procedures are:

'Between 9:30 and 10:00 call the statistics summary screen. Insert the three aggregates at the bottom of the screen in form T25. From the Management Summary screen, copy the totals of the four columns into the same form. Pass this form on to the team supervisor before 11:00.'

Your job is to organize whatever it takes to help people feel comfortable with your system and thus get it to work successfully.

12.7 TRAINING, SUPPORT AND MAINTENANCE

Projects are set up because the existing functional organization faces a change which cannot be managed within the existing structure. Projects in the IT industry can have a major impact on the existing user organization. The impact is heavily influenced by the amount of new technology chosen to address specific business needs. The integration of this new technology into the users' organization is part of the change which the project was set up to achieve.

Within your project you will need to provide the basis for someone (possibly yourself) to:

- *Provide adequate training and operations procedures so that the operations staff can use the system* In addition to training, someone will need to modify existing operations procedures and, where necessary, develop new procedures. The success of any project is largely determined by the success of the products after their delivery.
- *Set up preventative and corrective maintenance facilities so that the system is kept running* An environment is needed in which the system can continue to operate and be used. In some cases, the system may fit into an existing support organization which can adopt the newcomer into the family and will know how to look after it. This will not always be so, in which case you must ensure that the system is well looked after and cared for.
- *Provide technical support to address the evolving users' needs* A specific aspect of the support organization is the ability to enhance the system to address the evolving needs of the users. These enhancements may be simple changes to the functionality or major new releases of the functionality requiring the setting up of a new project.

SUMMARY OF THE FINISHING TOUCHES

1. Integration of systems is generally underestimated by most system builders. It can be made easier when you:
   - Define the integration strategy as part of the project planning
   - Produce the integration plan very early in the project, preferably as part of the project planning tool
   - Use the integration strategy and plans to derive the production process of the system components
   - Wherever possible, make sure that the users are involved in the integration of the system.

2. Maintaining momentum is important because
   - There is more pressure on resources and on time scales
   - Team members leave for new projects
   - The team can feel isolated and tired
3. Delivery of the product
   - Delivery to the users should be planned, with the users, as early as possible
   - Produce the user acceptance specification as early as possible
   - The users should be involved in producing this specification
4. Setting up the operations organization:
   - Train the users
   - Remember that their needs and background will be different
   - Set up new procedures and modify existing ones
   - Ensure that the future needs of the users are addressed

13

PROJECT CLOSE-DOWN

13.1 WHEN IT IS ALL OVER

When the day finally comes to deliver the system to the users we need to take all measures possible to make the event memorable and enjoyable for everybody. It is a creative process with its end marked by a satisfied client, a happy and proud team and a celebration for all.

When the project is over everything must be tidied up and left as we originally found it. The documentation must be finished off according to the documentation plan and, where necessary, archived following the agreed procedures. Long-duration projects tend to borrow and lease lots of equipment. This equipment must be clearly inventorized and returned to its rightful owner(s) and any associated accounts must be closed. Finally, the project management must ensure that each team member has the right references and support to take the next step in his or her career.

This chapter is dedicated to looking at project close-down and how to make the closing moments of the project as memorable as possible. We will do that by first looking at how to use the end of the project celebration as a focal point for the team. We will then discuss the lessons and learning opportunities in projects, how to wind down the organization and disband the team. Finally, we will address closing the project down and the formal hand-over to the production and support organizations.

13.2 PLANNING THE CELEBRATION

Every project comes to an end, although some ends are happier than others. There are many reasons why some projects succeed while others don't. The right team, a clear vision and a healthy relationship with the users are just some of the project success factors.

One of the main success factors for any undertaking, and projects are no exception, is focusing on success and planning for it. Planning, at any early stage, to celebrate success demands courage and team confidence. More importantly, it requires a deep belief in the plans and a strong commitment to achieving them.

The project success party should be one of the main milestones that should be clearly identified in the project plan as early as possible. You may choose to celebrate intermediate milestones spontaneously and as they are achieved, but celebrating the completion of the project must be well prepared for and widely advertised in advance.

Three years is very long in the world of IT projects where staff seek variety of work and enjoy the challenge of stretching themselves to acquire new skills in the ever-expanding world of technology. Projects that continue for this length of time would witness career changes, developments and setbacks. People may change employers, may emigrate to far-away places or may face all kinds of changes of fortunes. The project management has to understand and deal with these developments to ensure that the consequences for the project are kept to a minimum and to maintain motivation and commitment in the rest of the team.

We had planned to achieve a major milestone approximately every six months. Every time we reached one of these milestones we would organize a party where we let our hair down and simply enjoyed ourselves. In some of these parties, we would present each team member with a little something as a souvenir to remember the occasion. Once we presented a T-shirt with the project logo while another time we would hand out certificates for the contribution the team had made.

In each one of these parties the team would hear a new piece of information on the final project success party which was a closely guarded secret within a small group of individuals. Some team members were almost obsessed about trying to find out more about this party, giving us countless opportunities for some gentle teasing. What form the party would take, where it would be, who would be present and so on were some of the questions that would be asked. The only piece of information that was available was the date which was set to be just two weeks after the official end of the project.

13.3 DOCUMENTING THE LESSONS

The more experience we have as individuals and as a profession, the more control we have over the way our projects develop. The professional disciplines that we know and trust now are the outcome of a large number of project years in a variety of situations and environments. Observations are made, analysed, passed on and evaluated by others. This is a learning and a maturing process that is going on all the time within the project managers' community.

This process usually happens in an *ad hoc* and undirected fashion. If we make this process more conscious and visible, learning takes place faster and more effectively.

Projects, whatever size, shape or complexity, have many learning opportunities for the project team and for others who are not directly connected with them. Wise project managers tend to learn from other people's fortunes and misfortunes as well as from their own. It is difficult when we are under daily pressures to make the time to take a few notes to document daily experiences. It is also difficult under such circumstances to distinguish the lessons that should be documented from the mass of daily events that we go through.

We suggest that you start noting down the lessons now if you are in the middle of a project or as soon as possible if you are about to start another. Once you have noted a few lessons and reviewed them you should find that you very quickly start to single out the real lessons from the mundane everyday events.

Create a learning culture by making it part of the standard agenda of formal as well as informal discussions. Suppose you have a standard item in every meeting where everybody describes a recent experience and the lessons learnt from it. In the beginning, the cynics in the team may try to shoot down the idea. Persevere: novel and creative ideas will always be met with resistance until they prove themselves and until the benefits become evident.

The lessons that are gathered during the course of the project should be integrated into one report at the end. This report should be discussed and agreed with all the key players in the project, within the team and outside it. Group discussions should be organized to invite feedback and to seek consensus on the major issues before the report is presented to the outside world.

One problem that can arise at this point is that these group discussions invariably highlight intense emotions, ranging from fear of reprisal to a witch-hunt and cover-ups within the project. You will need to act as a leader and a facilitator with your team, to encourage everyone to focus on the learning for the future not on the mistakes of the past.

Your example and the culture of your organization will determine whether this exercise is effective. A sensitively handled project review meeting can be very constructive for both the individuals and the organization. Lessons can be learnt, people's contributions can be recognized, team members can acknowledge and express feelings which at the time were repressed and thus 'let go' of some of the difficult memories and retain the memory of the good times which will support them in future projects.

The production of the project-evaluation report and the associated group discussions should be planned well in advance to provide the opportunity for adequate preparation. Large projects set up this activity of learning from the experience as a separate project in its own right. You can do this early in the project by identifying a group of people who have the objective of producing the evaluation report and reaching consensus on it. At the end of this chapter, we give extracts from such an evaluation report.

13.4 WINDING DOWN THE PROJECT ORGANIZATION

In your project planning you will have identified the staffing profile which would typically look like a normal distribution curve (Fig. 13.1). This staffing profile would be the basis for all agreements the project makes with the staff and their managers on the length of assignments to the project.

The saddest part of a project is having to dismantle a team in which you have invested so much time, effort and resources to make it grow into a super-organism. The team bond that is created, nurtured and strengthened will be broken by the same people who built it. This is not easy for the project team nor for the managers who have to carry out the action.

Next to the commercial realities which dictate winding down the project team, there are other forces at work. When the project nears completion team members begin to look

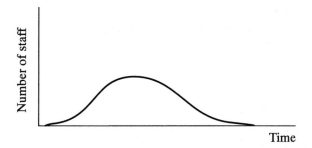

Figure 13.1   A typical staffing profile.

outside the project for other career opportunities. For some members, leaving the team may be painful, for others their career ambitions will work the other way. These complex relationships and the interactions among the various forces that come into play at this stage of the project put additional demands on project managers. Care, sensitivity and understanding are prerequisites for the successful management of winding down the project organization. In large and long-duration projects human relationships of all kinds evolve that must be taken into consideration during this process, requiring another level of understanding and respect.

The project manager has obligations towards each individual in the team. You must work with your team members to help them to recognize the contributions they made during the project and to allow them to build on these contributions to take their career ambitions a step further. Where necessary, references should be sent to their new project managers and/or employers.

You should also make time to assess and discuss the performance of your team members so that they get well-balanced feedback on their experiences in the project and a basis on which they can develop their skills further.

13.5 PROJECT CLOSE-DOWN

Project close-downs are often grossly underestimated, which is why some project managers continue to carry out many thankless tasks long after the project has delivered its products. This is to be expected since the closing stages of projects are dominated by very detailed actions which most people find difficult to identify and plan at the beginning of the project. Additionally, these finishing touches are often considered to be unimportant and uninteresting unless natural finishers happened to be clearly present in the team.

These finishing touches are mostly invisible to senior management or the users, who tend to lose interest as soon the main products are delivered. The project manager and the team members who are left at the end are often desperately short of resources to finish off the job, unless the activity is very well planned and organized at the beginning.

The time and resources required to write references and career-assessment reports and talk to future project managers for a 30-person team (say) can be significant. You will have difficulties if you have not planned for it or if you are starting another project. Tidying up the project area, finishing off the documentation and closing the project accounts can also cost a substantial amount of unplanned effort.

There are also other major actions that may amount to small projects in their own right with which the team may be unexpectedly confronted at the end of the project. We will cover the most common of these actions.

Transfer of experience

Post-delivery, operations and maintenance support organizations need to be set up and trained until they are self-sufficient. The skills and experience that these organizations need are available within the project team. As part of the project close-down actions you must make sure that this experience and knowledge is passed on to the permanent organizations in an efficient and sensitive manner.

The team members who stay until the closing stages are, by definition, the longest-surviving members in the project. They could have been doing similar tasks for a long time. It is tempting for management and users to move these members to the operation or support organizations for long periods of time, without any consideration for the individuals' own wishes and career aspirations.

In some cases team members may find new and interesting challenges in moving over to the permanent organizations. In others, however, these team members may be looking forward to being involved in different projects and to doing tasks that are different in nature such as moving from technical to management tasks. In planning the knowledge transfer you must take the individuals' wishes into consideration well in advance to avoid the conflict between the career ambitions of the individuals and the needs of the permanent organizations.

Future releases

The system you have delivered will, over the course of time, be modified and improved. Whether these improvements are carried out as part of your current project or not, it is your responsibility that they can happen. If the system goes live before these improvements are implemented the need for detailed knowledge of the system becomes more crucial, to manage the risk of serious operational difficulties that may lead to an interruption of the service, loss of revenue or both.

The continuity of project knowledge and experience is vital for future releases of the system. Fortunately, phased delivery of systems offers good career-development opportunities for the team, unlike operation and maintenance. This makes it easier for managers to recruit candidates from the project team for these activities. Subsequent system deliveries can be set as projects on the back of the current project, offering team leaders, for example, the opportunity to move on to project management.

Future projects

Projects are often part of a programme of projects, and even if they are not, it is likely that new programmes are initiated as a result. Therefore, the end of the project could well lead to other projects that must be set up and planned. The skills and experience to produce the project estimates and proposals and to set up the new projects are within the current project team.

As part of the project close-down plan you must take into consideration these future developments. These activities offer new career-development opportunities for the team.

13.6 LASTING RELATIONSHIPS

A successful project makes for lasting professional and personal relationships, as a colleague described.

As soon as the project ended I took over a project on a client's site, so I lost contact with the previous project team. Although, on occasions, I received telephone calls on career management and staff assessment matters involving team members of the previous project, I felt I was out of touch. In the early days in this new project, I felt a sense of isolation, since I had to be on my own for long periods of time. I had moments of flashbacks reliving some moments of the previous project, confirming the sense of friendship and closeness I felt towards that team. I often wondered if those feelings were shared by other team members towards me and towards each other.

Six months after the project ended there was an all-staff general meeting with 200–250 people. I hoped to meet most of the project team during that meeting. I knew that most of the team members were also working away from the main office, and this would make it difficult for some of them to be on time or even attend. The presentations and the formal parts of the meeting were finally over. A buffet meal was laid out for the social informal part. Having been six months away from the office, I felt like a newcomer to the company. However, I came across many colleagues outside the project who wanted to talk to me and to catch up with what I had been doing in my new project.

Then I noticed the technical manager of my previous project sitting at a table with several others. When I reached him I realized that everyone at that table was in the project team. Suddenly, I felt a strong sense of belonging. There was a lot to listen to and many stories to exchange and enjoy. Altogether we had a very enjoyable evening.

When we parted company at the end of that evening one member of the team, who had never been one for expressing his emotions, suddenly looked at us all and said: 'You know something? This project has made us friends for life!'

Projects go through many emotional experiences involving hope, fear, pride, disappointments and so on. When it is all over the pains and pleasures tend to merge into a binding force that keeps at least some of the individuals close to each other long after they part company.

We finish with some extracts from a project-evaluation report that demonstrates some of the typical but significant memories and lessons from a successful project.

We planned a relatively large project with many risks and uncertainties and zero contingency and yet we achieved the project objectives only days away from the original plan. Part of the reason for our achievement was that right from the start we were aware of most of the risks and set out together to deal with them.

We were very fortunate in the quality of our team members both as technicians and as human beings; we 'managed each other to manage the project' and the rest seemed to fall into place. Despite the very difficult circumstances and the extreme time pressure, our spirits were high throughout, mainly because of the supportive atmosphere we had.

Everything has a price and the price of this achievement was an enormous amount of hard work, heartache and, at times, frustrations. However, when the system went live, it did so almost faultlessly. This success made us forget the pains of the experience and turn those frustrating moments into fond memories.

We have all developed and learned many lessons:

1. If you believe that the project objectives are not realistic, say so and keep saying so until somebody listens.
2. Indirect relationship with the users is not enough; you must have direct contacts.
3. Even if you think that the individual parts of the project are perfect, integrating them will cost more time than you think!
4. The number of errors in a document is proportional to the square of the number of the authors.
5. Project set-up is more costly and time consuming than you think!
6. Stocktaking sessions are a very useful mechanism of determining where the project is when you start losing the your overview.
7. Don't start low-level planning until your high-level plans are stable.
8. Well-planned brainstorming sessions are catalysts for team building.

Which lessons from your last project or your current project come to mind for you?

SUMMARY OF PROJECT CLOSE-DOWN

1. Use the end celebration as a focal point throughout the project.
2. Document the lessons as you go.
3. Plan a project review meeting at the end.
4. Make time to give feedback to your team individually.
5. Give references to your team members' new managers.
6. Help operations and support organizations to take over the system.
7. Encourage some team members to help with future releases.
8. Good projects make for lasting relationships.

14

PLANNING YOUR CAREER

14.1 INTRODUCTION

Project managers are very special. The number of really excellent project managers is small, and even in times of recession there is still a considerable demand in the industry for their skills.

This chapter is an opportunity for you to put your project management role in the context of your career and your personal values. We each have to make our own choices; our intention here is to share some personal views and experience in the hope that these ideas will offer you additional support in deciding what is right for you.

We look first at the relationship between project management and line management, and the career possibilities over the long term. We then consider in more depth what makes project management particularly rewarding, and how the project manager's role differs from that of the line manager. In our final section we discuss the link between your personal values and your search for job satisfaction in your career.

14.2 REVIEWING YOUR CAREER

The end of a project is a natural moment for us to take stock of where we are with regard to our skills, experience and career ambitions. This is the time to stand back and take a look at yourself to determine the next step in your career.

The project had lasted over three years and peaked at several hundred people. It was described as the biggest business change the organization had ever faced in its entire history of nearly a hundred years. The project was an astounding success. Because of its complexity, size and ambitious nature, the project offered career transformations on a huge scale for the whole team, including the project manager.

When the project was nearing completion, the project manager asked the obvious question: what next? The project's long duration and its multi-layered management structure, and the contact with senior managers of many different disciplines, had given the project manager the opportunity to operate more like a business director. He had developed advanced management skills which he wanted to apply.

He was given several options: he could take over another big project, manage a large business unit or run a small unit which supported major projects in the organization. He chose the last option which made him a member of the board, something he had always wanted.

Most people have dreams and want their dreams to come true. However, only those with clear visions and with the understanding of what really motivates them succeed in achieving those dreams. Clarity of vision must be supported by a realistic assessment of talents and strengths and a deep understanding of the values that guide us consciously or subconsciously through life. We also need to have a sense of realism, without being pessimistic, of what is feasible in the world around us. In the next few sections we will review these elements in more detail.

14.3 CAREER POSSIBILITIES IN PROJECT MANAGEMENT AND LINE MANAGEMENT

Career paths in organizations are rarely clearly defined, but Fig. 14.1 shows some of the options. Typically, as you move from managing a small to a medium-sized project the question 'what next?' will keep coming up in your head. For most project managers the major choice will arise after they have completed their next project: should they become a line manager or not?

This decision can be unduly influenced by factors outside the job itself. Young managers often feel under pressure to increase their status and their salary via the line management route. The pressure comes from a number of sources: the social and economic environment, the expectations of others, the expectations you may have been brought up to have about yourself and your future. The result is that some managers make the transition to line management for the wrong reasons, and end up not being able to cope in their new role and unhappy in themselves.

Think carefully about what you want. Line management offers you different challenges; if you think you will enjoy them, and you have the skills and capacities to meet them successfully, then line management offers you an exciting next step. You will need to enjoy 'bottom-line responsibility', possess strong commercial skills and demonstrate a thorough understanding of and interest in the market. You will also need the analytical ability and vision to plan ahead over longer periods of time and deal effectively with high levels of uncertainty. In exchange for the different challenges and increased status you will almost certainly have to trade the close contact with your team and the sense of ownership that goes with the feeling 'this is my project'.

The decision is not irreversible. Some project managers have moved into line management, discovered that they did not enjoy it and moved back to managing projects,

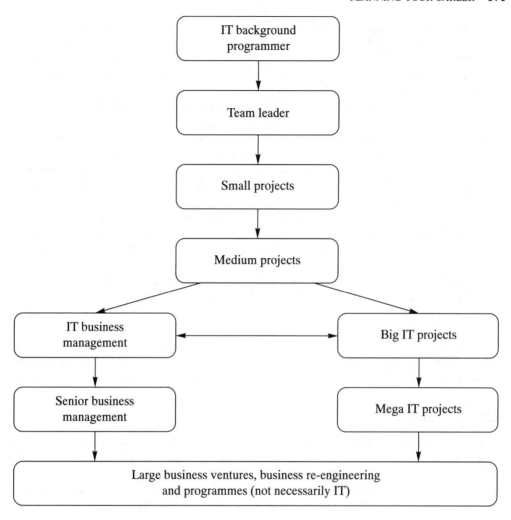

Figure 14.1 Career path of an IT project manager

having benefited from the broader experience. However, in difficult economic climates with fewer jobs available this entails a risk, so it is advisable to think ahead and make a carefully considered decision.

At the level of IT business management on one side and big IT projects on the other, there are sometimes considerable similarities in the managers' roles, although the emphasis will be different. Managers will be networking throughout the organization, playing an important role in influencing key decisions. They will need a strong awareness of economic factors in the environment. The business manager will be primarily an entrepreneur, however, looking outwards. The senior project manager will be primarily responsible for the success of his or her project team.

The final stage in Fig. 14.1 shows a merging of the career paths, where the mega-project manager is experienced enough to start to tackle programmes which are not necessarily IT-related, in partnership with senior business manager colleagues. To run these programmes, the senior project manager would need the ability to develop strategies and produce programme plans that form an integral part of business strategic plans. Programmes often have much longer time scales than single projects. To be able to produce stable plans for these programmes he or she will also require long-term vision and the talent to communicate this vision to the team.

As the programmes becomes larger and more complex, you will need to operate across broader organizational boundaries requiring different communication skills and political sensitivity and understanding.

This variety and progression of jobs, at the very senior level, will only be available to a limited number of project managers, because of the economic realities. Nonetheless, our starting point should be to think about what we would like to do, so that when the opportunity arises we are ready to grasp it. When you like what you do and are motivated at work you will continue to grow and improve and go from strength to strength. You may even end up earning a lot of money and having a lot of power, although most project managers will not place money and power at the top of their priorities.

14.4 SHOULD I STAY IN PROJECT MANAGEMENT?

Suppose the mention of the bottom-line responsibility does not fill you with entrepreneurial zeal but a small, cold chill – what then? We suggest that you look more closely at the advantages of project management as a longer-term stage in your career. The following are some of the special features which make project management so rewarding.

Being close to the team

As a project manager you have to stay *close to the team* – you have to nurture the super-organism. If you get it right, this is immensely fulfilling. You can watch your team members grow and mature in their role, knowing that you have helped them to exploit their considerable talents. You can sometimes even turn 'difficult ' colleagues round and enjoy the results of a relationship which has been brought back on track as in the following example.

> Pierre was an academic in his early years, and he had a reputation for being moody and difficult to work with. He'd got to his current post as a project manager of a large project because he'd been the protégé of a very senior manager. 'You've got to replace him,' they told me, 'he's a disaster, the team is stressed, his results are appalling. He'll bring the whole programme down.' I scheduled a meeting with him – I wanted to form my own view first.
>
> He got very angry when I asked him how the project was going. 'I know what you're doing,' he said, 'just get it over with.' I asked him what experience he'd had in project management – it turned out to be none. He'd also had very little help or coaching. The picture that emerged was of someone who would make an easy scapegoat. The question that came into my head – was this fair?
>
> Project managers have to make up their own minds about members of their team. I decided he deserved another chance – in spite of the pressure from my own colleagues in the organization. Of course, when I suggested that he should take a more experienced

member to help him, he hit the roof. 'I can't do that,' he said, 'it would be a real admission of failure.' I went straight to the point, and told him that I understood he wanted to save face, but he had to have help and have it now. 'Suggest it yourself.' I said, 'present it as your request. I will stay out of it.'

Within a very short time the team was beginning to relax and the atmosphere improved very quickly. The following two milestones were met on time and we brought most of the fires in his project under control. He continued for a while to get into the odd fight within the team, but gradually he became more aware of his behaviour and began to do something about it.

The important thing is to stick to your values as a project manager. People are important – you can't just throw them away. I took a risk and it paid off. It was a very rewarding moment for me when he came back to me months later to thank me for the support I had given him and to tell me how much he had learnt since our first discussion.

People are not just another resource – they have dreams and ambitions, and the manager has the responsibility to help. If you enjoy this long-term contact, and have the judgement and the maturity to make sound decisions, then project management offers you unique opportunities to use your skills.

Coach and facilitator

A good project manager is a coach and a facilitator. The talents, skills and creativity in the team have to be unleashed, channelled and focused if the super-organism is to develop quickly. There is also a joy in passing on knowledge and experience to your less experienced colleagues.

Deepak was one of those people who was a knowledge sponge. He was a pleasure to work with. The decisions I took and the meetings I ran were nothing special until he took part in them. He would ask to come to talk to me and then ask questions about many things.

In the beginning I felt that he was making unfair demands on my time. Sometimes I also felt self-conscious under Deepak's microscope until I became accustomed to his learning style. Then I noticed how he would immediately apply whatever we discussed with enthusiasm and commitment. His response provided me with a mirror to view my own actions, and, oddly enough, this motivated me to invest more time in talking to him. He was a perceptive young man who helped me to be conscious of my own competence and incompetence.

At times, Deepak would ask me to take part in discussions with his peer group to talk about fresh experiences in our project. He was unique in his almost unlimited desire to learn from every experience.

Consensus building

Another key feature of project management is the balancing out it entails. Throughout the book we have stressed the importance of weighing up and reconciling the different interests of the client, the team and your management. A good project manager will enjoy this process of alignment – stressing the common goal, building consensus, leading from the middle. To some people this could be immensely stressing, but to the project manager it is a genuine challenge.

The joy of completion

Project management also offers the satisfaction of seeing 'your' project through to the end. In some ways this is a luxury. Consultants have to learn to pull out of their client organization sometimes just at the point when they'd love to manage the implementation of their carefully selected proposal. They can't 'finish the job' and experience the joy of completion. Business managers on a bad day could see life as a treadmill or a never-ending uphill grind. The project manager who completes the job well will actually be able to watch her system running, and receive the congratulations of her client and her manager. She can enjoy the excitement of the start and the satisfaction (and sometimes sadness) at the end. If you like being in control of the process right the way through, then few other jobs will compare in this respect to project management. As one project manager put it:

> When I go past the building, even though it's two years now since the project was completed, I still feel a warm glow. 'That's my baby,' I think to myself. It may sound silly, but it's great to know that the system's still up and running and providing value.

The following is another account from a different manager.

> When I joined the project it had been going for nearly a year and it was entering a very critical stage. The time scales were challenging and a recent audit confirmed that the project was likely to take 12 months longer than planned. The team was concerned about this – they'd got demotivated and were virtually at a standstill.
>
> We spent the first three weeks brainstorming, discussing and sometimes arguing. Out of this emotionally charged atmosphere a clear vision of how to achieve the project objectives began to emerge. The tension gave way to hope and enthusiasm. That time when we turned the team round from the original state of defeat to a state of hope is one that I won't forget.
>
> When the project ended, 100 per cent according to plan, each team member was asked to express his or her own feelings about the way things went. Every contribution was full of praise for the support of the rest of the team. This gave me a feeling of immense satisfaction and pride – at that moment we felt like gold medallists. Such moments confirmed to me that there was nothing like projects and project management!

14.5 CAREERS, A CHANCE TO MAKE A DIFFERENCE

If somebody was to ask you what you did for a living, your answer would consist of your role or title and perhaps the name of the organization where you work. But what we do for a living is more than those bare details.

We all like to feel that we are in some way helping and making a difference. Success is measured not only in terms of power and financial rewards. If we feel that we are in some way making the world a better place, we are happier, more motivated and contented. This feeling of making a difference will give us higher self-esteem, which in turn will help us to improve further.

The choices we make in the course of our career are dictated not only by the strengths and talents we have but also by the instinctive desire to stay in alignment with our deepest values. The following is one project manager's description of how he works in alignment with values he learned from his grandfather.

> My grandfather was a very wise man who instinctively knew the right answer to any question I had as a little boy. I thought he was some kind of a super-being who knew everything and I wanted to grow up to be like him.
>
> If you make any agreement, you must respect it, whatever the price,' he used to say. 'If you don't, life will turn against you in one way or another.' These statements stuck in my mind and must have affected me very deeply. I didn't realize this until very recently when we were having a casual chat on the subject of agreements. I realized then that I was almost extreme in expressing my views on the subject. But now I know not to put myself in a position where I can't keep to my agreements. Project management is about making agreements and keeping to them; I wonder whether this is why I made my choice.

When you stand back to review your career in order to determine the next step consider the things that *really* matter to you. They are the things that you will remember with fondness and affection when you look back on your working life: the things that give you the feeling that you have made a difference.

14.6 A FINAL NOTE

Project managers are becoming more and more crucial for managing the inevitable business changes or business re-engineering. We need to be aware of the overlaps and differences between project management and line, functional or business managers. At the senior level of project management the differences with senior management may not be very noticeable and migration from one side to the other is common. In making the final choice in our careers we must be aware of these differences and overlaps. We must also be aware of our values and beliefs. We must look for the way to find the balance between these values and beliefs and the roles we play in life and at work.

We hope that you can find your direction and that you have the opportunity to have a fulfilling and satisfying career. It has been a pleasure to share our ideas with you, and we hope that you have found them useful. We wish you success in your life.

FURTHER READING

CHAPTERS 1 AND 2

Adams, J. R. and Martin D. (1987). *Professional Project Management*. Universal Technology Corporation. Includes a good section on planning and control.

Anwan, A. O. (1993). *Project Management Techniques*. Petrocelli, New York. Covers many scheduling techniques.

Bergen, S. A. (1986). *Project Management*. Blackwell, Oxford. Has a good section on project organization.

Boddie, J. (1982). *Crunch Mode: building effective systems on tight schedules*. Yourdon Press, New York. Worth reading if you are managing a software development project.

Bruce, P. and Pederson, S. (1987). *The Software Development Project: planning and development*. John Wiley, Chichester. Another good reference on software development.

Cleland, D. I. and King, W. R. (1983). *System Analysis and Project Management*. McGraw-Hill, New York. More on project organizations.

Davidson Frame, J. (1987). *Managing Projects in Organizations*. Jossey-Bass, San Francisco, CA. Covers project organizations, vision building and scope definition of projects.

Fox, J. M. (1982). *Software and its Development*. Prentice-Hall, Englewood Cliffs, NJ. Another good text on the subject.

Gilbreath, R. D. (1986). *Winning at Project Management*. John Wiley, Chichester. Covers expectation management and people management.

Kerzner, H. (1984). *Project Management*. Van Nostrand Reinhold, New York. Deals with planning and control.

Kerzner, H. (1989). *Managing projects and programs*. Harvard Business Review Press, Boston, MA. Covers risk management and the skills of project managers.

Meredith, J. R. and Mantel, S. J. (1987). *Project Management, a managerial approach*. John Wiley, Chichester. Deals with project organizations, project planning and control, project termination and the present and future states of project management.

Randolph, W. A. and Posner, B. Z. (1987). *Effective Project Management and Planning*. Prentice-Hall, Englewood Cliffs, NJ. A good reference for vision building and team management.

Weiss, W. and Wysocki, R. K. (1992). *5 Phase Project*. Addison-Wesley, Reading, MA. Contains good sections on project close-down and the future of project management.

CHAPTER 3

Albrecht, A. J. (1979). *Proceedings Joint Share/Guide/IBM Application Development Symposium*. The original publication on Functions Point Analysis (FPA). Another classic reference on FPA is Albrecht, A. J. and Gaffney, J. E. Software function, source lines of code and development effort prediction: a software science validation. *IEE Transactions on Software Engineering*, **SE-9**, 6.

Boehm, B. W. (1981). *Software Engineering Economics*. Prentice-Hall, Englewood Cliffs, NJ. Contains good coverage of Cocomo.

Kerzner, H. (1984). *Project Management*. Van Nostrand Reinhold, New York.

Meredith, J. R. and Mantel, S. J. (1987). *Project Management, a managerial approach*. John Wiley, Chichester.

CHAPTER 4

Baker, W. E. (1994). *Networking Smart*. McGraw-Hill, New York. Has a section promisingly entitled 'Managing up, down and sideways'.

Bramson, R. (1992). *Coping with Difficult Bosses*. Nicholas Brealey, London. Try some of the author's ideas if you are unlucky enough to have a really awkward manager.

Davidson Frame, J. (1987). *Managing Projects in Organizations*. Jossey-Bass, San Francisco, CA.

Gabarro, J. and Kotter, J. (1992). Managing your boss, in *People: Managing Your Most Important Asset*, Harvard Business Review Press, Boston, MA. Covers the manager/subordinate relationship in detail.

Meredith, J. R. and Mantel, S. J. (1987). *Project Management, a managerial approach*. John Wiley, Chichester.

Sizemore House, R. (1988). *The Human Side of Project Management*. Addison-Wesley, Reading, MA. Offers a good coverage of vision building and people management.

Turner, W. S., Langerhorst, R. P., Hice, G. F., Eilers, H. B. and Uijttenbroek, A. A. (1988). *System Development Methodology*. Pandata. Rijswijk, Holland.

CHAPTER 5

Adams, J. R. and Martin, D. (1987). *Professional Project Management*. Universal Technology Corporation.

Belbin, R. M. (1981). *Management Teams – why they succeed or fail*. Butterworth-Heinemann, Oxford. Contains some of the best-known research on the contributions of team members and on team composition.

Belbin, R. M. (1993). *Team Roles at Work*. Butterworth-Heinemann, Oxford.

Bennis, W. (1989). *On Becoming a Leader*. Addison-Wesley, Reading, MA. One of the most inspiring books on leadership.

Bergen, S. A. (1986). *Project Management*. Blackwell, Oxford. Has good sections on team motivations.

Bird, M. (1992). *Effective Leadership*. BBC Publications, London. Motivation is a particularly complex area, and much of the literature can seem very abstract. This book is a clear summary of conclusions from the motivation 'gurus'.

Blanchard, K., Oncken, W. and Burrows, H. (1990). *The One Minute Manager Meets the Monkey*. Collins, London. Covers the concept and the dangers of under-delegation and 'delegating up' in a very readable way.

Block, P. (1993). *Stewardship: choosing service over self-interest*. Berrett Koehler, San Francisco, CA. A thought-provoking view of the pitfalls of the leadership and empowerment concepts, together with an alternative approach.

Davidson Frame, J. (1987). *Managing Projects in Organizations*. Jossey-Bass, San Francisco, CA.

Gilbreath, R. D. (1986). *Winning at Project Management*. John Wiley, Chichester.

Handy, C. (1990). *Inside Organizations – 21 ideas for managers*. BBC Publications, London. A readable overview of managerial and leadership skills.

Hersey, P. and Blanchard, K. (1988). *Management of Organization Behaviour*. Prentice-Hall, Englewood Cliffs, NJ. Contains material on adjusting your style to the experience and motivation of the subordinate.

Maddux, R. B. (1990). *Delegating for Results*. Kogan Page, London. Offers some useful checklists.

Randolph, W. A. and Posner, B. Z. (1987). *Effective Project Management and Planning*. Prentice-Hall, Englewood Cliffs, NJ.

Scott, C. D. and Jaffe, D. T. (1991). *Empowerment – building a committed workforce*. Kogan Page, London. Includes a, concise overview of the changes in the expectations between the employee and the organization.

Sizemore House, R. (1988). *The Human Side of Project Management*. Addison-Wesley, Reading, MA.

Video Arts (1983, 1985). *The Unorganised Manager*, Parts 1–4. An entertaining introduction to the principles of time management and delegation, although the roles of women now look decidedly dated. (Tel. 071–637–7288)

Specialized workshops based on the work of Dr David McClelland, one of the most famous researchers into motivation, are run and organized by Dr David Cormack (tel. (44) 035072 8715). McClelland's research provides much more detail on the 'results-oriented', 'power-oriented' and 'relationship-oriented' motivation patterns described very briefly in this chapter.

CHAPTER 6

Adams, J. R. and Martin, D. (1987). *Professional Project Management*. Universal Technology Corporation.

Back, K. and Back, K. (1982). *Assertiveness at Work*. McGraw-Hill, London. Assertiveness skills are an essential part of motivating staff. This is the classic text, although the examples are very British. You would have to adapt them to your own style.

Bruce, P. and Pederson, S. (1987). *The Software Development Project: planning and development*. John Wiley, Chichester.

Mole, J. (1992). *Mind Your Manners – managing culture clash in the single European market*. Nicholas Brealey, London. Describes the cultural aspects of meetings.

O'Brien, P. (1992). *Positive Management – assertiveness for managers*. Nicholas Brealey, London. Offers an attractive, wide-ranging overview of the subject.

Randolph, W. A. and Posner, B. Z. (1987). *Effective Project Management and Planning*. Prentice-Hall, Englewood Cliffs, NJ.

Trompenaars, F. (1993). *Riding the Waves of Culture*. Economist Books, London. Describes the cultural aspects of feedback and other techniques.

Weiss, W. and Wysocki, R. K. (1992). *5 Phase Project*. Addison-Wesley, Reading, MA.

CHAPTER 7

Crosby, C. (1979). *Quality is Free – the art of making quality certain*. Mentor, New York. The famous all-round text on quality.

Macro, A. (1991). *Software Engineering, Concepts and Management*. Prentice-Hall, Englewood Cliffs, NJ.

CHAPTER 8

Honey, P. and Mumford, A. (1992). *The Manual of Learning Styles*. Peter Honey, Ardingly House, 10 Linden Avenue, Maidenhead, Berkshire SL6 6HB. Gives more information on learning styles and selecting learning methods.

Video Arts (1987). *Can You Spare a Moment?* A good introduction to the principles of counselling. (Tel: 071–637–7288)

Whitmore, J. (1992). *Coaching for Performance – a practical guide for growing your own skills*. Nicholas Brealey, London. Offers some excellent sections on questioning techniques for both coaching and counselling sessions.

CHAPTER 9

Crawley, J. (1992). *Constructive Conflict Management – managing to make a difference*. Nicholas Brealey, London. Gives a range of practical techniques for coping with conflict.

Fisher, R., Ury, W. and Patterson, B. (1991). *Getting to Yes*. Century Business, London. An excellent, readable book on influencing and negotiating.

Laborde, G. Z. (1987). *Influencing with Integrity*. Syntony, California. More on non-verbal matching and the concept of rapport.

Pfeffer, J. (1992). *Managing with Power: politics and influence in organisations*. Harvard Business School Press, Boston, MA. Describes managing the politics of an organization.

CHAPTER 10

Bridges, W. (1991). *Managing Transitions – making the most of change*. Addison-Wesley, Reading, MA. Gives a powerful insight into the effects of organizational change and offers practical suggestions for supporting your staff through periods of organizational and personal turmoil.

Cormack, D. (1986). *Seconds Away*. Monarch Publications, Eastbourne. Much of the material for this chapter has been drawn with permission from this book, which gives an excellent overview of time management.

Cranwell Ward, J. (1990). *Thriving on Stress*. Routledge, London. Offers a number of self-help questionnaires and a good section on strategies for making stress work for you.

DeMarco, T. and Lister, T. (1987). *Peopleware*. Dorset House, New York. A readable but idiosyncratic view of managing people and time.

O'Brien, P. (1992). *Positive Management–assertiveness for managers*. Nicholas Brealey, London. Readable, practical guide to assertiveness.

Patel, C. (1989). *The Complete Guide to Stress Management*. Macdonald Optima, London. One of the best overviews of stress management.

The authors are grateful to Peter Callender of Balance Consultants for permission to use his list of stress management strategies.

CHAPTER 11

Boddie, J. (1982). *Crunch Mode: building effective systems on tight schedules*. Yourdon Press, New York.

Bruce, P. and Pederson, S. (1987). *The Software Development Project: planning and development*. John Wiley, Chichester.

Fox, J. M. (1982). *Software and its Development*. Prentice-Hall, Englewood Cliffs, NJ.

Keen, J. (1987). *Managing System Development*. John Wiley, Chichester. Covers people management, the consolidation of plans, prototyping, and the advantages and disadvantages of project management.

Kerzner, H. (1989). *Managing projects and programs*. Harvard Business Review Press, Boston, MA.

Macro, A. (1991). *Software Engineering, Concepts and Management*. Prentice-Hall, Englewood Cliffs, NJ.

Metzger, P. W. (1991). *Managing a Programming Project*. Prentice-Hall, Englewood Cliffs, NJ.

CHAPTER 12

Boddie, J. (1982). *Crunch Mode: building effective systems on tight schedules*. Yourdon Press, New York.

Bruce, P. and Pederson, S. (1987). *The Software Development Project: planning and development*. John Wiley, Chichester.

Fox, J. M. (1982). *Software and its Development*. Prentice-Hall, Englewood Cliffs, NJ.

Gilbreath, R. D. (1986). *Winning at Project Management*. John Wiley, Chichester.

Keen, J. (1987). *Managing System Development*. John Wiley, Chichester.

Macro, A. (1991). *Software Engineering, Concepts and Management*. Prentice-Hall, Englewood Cliffs, NJ.

Metzger, P. W. (1981). *Managing a Programming Project*. Prentice-Hall, Englewood Cliffs, NJ.

CHAPTER 13

Keen, J. (1987). *Managing System Development*. John Wiley, Chichester.

Meredith, J. R. and Mantel, S. J. (1987). *Project Management, a managerial approach*. John Wiley, Chichester.

Metzger, P. W. (1981). *Managing a Programming Project*. Prentice-Hall, Englewood Cliffs, NJ.

Weiss, W. and Wysocki, R. K. (1992). *5 Phase Project*. Addison-Wesley, Reading, MA.

CHAPTER 14

Adams, J. R. and Martin, D. (1987). *Professional Project Management*. Universal Technology Corporation. See the section on career management.

Hudson, F. M. (1991). *The Adult Years – mastering the art of self-renewal.* Jossey-Bass, San Francisco, CA. Covers the psychology of adult development.

Johnson, S. (1993). *Yes or No – the guide to better decisions.* Fontana, London. A short but powerful book that guides the reader through the more personal aspects of decision making.

Kerzner, H. (1984). *Project Management.* Van Nostrand Reinhold. New York.

Kerzner, H. (1989). *Managing projects and programs.* Harvard Business Review Press, Boston, MA.

Smith, M. (1992). *Changing Course.* You can find a number of books on making career choices. This is a good example.

CHAPTER 2   PLANNING

Before you start

1. Have you made time to plan? Does your organization understand and support the planning process? Do you need any help? Where can you get it?
2. Do you know the purpose of your project? Why has it been set up? Who is paying for it – and what do they expect? What are their criteria for success? What are the expectations of the other stakeholders? Who is the client?
3. Have you ever done anything like this before? Are you confident that you understand the scope of your responsibilities?

Stage 1 – The overall plan

4. What's the purpose of your plan? (For instance, to get a feel for costs? Ask for budget? Assess how to deliver within key constraints?)
5. Have you formulated your SMART objectives?
6. Have you identified your conditions, prerequisites, risks and exclusions?
7. Have you involved your team in identifying the production process (how and who)? Have you thought about the organization of your team, and the key tasks and interfaces?
8. Have you communicated your Stage 1 plan and consulted your client, your team and your management? Do they all think it makes sense? Have you distributed it?
9. Have you defined your integration strategy?

Stage 2 – The detailed plan

10. Have you produced a high-level plan ('the head of the snake')?
11. Have you completed your estimates, so that you now have the project baseline and agreed scope of supply, together with your production process description, your rough organization, the cost and effort estimates, risk analysis, prerequisites and contingency estimates?
12. Have you organized your team members to work on different parts of the detailed plan?
13. Does your plan include a summary, a description of the scope and objectives, methodology, organization, quality, monitoring and reporting, documentation, change control, time scales, cost plan, risk analysis and contingency planning? Have you planned to manage the risks?
14. Have you organized a meeting with the rest of the team to resolve any differences and overlaps and to agree a common vision? Are you encouraging openness during these discussions, to promote team spirit?
15. Have you planned how to present your plan to the outside world? Do you feel excited and confident about running this project?

CHAPTER 3   ESTIMATING

1. Have you defined the scope of the project, and agreed it with your client?
2. Have you listed the materials and project expenses (List 1)?
3. Have you broken down the project life-cycle into phases, each with products that are certifiable and/or auditable?
4. Have you broken down each phase into subactivities, with clear completion criteria, in order to produce your list of activities (your Work Breakdown Structure: List 2)?
5. Lists 1 and 2 form your estimating baseline. Have you reviewed this baseline against the scope of supply defined in question 1?
6. Have you consulted the specialist literature and the Further Reading in this book to help you to select any appropriate tools and techniques?
7. Have you identified some experienced colleagues who can work in your estimating team?
8. Has your estimating team agreed on a set of assumptions?
9. Have they produced as many estimates as possible, using a variety of methods? Has each estimator worked independently?
10. Have you reached a consensus to consolidate your estimates, and written a consolidation report?
11. Have you produced a list of costs with associated risks?
12. If you have had to adjust your estimates in order to meet particular constraints, have you really thought creatively about different scenarios (e.g. reducing the functionality in consultation with the client)?
13. If you have any doubts about the realism and accuracy of your estimates, have you raised these with your manager and discussed how to resolve any problems? Have you recorded your concerns?
14. Are you now feeling realistically confident about your estimates?

CHAPTER 4   PROJECT SET-UP

1. Have you recruited your core team first – those with the special technical and/or managerial skills required for your project?
2. Have you selected a methodology which is easy to communicate and which involves the users from the start?
3. Have you defined all the inputs and outputs for each stage of your production process?
4. Have you delegated to your technical staff the choice of tools (development tools, test tools, monitoring and control tools, etc.)?
5. Have you devised appropriate and, if need be, original ways of helping your team to understand the users' needs?
6. Have you organized appropriate training?
7. Have you discussed with your manager what you can both reasonably expect of each other in a productive and professional working relationship?
8. Have you identified your manager's personal and professional objectives?
9. Have you agreed with your manager how you will work together – including your pattern of reporting, when you can come for help, etc.?
10. If there are any aspects of your working relationship which bother you, have you been able to raise these promptly and diplomatically?
11. Have you done the same preparatory work to set up a good relationship with your client? Have you identified your client's personal and professional objectives?
12. What is the key output from your project that will contribute most to his or her long-term organizational goals?
13. What aspect of your project will your client be most concerned about?
14. How much IT experience does your client have? How will this affect your working relationship?
15. What are the key strengths of both your manager and your client? How will you best be able to use these strengths during your project?

CHAPTER 5   TEAM BUILDING

1. Have you identified the kinds of organizational support you will need for your project?
2. Have you identified your key support functions, and made their purpose and authority levels clear to all the people concerned with your project?
3. Have you defined all the important interfaces both inside your project and with the 'outside world'?
4. Have you taken into account both the technical and the personal strengths of your team members?
5. Are you comfortable about your own role as leader? Are you able to maintain the project vision and 'lead from the middle'?
6. Do you feel reluctant to delegate? If so, what are the blocks you can recognize in yourself?
7. Are you ever guilty of over-delegating and dumping?

8. Have you prepared your delegation carefully, by first identifying those tasks that are essential to the project success and which only you are qualified to do?
9. Have you delegated tasks to your team that will help them to develop their skills?
10. Have you tailored your delegation style to the expertise, confidence, etc. of the individuals?
11. Have you briefed them thoroughly and ensured that they get the necessary resources and support?
12. How do you measure up against the *ideal* manager? Do you give your team the information they require? Is there any information they may currently be lacking?
13. Are you able to Delegate and Encourage them by adapting your approach to their individual needs? Are you able to Accept their strengths and work round their weaknesses?
14. Do you Listen attentively, to pick up early warning signs, for instance?
15. Do your staff leave your meetings feeling more motivated and enthusiastic?
16. Do you prepare for all your meetings thoroughly – with objectives, agenda, etc.?
17. Are you consistent and explicit about the ground rules to promote a constructive team culture?

CHAPTER 6   STAYING ON TRACK

1. Did you cover monitoring, reporting and quality adequately in your project plan?
2. Have you thought about your baselines (States A, B, etc.) as in the process control analogy?
3. Have you defined the key variables you want to measure?
4. Have you worked out a system of cost monitoring which will enable you to make efficient trade-offs?
5. When you report, have you thought about your different sets of readers and their needs?
6. Are you able to separate out the short-term from the longer-term perspective?
7. Have you set up a good action follow-up system for yourself?
8. When you monitor your team's performance, are you able both to avoid blame and to stand up to counter-attacks?
9. Are you able to pick up the verbal and non-verbal clues when you are talking to a team member?
10. Can you help your team members to identify for themselves realistic action plans?
11. Are you able to adjust the frequency of monitoring to the experience and needs of your staff?
12. Do you monitor all team members, including those who are more senior?
13. When you give feedback, do you prepare the facts carefully beforehand?
14. Are you able to avoid judgemental remarks and give a fair mixture of praise and criticism?
15. Do you limit constructive criticism to about three items?
16. Do you check that the team member agrees with your feedback before discussing further actions?
17. Are you able to use alternative approaches if you think criticism is too risky?
18. In review meetings do you emphasize that the purpose is to review the *team's* work?

19. Have you the skill and confidence to implement timely stocktaking sessions if necessary?

CHAPTER 7 THE FUNDAMENTALS OF QUALITY

1. Are you one of the supporters of the quality department? Do you take initiatives to improve the quality procedures in your projects and in the company at large?
2. Is quality planning an integral part of your project planning?
3. Do you understand how quality attributes, criteria and procedures relate to each other?
4. Can you explain easily in layperson's terms why the products and services of your project are of high or low quality?
5. Can you define simple and pragmatic working (quality) procedures in your project? Are you open to suggestions for improvements from the team, users and management?
6. Do you feel confident that you can translate the 'subjective' quality expectations of the users and others into objective measurable criteria?
7. Can you identify the quality criteria of your products and services? Can you devise relatively simple ways of checking these criteria?
8. Have you defined completion criteria for your products?
9. Do you always congratulate your team members when they complete products?
10. Can you implement simple but effective quality systems in your projects? Are you able to use original but practical ideas?
11. Can you motivate your team easily to adopt quality procedures?

CHAPTER 8 COACHING AND COUNSELLING

1. Do you use a systematic approach to coaching? Do you always take the time to set and agree realistic objectives, for instance?
2. Have you identified your own preferred learning style (your own combination of Activist, Reflector, Theorist, Pragmatist)?
3. Do you discuss with the person you are coaching how he or she likes to learn so that you can identify the most effective approach?
4. Are you good at following through your coaching sessions by identifying or setting up specific opportunities for the other person to practise and apply new skills?
5. Do you ensure that the person gets specific and constructive feedback? Do you make time to give a review?
6. Have you done any thinking recently about your own development, and how you can apply these ideas for yourself?
7. Do you agree that counselling is part of your job?
8. Are you able to offer people support in a number of ways – not just with suggestions or information, for instance, but also by acting as a sounding board?
9. Are you sensitive to the cultural differences that can emerge in counselling situations?
10. Are you able to pick up the signs that someone is suffering from stress and may need you to initiate a counselling session?

11. Are you open-minded to the idea that some work-related stress can be induced by the manager's style? That your way of working may be part of the problem?
12. Do you listen attentively without being critical and passing judgements?
13. Do you summarize regularly to check that you really understand the problem?
14. Are you able tactfully to help the other person to express his or her feelings?
15. Do you encourage the other person to explore a range of options without trying to steer him or her towards your preferred outcome?
16. Do you feel reasonably confident that you can also help people when they are very distressed simply by listening and acting as a sounding board?

CHAPTER 9   INFLUENCING AND CONFLICT HANDLING

1. Do you regularly take time to present ideas in a way which is easy for your target audience to absorb?
2. Do you try wherever possible to present your ideas in one-to-one meetings?
3. Do you formulate specific objectives for each stage of your influencing process?
4. Are you skilled at accurately identifying the needs and agendas of others?
5. Do you 'desk check' your influencing strategy first to ensure that there is enough overlap of needs and a strong enough benefit for the other party to give you a good chance of success?
6. When confronted with an unexpected conflict, are you able to change direction and ask about the other person's underlying needs and pressures in a way that helps both parties to progress?
7. If you are in the middle of an ongoing conflict situation, are you able to detach yourself and raise your concerns in a neutral way? Can you keep an open mind and listen to the other person's point of view – even if you feel that the situation is unfair?
8. Do you consistently invest time in specifying a clear objective and identifying what the audience needs to hear?
9. Do you sketch out an overview of the content and the schedule so that you are able to stay concise and to the point?
10. Have you developed your own 'on-stage' style which is confident and natural? If not, do you organize support from colleagues, in 'dry runs' for instance, so that you can practise until you feel reasonably at ease?
11. Do you 'signpost' your reports with a clear, attractive layout, designed to meet the needs of your different sets of readers?
12. How does your writing measure up under the readability tests? Can your colleagues pick up your key ideas quickly and accurately?
13. Do you use consensus for the decisions which need the wholehearted support of the team?
14. Do you stress points of agreement, so that the team can move on confidently to address the more difficult areas? Do you summarize regularly?

CHAPTER 10   MANAGING YOURSELF

1. How effective is your time management currently? What do you think could be your weak areas?
2. Are you able to keep in mind the purpose of the project and your Key Results Areas in order to set priorities – even when you are under time pressure?
3. Have you sorted out your proactive from your reactive tasks? How is the balance? Do you need to discuss or negotiate anything with your manager?
4. Are you able to distinguish between urgent and important tasks?
5. Do you find time for your C tasks?
6. Do you use regular daily action lists?
7. Have you set up some system for promoting 'flow' time in your team for those tasks which require uninterrupted concentration?
8. Are you able to refuse requests when necessary in a firm but friendly manner?
9. Have you got an efficient system for handling your incoming mail?
10. Which indicators (physical, emotional, intellectual) are most helpful for you in monitoring your own stress level?
11. Do you feel that you are operating in the Peak Performance Zone?
12. If not, can you identify the causes of under- or overstress at work or outside work?
13. Are you able to confront problems directly, at source, rather than pretending that the problems don't exist or taking out your tension on someone else?
14. Have you got a solid network of family and friends who will support you when times are difficult? If not, what simple actions could you take to build new friendships or renew old contacts?
15. Do you look after yourself even when you are busy by building in a routine of regular exercise, relaxation and a balanced diet?
16. If you are lucky enough to be particularly stress resistant, do you feel able to recognize signs of stress in others and to help them cope?
17. Is there one single action you can identify which could contribute to your overall health in the long term?

CHAPTER 11   MANAGING COMMON RISKS

1. Have you kept the client closely involved in defining the delivery process?
2. Have you ensured that the user is aware of the main project risks? Do you have a plan to deal with these risks?
3. Do you have alternative scenarios and 'work-arounds' if these risks turn into real problems?
4. Do you understand the users' expectations? Have you translated these expectations into concrete needs?
5. Have you agreed with the users a priority rating for their requirements?
6. Have you committed to review your plans at the end of the design phase?
7. Do you have a good constructive relationship with the users?
8. Have you talked through your detailed design of the operator interface with the users?
9. Have you identified the minimum requirements of the user? Do you have a plan to phase the delivery of the system in case you come under time pressure?

10. Have you identified the functions where close interaction with the users is necessary? Have you planned to prototype these functions?
11. Have you assigned someone in your team to keep an eye on the performance risk?
12. Have you identified the main performance risks? Have you planned to use benchmarking to assess these risks? Have you involved the users?
13. Do you regularly review your project risks with the client and management?

CHAPTER 12   THE FINISHING TOUCHES

1. Have you planned to deal with the lack of attention and the team demotivation that come at the end of the project?
2. Have you planned the integration early in the project?
3. Do you have a clear integration strategy – for example, incremental or big bang? Are the users involved in the decision?
4. Are you producing the system components to satisfy this strategy?
5. Are the time scales for integration realistic? Have you planned to deal with the last-minute panics that come close to the delivery?
6. Have you defined clear and measurable project baselines?
7. Are the users involved in the preparations for delivery and do they understand the risks?
8. Are the acceptance criteria part of the integration and pre-acceptance preparations?
9. Have you produced the Acceptance Test Specification? Have you involved the users in the production of this document?
10. Do you watch out for signs of complacency inside and outside your team? Do you take visible measures to maintain momentum?
11. Have you planned to train the operators of the system?
12. Have you set up the support and the maintenance organization? Have you identified the follow-on projects? Have you advised management on how to tackle these projects?

CHAPTER 13   PROJECT CLOSE-DOWN

1. Have you identified all the close-down actions? Have you produced a project close-down plan?
2. Do you plan to leave everything neat and tidy?
3. Have you planned to celebrate the project completion? Have you acknowledged all those who helped you?
4. Do you encourage the team to note the daily lessons to stimulate the learning process?
5. Do you use the lessons as opportunities to improve the way you and your team work?
6. Does the atmosphere in the project allow for suggestions for improvements without fear of reprisal or unhealthy rivalry?
7. Have you planned to wind down the organization? Have you planned to prepare references for the team members?
8. Have you helped the team members to update their curricula vitae?

9. Do you show care, sensitivity and understanding when winding down the organization?
10. Have you planned to transfer the relevant knowledge and experience to the users?
11. Have you identified the future releases of the system and helped the users to plan for them?
12. Do you encourage your team members to make use of the project follow-on opportunities to develop their career further?
13. Do you know what every team member is going to do after the project? Do you plan to stay in touch with them?
14. Have you documented the lessons you learned?
15. Are you certain that there are no open actions or loose ends remaining?
16. Do you feel proud of the results of your project?

CHAPTER 14   PLANNING YOUR CAREER

1. Have you thought about the wider role project managers play in managing the changes in the business?
2. Do you actively demonstrate to your team and the outside world the business contribution of your projects?
3. Are you aware of the 'what next' question that poses itself at the end of the project? Are you prepared to deal with this question?
4. Do you take stock of the new skills and strengths you develop in each project?
5. Do you capitalize on the career opportunities your project presents to you?
6. Have you made a realistic inventory of your strengths? Have you taken the time to review your likes and dislikes?
7. Do you have a clear vision of where you want to go in your career?
8. Are you aware of the differences and similarities between project managers and line managers? Do you know which path appeals most to you?
9. Do you enjoy being close to the team?
10. Do you enjoy passing on knowledge and experience?
11. Can you deal with conflicts easily?
12. Do you enjoy seeing things through to the end?
13. Are you conscious of your deepest values? Does your current function support these values? Are you happy with your current job?
14. Can you identify one single action which will help you on your way forward to building a happy and rewarding career?

INDEX

Further titles in this Series

Practical Formal Methods with VDM	Andrews and Ince
Portable Modula-2 Programming	Woodman, Griffiths, Souter and Davies
Software Engineering: Analysis and Design	Easteal and Davies
Systems Construction and Analysis: A Mathematical and Logical Framework	Fenton and Hill
SSADM Version 4 Project Manager's Handbook	Hammer
Introduction to Compiling Techniques: A First Course Using ANSI C, LEX and YACC	Bennett
An Introduction to Program Design	Sargent
Expert Database Systems: A Gentle Introduction	Beynon-Davies
A Structured Approach to Systems Development	Heap, Stanway and Windsor
Rapid Information Systems Development	Bell and Wood-Harper
Software Engineering Environments: Automated Support for Software Engineering	Brown, Earl and McDermid
Knowledge Engineering for Information Systems	Beynon-Davies

Related titles are available in McGraw-Hill's International Software Quality Assurance Series